# Economics

*An Introduction for Students
of Business and Marketing*

The Marketing Series is one of the most comprehensive collections of books in marketing and sales available from the UK today

Published by Butterworth-Heinemann on behalf of the Chartered Institute of Marketing, the series is divided into three distinct groups: *Student* (fulfilling the needs of those taking the Institute's certificate and diploma qualifications); *Professional Development* (for those on formal or self-study vocational training programmes); and *Practitioner* (presented in a more informal, motivating and highly practical manner for the busy marketer).

Formed in 1911, the Chartered Institute of Marketing is now the largest professional marketing management body in Europe with over 22,000 members and 25,000 students located worldwide. Its primary objectives are focused on the development of awareness and understanding of marketing throughout UK industry and commerce and on the raising of standards of professionalism in the education, training and practice of this key business discipline.

**Other titles in the series**

*Students series*

*Behavioural Aspects of Marketing*
K. C. Williams

*Business Law*
A. A. Painter and R. G. Lawson

*Effective Sales Management*
John Strafford and Colin Grant

*Financial Aspects of Marketing*
Keith Ward

*International Marketing*
S. J. Paliwoda

*Marketing Communications*
C. L. Coulson-Thomas

*Marketing Financial Services*
Edited by Chris Ennew, Trevor Watkins and Mike Wright

*Marketing-Led, Sales Driven*
Keith Steward

*Mini Cases in Marketing*
Lester Massingham and Geoff Lancaster

*The Fundamentals of Advertising*
John Wilmshurst

*The Fundamentals and Practice of Marketing*
John Wilmshurst

*The Marketing Primer: Key Issues and Topics Explained*
Geoff A. Lancaster and Lester Massingham

*The Principles and Practice of Selling*
A. Gillam

*Strategic Marketing Management: Planning, Implementation and Control*
R. M. S. Wilson, C. T. Gilligan and D. Pearson

*Books by Frank Livesey*

# Economics

*An Introduction for Students
of Business and Marketing*

Third Edition

FRANK LIVESEY

*Published on behalf of
the Chartered Institute of Marketing*

Butterworth-Heinemann Ltd
Linacre House, Jordan Hill, Oxford OX2 8DP

PART OF REED INTERNATIONAL BOOKS

OXFORD   LONDON   BOSTON
MUNICH   NEW DELHI   SINGAPORE   SYDNEY
TOKYO   TORONTO   WELLINGTON

First published 1977
Reprinted 1981
Second edition 1986
Reprinted 1987, 1989
Third edition 1990
Reprinted 1990, 1991

**British Library Cataloguing in Publication Data**
Livesey, Frank
Economics: an introduction for students of business and
marketing – 3rd edition.
1. Economics
I. Title   II. Chartered Institute of Marketing
330'.024658'8   HB171.5

ISBN 0 7506 0081 0

Printed and bound in Great Britain by
Redwood Press Limited, Melksham, Wiltshire

To Shauna, Karen, Susan, and St John,
with love

# Contents

# *Preface*

The commission from the Chartered Institute of Marketing to write a textbook in connection with the new Economics for Marketing syllabus has given me the opportunity to develop a theme I believe to be neglected in most economics textbooks. This is that the activities of producers, including marketing activities, are extremely important in meeting two of the community's greatest needs – the need for consumption and the need for employment. Writing this book has also allowed me to demonstrate the close interrelations that exist between producers and consumers on the one hand, and producers and the State or government on the other.

While a book that puts producers at the centre of the stage must have a particular appeal to marketing students, it will also be suitable for those taking Ordinary or Higher National Certificates or Diplomas in business studies, or the intermediate examinations set by many of the professional bodies, including:

> The Chartered Institute of Bankers,
> The Chartered Association of Certified Accountants,
> The Institute of Chartered Secretaries and
>     Administrators,
> The Chartered Institute of Transport,
> The Institute of Personnel Management.

I would like to acknowledge the assistance given by Martin Rogers. As chief examiner with the Chartered Institute of Marketing, Mr Rogers is in the best position to know what students require from a textbook, and he put this knowledge to good use when reading the manuscript. I am sure that students will benefit as much as I did from the very extensive advice he offered. I also benefited substantially from the advice provided by Malcolm Stern, my editor at Heinemann. Finally the manuscript was read by my wife. She has now performed this function on several occasions, and remains as helpfully critical as ever.

The manuscript was typed by Mrs Muriel Shingler so efficiently and cheerfully as to provide every incentive to the author to meet his deadlines.

F.L.

# Preface to the Second Edition

The book, first published as *A Modern Approach to Economics*, has been extensively revised to meet the requirements of the new Joint Syllabus introduced by the Chartered Institute of Marketing, the Institute of Purchasing and the Institute of Chartered Secretaries and Administrators. Account has been taken of the dramatic changes in government policy that have occurred since the first edition. Recent developments in international economic relationships are also documented. However, the activities of producers remains as a major theme in the second edition.

F.L.

# Preface to the Third Edition

Although the Joint Syllabus has remained unchanged since the publication of the previous edition of the book, various changes have been incorporated in this new edition. There are several reasons for this. The first reason is the many changes that have occurred in the economic scene in the last few years. It seems that the pace of change in national and international economies accelerates year by year, and one manifestation of this is the shorter intervals between new editions of textbooks. All the tables of actual data have been updated, together with the discussion of those tables. Changes in government policy have also been incorporated, even if this has not been strictly required by the Syllabus.

Examiners are not always fully bound by the Syllabus, and a second reason for change has been to incorporate topics which are not spelled out in detail in the Syllabus but which have appeared in examination papers during the past three years.

Finally, major changes have been made in order to improve the chapter layout. The material in Chapter 1, The Economic System, has been divided to make two separate chapters. Economic resources are still discussed in Chapter 1, together with new material on alternative economic systems. But the discussion of the measurement of economic activity (national income etc.) now forms the basis of a new Chapter 12. Although it appears as the first topic in the Syllabus, experience has shown that for teaching and learning purposes, this topic is best presented as a lead-in to the discussion of the elements of national income: consumption, investment etc. (Chapters 13, 14, ff.).

The previous Chapter 12, Public Sector Producers, is now Chapter 11, and also includes an expanded discussion of Privatization. Finally, Small Firms and Economic Efficiency, previously Chapter 11, has been incorporated in the examination of Competition Policy in Chapter 10.

As before, the book contains revision exercises and objective tests (the latter with answers) to help students to test their understanding. New questions of both kinds have been included in this edition.

F.L.

# 1. *The Economic System*

## 1.1 Introduction: the Allocation of Scarce Resources among Competing Ends

Consider the following statements: (1) as a result of an increase in the price of oranges, Mrs Jones buys fewer oranges, but more apples, than she did last week; (2) the Insulex Manufacturing Co. decides to advertise on television rather than in the press because it believes the former to be more cost-effective; (3) Mr Green, a farmer, buys a combine harvester, since it will enable him to reduce the size of his labour force; (4) in order to be able to buy a car, Mr Smith decides to look for a new job that will offer more overtime than his present job. The four decisions referred to in these statements are very different in kind. Nevertheless they all refer to the allocation of scarce resources among competing ends. The first three decisions relate to alternative forms of expenditure, and these reflect the fact that in modern economies many transactions include the payment of money. The choice facing Mr Smith is somewhat different, namely how he should allocate his time. But even here the same principle is brought into play. Mr Smith's time is a scarce resource; he cannot have both more leisure and a new car.

We shall see that an analysis of the factors influencing individual decisions of this kind forms a very important part of economics. Also of great importance is the analysis of how these individual decisions interact. The economic system comprises a complex web of interrelations. Probably a single example is sufficient to give an indication of this complexity.

Between 1983 and 1988 the number of employees in employment in manufacturing industry fell by 8 per cent, while the number in service industries rose by 17 per cent. These changes resulted from decisions by consumers (households and firms) to spend a smaller proportion of their income on manufactured goods and a higher proportion on services, and decisions by workers to leave manufacturing and enter the service industries. These decisions were themselves influenced by a whole range of other factors including changes in relative wage rates, technological change, and government policy.

In order to try to unravel this complex web economists adopt a systematic approach based on classifying economic phenomena. We have identified the allocation of scarce resources among competing ends as one of the central concerns of economics, and we shall therefore discuss in this chapter the classification of both resources and ends. We begin with resources, as seen from the viewpoint of a national economy.

## 1.2 The Nature of Economic Resources

Economic resources include anything that can be utilized in the production and distribution of goods or services. This definition has the advantage of being comprehensive, but for the purposes of economic analysis we need to go further, and to divide resources into the three basic categories of land, labour and capital.

### 1.21 Land

At the national level the most obvious characteristic of land is that its *quantity* is virtually fixed in supply. Changes in quantity, either negative (e.g. due to flooding) or positive (e.g. due to land-reclamation schemes), usually take place only over long periods of time, and even then are insignificant.

On the other hand, substantial changes may occur in the *quality* of land. Bad husbandry turned once fertile plains in the United States into dust bowls. Easily worked deposits of minerals become exhausted. On the credit side good husbandry has improved the fertility of some land, and improved communications have led to the unlocking of the potential of hitherto inaccessible areas.

A second important characteristic of land is that its nature varies considerably from country to country. Although, as we have indicated, its quality can be changed over time by the activities of man, substantial differences in its nature will always remain. Some countries will always be richer in minerals than others; some will always be more suitable for growing certain crops than others (climate, which is more impervious to the activities of man than is the fertility of the soil, is important here, of course); some countries will always have a land formation that is more suitable for shipbuilding than others; and so forth.

These differences in the nature of land, allied to differences in climate, help to explain differences in industrial structure, at both the international and the regional level. The implications of these differences in industrial structure are discussed in Chapters 19 and 20.

### 1.22 Labour

An upper limit is set to the number of workers employed at any given time by the population of the country. However, in practice the number of people available for work is considerably less than the total population. At present the working population in the U.K. is about 27 million people, less than 50 per cent of the total population. The remainder, who are not seeking employment, comprise children, full-time students, retired people and housewives.

It follows that even if the total population remained constant, the size of the working population would be likely to change if changes occurred in the age and sex distribution. Other influences include social customs (especially in relation to the place of women in society), laws (especially those governing the employment of young people), and welfare provisions (especially relating to retirement pensions and unemployment benefits).

Finally, note that, given the working population, the supply of labour is affected by the hours of work and the number of holidays.

The quality of labour is to some extent amenable to improvement by education and training. It is often asserted that international differences in rates of economic growth are partly due to differences in the quality of labour. This would certainly seem to be true as between the developed and the under-developed nations.

An obvious difference between labour and land is that labour is more mobile geographically. At the international level, restrictions have sometimes been placed on the movement of population, usually because of the social problems which it is feared might follow from high levels of immigration. On the other hand, some countries have encouraged immigration in order to enable their economies to grow faster than they would otherwise do. Perhaps the best example of a country that followed this policy in the postwar period was West Germany, where output was restricted by a shortage of labour. Technically we would say that the best or optimum mix of resources did not exist; there was insufficient labour in relation to the amount of land and capital.

Many of the immigrants to West Germany were relatively unskilled manual workers. In other instances the flow largely comprised workers with very specific skills that were in greater demand in some countries than others. A good example is the so-called 'brain drain' of the 1960s, when thousands of British scientists and technologists left the U.K. for employment in the booming aerospace industries of the U.S.A.

## 1.23 *Capital*

Capital can be defined as any material resource, other than land, which can be utilized in the production and distribution of goods and services. This definition implies that capital does *not* include money, since money is not in itself useful in production, and can be regarded merely as a facility which lubricates the economic system. 'Real' capital includes factories, the machines that are housed in those factories, the vehicles that transport raw materials and finished products, etc. Some other examples are perhaps rather less obvious, and are certainly more difficult to identify in practice. So, for instance, although we would normally consider a field as land, if this field's fertility has been increased by the application of fertilizer, then, strictly speaking, it should be seen as comprising both land and capital. Similarly capital, in the form of shafts, drainage works, etc., often has to be applied before minerals can be worked.

However, other examples are less straightforward. We have already shown that education may enhance the quality of labour, thus leading to a faster rate of economic growth. Thus expenditure on education *could* be considered to be similar to expenditure on a machine that leads to higher output, and school and university buildings could be seen as capital in the same way as factory buildings. But note that an improvement in efficiency is only one, and not necessarily the most important, of the goals of education. Indeed some educationalists would not accept this as a goal, and might be quite happy if education had the effect of reducing the rate of economic growth, perhaps because people have come to attach greater importance to leisure.

Changes in the quantity of resources will normally be easier to accomplish in the case of capital than of either land or labour. Capital also tends to be more mobile than labour, and certainly than land. For example, when I.C.I. decided to build a chemical plant in Italy, it utilized materials from many different countries, whereas the vast majority of the labour force were Italians.

Finally, efforts are constantly being made to improve the quality of capital, by the introduction of machines capable of higher speeds, greater accuracy and so forth. Much of the increase in efficiency represents the cumulative effect of many small improvements. Sometimes, however, more significant developments occur dramatically in certain sectors of industry, such as the dry copying process pioneered by Xerox, the computer, the jet engine, etc.

## 1.3 Competing Ends – Effective Demand

Production invariably brings about the utilization of all three types of resource, or factors of production – land, labour and capital. The owners who make resources available to producers receive payment in the form of rent, wages (including salaries) and interest.

Producers decide which resources shall be utilized and how they shall be utilized. These decisions are in turn strongly influenced by the pattern of effective demand, i.e. by the competing ends. Let us return to the statements at the beginning of the chapter. If all farmers have the same views as our Mr Green, producers will be encouraged to manufacture more combine harvesters and to employ the additional resources that will be required. If the Insulex Manufacturing Company is typical of all advertisers, fewer newspaper pages will be devoted to advertising, and fewer resources will be employed in the newspaper industry. If Mr Smith, and others like him, earn sufficient money to buy a car, more cars will be produced.

As Mr Smith was aware, effective demand implies an ability to pay. Payments for goods and services are basically financed out of the rewards received by resources for participating in the production process. The nature of these resources has already been discussed, and the analysis has now come full circle.

The pattern of relations that we have discussed above is summarized in Figure 1.1, which is a simple model of a country's economic system. Flow A indicates the resources that are made available to producers in return for various types of reward (flow B). Producers utilize these resources in order to produce goods and services which are supplied (flow C) in exchange for payment (flow D).

## 1.4 Alternative Economic Systems

The economic system described above is a *free market economy*, the most important characteristics of such an economy being (a) that resources are owned by the private sector and not by the government or state, and (b) that these resources are allocated via the price mechanism.

In a fully *planned* or *command* economy, resources are allocated by a centralized administrative process. Decisions as to which goods and services should be produced may be influenced by the planning authorities' perceptions of consumers' desires. But the decisions are likely to be heavily influenced by

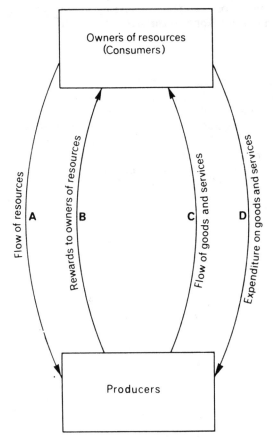

Fig. 1.1 A model of an economic system

the planners' view of what would be beneficial for the community and state as a whole.

To enable the planned output to be produced, the planners must ensure that the required inputs are available. Thus a series of production quotas is established for components and raw materials, as well as for final goods.

Implementation of the plans is very much easier if resources are owned by the state. Consequently, planned economies are characterized by extensive public ownership, as well as by the limited role accorded to the price mechanism. Indeed, in the pure form of the command economy all resources would be publicly owned and the price mechanism would not operate.

Today all economies are *mixed*. Resources are owned part privately and part publicly, and are allocated partly via the price mechanism (modified by government intervention) and partly in accordance with a centralized planning mechanism. But although all mixed economies have both free market and planned elements, these elements are found in very different proportions in different economies. For example, Albania is very close to the planned end of the spectrum and Hong Kong to the free market end.

## 1.5  Summary and Conclusions

In this introductory chapter we have considered the nature of economic resources and shown how these resources are allocated among competing ends. We presented a simple model of an economy, comprising four interlocking flows: of resources, rewards to the owners of resources, goods and services and expenditure on these goods and services. (The various factors influencing these economic flows are discussed in the following chapters.)

This model related to the free market economy, in which resources are owned privately and allocated via the price mechanism. In a planned or command economy resources are owned publicly and allocated by a centralized administrative process. Today all economies are mixed, having free market and planned elements.

## Further Reading

Begg, D., Fischer, S. and Dornbusch, R., *Economics* (London: McGraw-Hill, 2nd Edn, 1987), Ch. 11.

Livesey, F., *A Textbook of Economics* (London: Longman, 3rd Edn, 1989), Chs 2 and 3.

Maunder, P., Myers, D., Wall, N. and Miller, R. L., *Economics Explained* (London: Collins, 1987), Chs. 2 and 4.

## Revision Exercises

1  Economics has been defined as the study of the means by which scarce resources are allocated among competing ends. Does this mean that economics becomes a less important subject as societies become more affluent?

2  Since the total supply of land is virtually fixed, how do you explain the vast increase in the output of food that has occurred in recent years?

3  What are the major factors affecting the supply of labour?

4  Explain how resources are allocated in a mixed economy.

5  What reasons might explain the increase in the relative size of the service sector in recent years?

6  Outline the factors that influence the mobility of factors of production and explain why mobility is important.

7  Why might expenditure on education be considered as a form of capital expenditure?

8  Explain why a change in any of the flows shown in Figure 1.1 would mean that changes would occur in all the other flows.

9  Explain what is meant by the quality of capital, giving examples of recent changes in quality.

10  What are the main features of a free market, planned or command, and a mixed economy?

# 2. The Consumer's Demand

## 2.1 Introduction

The behaviour of consumers, and indeed all human behaviour, is influenced by attitudes, objectives and values – factors that are extremely difficult to measure. Faced with this difficulty, economists normally adopt a deductive approach. Assumptions are made about attitudes and objectives, and conclusions about behaviour are *deduced* from these assumptions. We examine in this chapter two alternative theories of demand based on two alternative sets of assumptions, beginning with the marginal utility theory.

## 2.2 Marginal Utility Theory

This theory postulates that products are bought because of the satisfaction or utility they yield to the purchaser. Central to the theory is the concept of marginal utility, i.e. the utility derived from an additional unit of any product purchased. The *law of diminishing marginal utility* states that the marginal utility of any product declines as the quantity of that product consumed in a given time increases.

As an illustration of the operation of this law let us consider a child's consumption of ice-cream. We assume that a second ice-cream consumed on a given day would yield less utility than the first. A third ice-cream would yield less utility than the second, and so on. For example, the child might value the first ice-cream at 30p, the second at 24p and the third at 18p, as shown in Figure 2.1.

When the child puts a valuation on any product, it takes into account the alternative products on which it might spend its money, and the utility that these products would yield. In fact we assume that the child (or indeed any consumer) wishes to maximize the total utility derived from a given expenditure. In order to achieve this objective the consumer must spend his (or her) money in such a way that the ratio of the marginal utilities derived from the various products that he (or she) buys equals the ratio of the prices of those products. Symbolically this can be expressed as:

$$MU_A/P_A = MU_B/P_B \text{ ---- } = MU_n/P_n$$

where A, B ---- n represents the range of products bought.

To illustrate this point let us assume that a consumer derives utility from different quantities of apples and pears, as shown in Table 2.1. If the apples and pears were the same price, the consumer would maximize her total utility by

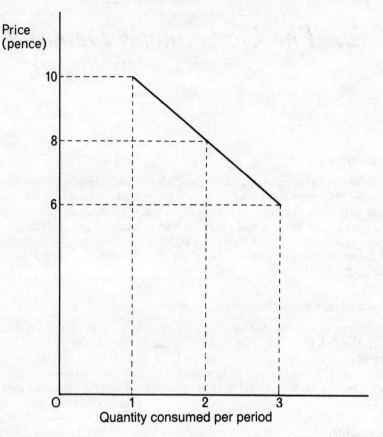

Fig. 2.1 Diminishing marginal utility

buying the same quantity of each. She might, for example, buy 3 kg of apples and 3 kg of pears at a price of 40p a kilo. We would then have:

MU apples/P apples = MU pears/P pears; 50/40 = 50/40

Consider now the situation where apples are twice as expensive as pears, say 50p and 25p respectively. In order to maximize the consumer's utility, her pattern of expenditure should be such that the ratio of the marginal utilities is also 2:1. This requirement would be met by buying either (a) 3 kg of apples and 6 kg of pears, or (b) 1 kg of apples and 3 kg of pears:

(a) 50/50 = 25/25    (b) 100/50 = 50/25

The fact that two alternative combinations satisfy the requirement that the ratio of marginal utilities should equal the ratio of prices indicates that this approach does not enable us to predict exactly how much of a product will be bought at a given price. What it does show is that, given the consumer's utility schedule, the higher the price of a product relative to that of other products, the less of that product will be bought.

*Table 2.1 A Hypothetical Utility Schedule*

| Quantity bought per week (kg) | Apples Total utility (utils) | Marginal utility (utils) | Quantity bought per week (kg) | Pears Total utility (utils) | Marginal utility (utils) |
|---|---|---|---|---|---|
| 1 | 100 | 100 | 1 | 100 | 100 |
| 2 | 175 | 75 | 2 | 175 | 75 |
| 3 | 225 | 50 | 3 | 225 | 50 |
| 4 | 265 | 40 | 4 | 265 | 40 |
| 5 | 300 | 35 | 5 | 300 | 35 |
| 6 | 325 | 25 | 6 | 325 | 25 |

In constructing a demand schedule, or drawing a demand curve, we make the assumption that all factors, other than the price of the product in question, do not change. In this instance, if we wished to construct a demand schedule for apples, we would assume that the price of pears remained constant, and vice versa.

One of the advantages of the marginal utility approach is that it helps to explain why products of an identical nature may command very different prices in different circumstances. The classic, if rather unreal, example is the valuation that would be put upon a glass of water by a man who was dying of thirst in the desert compared to one who was in danger of drowning. More realistic, if less dramatic, examples are presented in the exercises below.

The marginal utility approach also has the advantage of simplicity. On the other hand, it has some fairly obvious deficiencies. One is that it is difficult to envisage a consumer being able to weigh up the relative ratios of price to marginal utility for products having very different prices, e.g. 1 kg of apples and a car. An even more fundamental deficiency is the assumption that a consumer can give an *absolute* value to the utility derived from any product, i.e. not only can he say that he would derive more utility from 1 kg of peas than 1 kg of carrots, but he can place a precise value on the difference between the two.

The unrealistic nature of this assumption (i.e. that consumers are able to apply a *cardinal measure of utility*) is one of the reasons why an alternative theory, involving indifference analysis, was developed.

## 2.3 Indifference Curve Analysis

This approach is based on the supposition that it would be possible by experimentation to discover a consumer's valuation of various combinations of products. It is not necessary that consumers should be able to measure utility cardinally. Provided that they know they prefer one combination of goods to another (i.e. that they can measure utility *ordinally*), useful conclusions can be inferred about their behaviour.

In Figure 2.2 we have an indifference curve, I, which indicates the various combinations of apples and pears that would give the consumer identical total satisfaction or utility. Note that although it is claimed that the indifference curve can in principle be derived by experimentation, in practice it is based upon the assumption that the less the consumer has of a product, the less of that product he will be willing to give up in exchange for a given amount of any other product. (Technically we say that the *marginal rate of substitution* of product R for product S changes according to the amount of product R the consumer has.) This assumption accounts for the shape of the indifference curve; it is convex to the origin.

So in Figure 2.2, when the consumer is at Y, he is willing to give up 2 kg of pears (YZ) in order to obtain 1 kg of apples (ZX). (Remember that points Y and X represent combinations yielding identical total utilities, since they are on the same indifference curve.) But when the consumer is at B, he is willing to give up only 1 kg of pears (BC) in order to obtain an additional 1 kg of apples (CA).

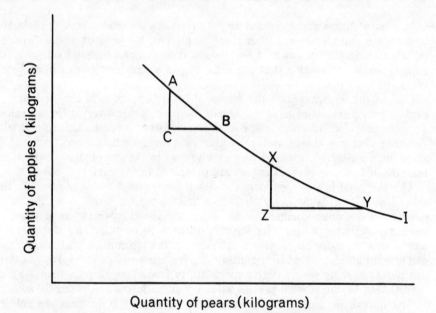

Fig. 2.2 Indifference curve

### 2.31 *The Budget Constraint*

In order to show the effect on quantity demanded of a change in price we introduce the concept of the budget constraint, i.e. we take account of the fact that the consumer's income is limited. Figure 2.3 shows that the consumer could buy any combination of apples and pears lying on the budget line AB.

The three indifference curves represent positions of successively greater total utility. The highest utility would be derived from any combination of apples and pears lying on $I_3$. However the consumer's income does not, of course, allow him to attain any of these combinations. The highest utility that he can obtain is at point X on $I_2$, which represents a combination of OD of apples and OE of pears.

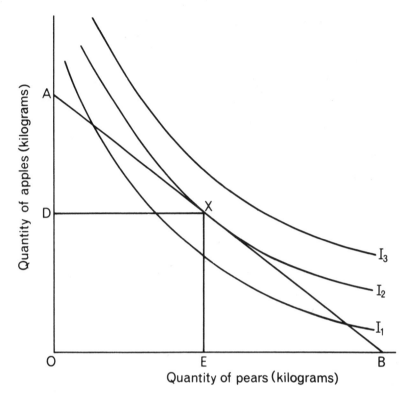

Fig. 2.3 The effect of a budget constraint

In Figure 2.4, with an initial budget line AB, the highest level of satisfaction that the consumer can attain is point X on indifference curve $I_1$. The price of pears is then halved, i.e. he can buy twice as many pears, $B^1$ as compared to B, from his given income. He is now able to attain a higher level of satisfaction $Y_1$ where his new budget line, $AB^1$, is tangential to indifference curve $I_2$. His consumption of pears has increased from OE to $OE^1$.

### 2.32 *Income and Substitution Effects*

Two factors combine to cause the price effect shown in Figure 2.4. First the consumer's *real* income has risen because of the fall in the price of pears. (The greater the proportion of spending accounted for by a product, the greater will be the change in real income following a given price change.) The effect of a change in real income is shown in Figure 2.5.

As income increases, the budget line shifts from AB to $A^1B^1$. The consumer moves from a point of equilibrium X, on indifference curve $I_1$, to Y on $I_2$. His consumption of apples increases from OD to $OD^1$, and of pears from OE to $OE^1$. This change in consumption indicates the income effect.

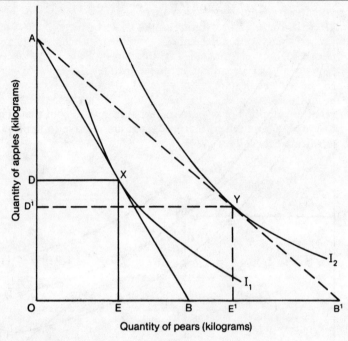

Fig. 2.4 Price change and budget constraint

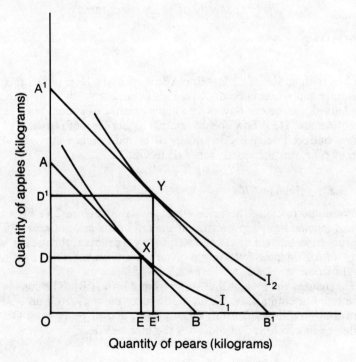

Fig. 2.5 The income effect

In order to demonstrate the substitution effect of a price change we cancel out the income effect. In Figure 2.6, with the initial budget line AB, the consumer is in equilibrium at X on indifference curve $I_1$. Following the fall in the price of pears, the budget line swivels to $AB^1$. The line RS indicates the choices that would have been open to the consumer at the new ratio of prices between apples and pears, had real income been maintained at its initial level. (Note that X and Y are both on indifference curve $I_1$.) In this situation, as the consumer moves from X to Y, the consumption of pears rises from OE to $OE^1$, but that of apples falls from OD to $OD^1$. The fall in the price of pears relative to apples causes pears to be substituted for apples.

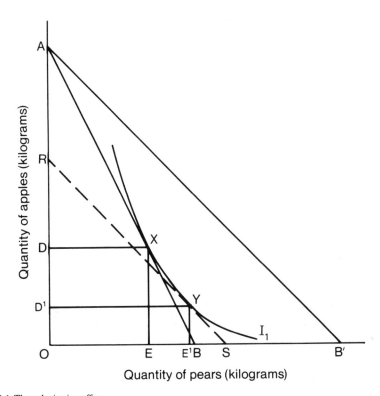

Fig. 2.6 The substitution effect

Figure 2.7 shows the overall effect of a price change. As before a fall in the price of pears causes the budget line to swivel from AB to $AB^1$. The substitution effect moves the consumer from X to Y on $I_1$. The income effect moves him from Y to Z on $I_2$. Both the income and the substitution effects cause an increase in the consumption of pears. This is the usual consequence of a fall in price. The quantity purchased would fall only if the substitution effect was outweighed by a *negative* income effect.

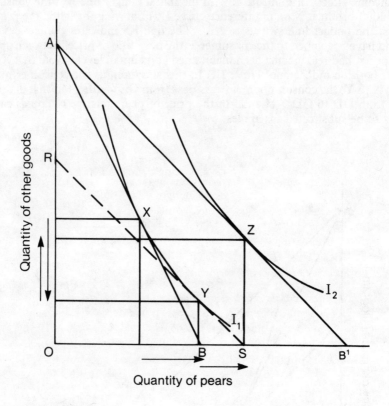

Fig. 2.7 Income and substitution effects

In Figure 2.7 we have made the analysis more general by measuring purchases of all goods other than pears on the vertical axis. It can be seen that the substitution effect causes a reduction in the consumption of other goods, but that the income effect causes an increase in their consumption. In the situation illustrated here the substitution effect outweighs the income effect, the overall effect being a reduction in consumption. In other instances the income effect may outweigh the substitution effect, causing an increase in consumption.

## 2.4 Summary and Conclusions

In this chapter we have shown that two alternative approaches to consumer behaviour both lead to the conclusion that an individual's demand for a given product usually varies inversely to its price, i.e. his demand curve slopes down from left to right. In the next chapter we use these individual demand curves to derive total or market demand curves.

**Further Reading**

Begg, D., Fischer, S. and Dornbusch R., *Economics* (London: McGraw-Hill, 2nd Edn, 1987), Ch. 5.
Lipsey, R. G. and Harbury, C., *First Principles of Economics* (London: Weidenfeld and Nicolson, 1988), Chs 11 and 12.
Livesey, F., *A Textbook of Economics* (London: Longman, 3rd Edn, 1989), Ch. 4.
Maunder, P., Myers, D., Wall, N. and Miller P. L., *Economics Explained* (London: Collins, 1987), Ch. 21.

**Revision Exercises**

1 Why has more than one theory of demand been advanced?
2 State and comment on the assumptions on which the marginal utility theory is based.
3 State and explain the pattern of expenditure that is required for a consumer to maximize his utility.
4 'Neither the marginal utility approach nor indifference analysis provides a satisfactory theory since both are based on concepts that cannot be identified and measured.' Discuss.
5 State what is shown by an indifference curve and explain why it is assumed that indifference curves are normally convex to the origin.
6 What do you understand by the term 'budget line'? What factors would result in (a) a change in the slope of the line, and (b) a change in the position of the line, the slope remaining unchanged?
7 Explain the statement that the consequences of a price change will depend upon the relative strength of the income and substitution effects.
8 Explain why indifference curves cannot cross.
9 Given the total utility schedules shown in Table 2.2, answer the following questions.

*Table 2.2*

| Meat | | Bread | |
|---|---|---|---|
| Quantity consumed per week (kg) | Total utility | Quantity consumed per week (kg) | Total utility |
| 1 | 100 | 1 | 40 |
| 2 | 180 | 2 | 65 |
| 3 | 240 | 3 | 75 |
| 4 | 280 | 4 | 80 |
| 5 | 300 | 5 | 82 |
| 6 | 310 | 6 | 83 |
| 7 | 308 | 7 | 82 |

(a) What combination of meat and bread could maximize the consumer's satisfaction from a given level of expenditure if 1 kg of meat cost as much as 1 kg of bread?

(b) What (two) combinations of meat and bread could maximize the consumer's satisfaction from a given level of expenditure if meat cost twice as much per kilo as bread?

(c) How much meat and bread would be consumed per week if both products were free?

10 Draw the total and marginal utility curves which you think would represent the change in satisfaction obtained by a family from different numbers of television sets. Explain briefly the shapes of the two curves and the relation between them.

# 3. Market Demand

## 3.1 Introduction

We presented in the previous chapter a justification for the view that the quantity of a product demanded by an individual consumer will normally vary inversely to the product's price. By a simple extension of this argument we can show that the total quantity of a product demanded will also normally be inversely related to its price.

*Table 3.1  A Hypothetical Demand Schedule*

| Price | Quantity demanded by: | | | Total quantity demanded |
| | Tom | Dick | Harry | |
|---|---|---|---|---|
| 1 | 10 | 8 | 6 | 24 |
| 2 | 8 | 6 | 4 | 18 |
| 3 | 6 | 4 | 2 | 12 |
| 4 | 4 | 2 | 0 | 6 |

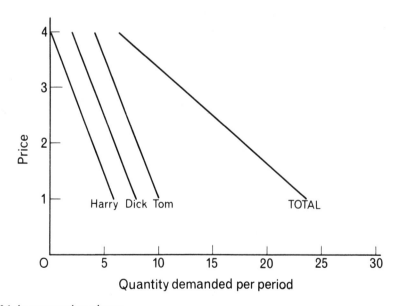

Fig. 3.1 An aggregate demand curve

17

Table 3.1 shows the quantity demanded of a hypothetical product by three consumers. The relation between price and total quantity demanded can also be expressed by means of a demand curve (Figure 3.1).

## 3.2 Elasticity of Demand

The price elasticity of demand (PED) is defined as:

$$\frac{\text{The percentage change in quantity demanded}}{\text{The percentage change in price}}$$

Algebraically, this is written

$$PED = \frac{d_q}{Q} \div \frac{d_p}{P}$$

where Q and P are the initial quantity demanded and price, and $d_q$ and $d_p$ are changes from these initial levels.

We can illustrate this formula by reference to the hypothetical demand schedule presented in Table 3.2. When price is reduced from 100 to 90, the quantity demanded rises from 200 to 240. Thus

$$PED = \frac{40}{200} \div \frac{-10}{100}$$

$$= 0{\cdot}2 \div -0{\cdot}1$$

$$= (-)\,2{\cdot}0$$

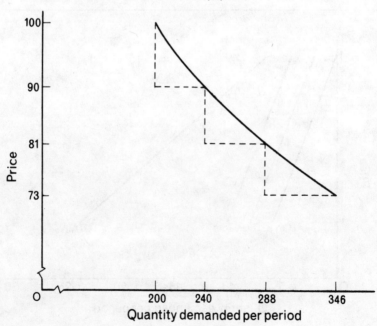

Fig. 3.2 Demand curve illustrating Table 3.2

*Table 3.2 Demand Schedule for Product X*

| Price | Quantity demanded |
|-------|-------------------|
| 100 | 200 |
| 90 | 240 |
| 81 | 288 |
| 73 | 346 |

The elasticity of demand is (negative) two. As we have seen, price and quantity demanded are usually inversely related, i.e. elasticity of demand is usually negative. Economists often adopt the convention of omitting the word 'negative' and the negative sign. We have included the negative in brackets in the above example, but hereafter we shall follow the usual convention and omit the negative.

In the above example we have used demand changes of 10 per cent. In fact, in order to obtain a precise measure of elasticity at any point, e.g. at a price of 100, we should specify a very small change in price. The choice of a relatively large change here can be justified on the ground that it makes the arithmetic (and the geometry of the accompanying diagram) easier to follow.

As price is reduced further, to 81 and to 73, in each case the elasticity is two. We have, therefore, a situation of constant price elasticity.

The demand curve derived from Table 3.2 is presented in Figure 3.2. It can be seen that when elasticity of demand is constant, the gradient of the demand curve differs at different points. The demand curve in Figure 3.3, a rectangular hyperbola, is of unitary elasticity (PED = 1) throughout its length. A change in price causes an identical percentage change in quantity demanded, so that revenue is the same whatever the price.

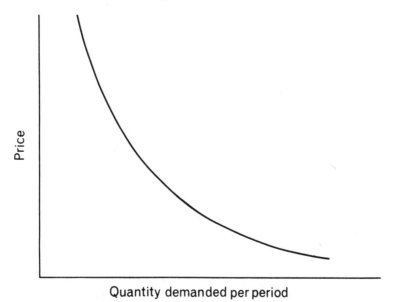

Quantity demanded per period

Fig. 3.3 Demand curve of unitary elasticity

### 3.21 *Straight-line Demand Curves*

Let us now briefly examine a demand curve of a different shape, namely a straight line (Figure 3.4). It can be seen that at all points a reduction in price of ten leads to an increase in the quantity demanded of twenty. But note that this change in price represents a fall of 10 per cent when the initial price is 100 but of 11 per cent when the initial price is 90. Similarly the change in quantity demanded represents an increase of 20 per cent from an initial demand of 100 but of 16·7 per cent from an initial demand of 120. As we have seen, demand elasticity is calculated from percentage, not absolute, changes, and so it is clear that the elasticity of a straight-line demand curve (except in the extreme cases of zero and of infinite elasticity) will be different at every point on that curve. More precisely, the elasticity will fall as one moves down the curve from left to right.

It will be useful to note for future reference that when we talk about a demand curve having a certain elasticity we are again using a form of shorthand. Strictly speaking, a particular value for elasticity can be attached only to a particular point on the curve (unless, of course, the curve is of constant elasticity).

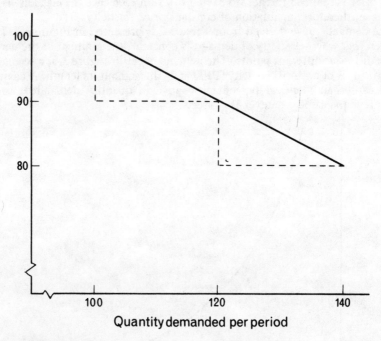

Fig. 3.4 Straight-line demand curve

### 3.22 *Elasticity of Demand: Summary*

When PED is one, we call this a situation of unit (or unitary) elastic demand. When PED is greater than one, we say that demand is elastic. When PED is less than one, we say that demand is inelastic. Note that even when demand is inelastic, the quantity demanded will change with a change in price, except in the limiting case where PED is zero. When PED is zero (i.e. when the same quantity is demanded at all prices) we say that demand is perfectly, or completely, inelastic.

### 3.23 *The Determinants of Elasticity*

Several factors influence the price elasticity of demand.

### 3.231 *Substitution*

The value of PED is strongly influenced by the existence and price of substitutes, *as perceived by the purchaser*. In general, we can say that the less willing or able purchasers are to substitute one product for another, the lower will be the PED. The classic example of a product with an inelastic demand is salt, for which no close substitute exists. On the other hand, the demand for peas is likely to be elastic because of the existence of close substitutes such as beans.

### 3.232 *The Classification of Products*

The value of PED is affected by the way we group or classify products. For example, if we considered food as a whole we would find the PED would be low; if the price of food increased relative to all other goods and services there would be a relatively small change in the quantity demanded since people must continue to eat. On the other hand, if we considered one type of food, say meat, we would find that demand was more elastic, as people could respond to a change in its relative price by switching consumption to or from substitutes such as fish, cheese and eggs. If we went on to consider one type of meat, say beef, demand would be even more elastic because purchasers now have the opportunity of substituting not only fish, etc., but also other types of meat. Finally, note that if only one producer of beef changed his price and other producers maintained their prices, elasticity would be very high indeed.

### 3.233 *The Price Level*

Elasticity may differ at different prices, i.e. at different points on the demand curve. For example, it is known that consumers are particularly prone to switch from butter to margarine when the price differential between the two reaches a certain level.

### 3.234 *The Importance of Time*

The value of PED may change over time. Sometimes purchasers react very sharply to a sudden price change, e.g. an increase in the price of cigarettes following a tax increase at budget time, but then slowly resume their former habits and purchasing patterns. On the other hand, the impact of a price change is frequently greater the longer the time period concerned. There are several reasons for this.

First, purchasers have more time to identify substitutes (this obviously applies following a price increase). Second, there may be technical obstacles to substitution that need time to overcome, e.g. when the price of oil rose it took time before purchasers could convert their equipment to use other fuels. Finally, the availability of substitutes may increase over time as producers respond to the increased demand from purchasers.

### 3.24 *Backward Sloping Demand Curves*

In some instances the quantity demanded rises as price rises, and falls as price falls, at least over a certain range of prices (Figure 3.5). There are several reasons why this may occur. First, a Giffen good is one for which the income effect is negative, and sufficiently strong to outweigh the substitution effect. Sir Robert Giffen was said to have observed in the nineteenth century that when the price of a product rose, its consumption by certain groups in society increased. The product in question is said by some writers to have been bread, and by others potatoes. In fact, it now seems unlikely that the alleged observation actually occurred. Nevertheless, the term Giffen good has been retained.

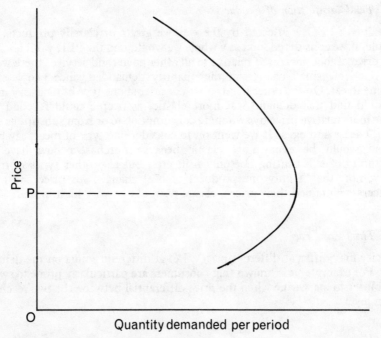

Fig. 3.5 A demand curve with a backward sloping segment

Two other groups of products which have sometimes been found to have a demand curve with an upward sloping portion are those whose price is taken by consumers as an indicator of the product's quality, and those which are bought for the purpose of conspicuous consumption, e.g. diamonds. In these instances the shape of the demand curve can be explained by a substitution effect different from usual. A lower price would now make consumers disposed to buy less of this product and more of substitute products. If this negative substitution effect is sufficiently strong to outweigh any positive income effect, consumption of that product will fall as its price is reduced.

## 3.3 The Conditions of Demand

Price is only one of the determinants of demand, and it is now time to examine the effects of other influences (i.e. to consider what happens when the conditions of demand change). We begin by examining the influence of income.

### 3.31 *Income as a Determinant of Demand*

As a community's real income increases, the demand for most products increases. However, the effect will vary considerably from product to product for several reasons. Especially important is the initial level of income. If the community's (or national) income is very low, increases will largely be used to increase the consumption of basic necessities, such as foodstuffs, housing and clothing. At higher initial levels, the demand for these basic necessities having been met to a greater extent, a greater proportion of the increase in income will be used for the purchase of consumer durables – cars, washing machines, etc. At still higher levels increases in income are reflected especially strongly in a greater demand for leisure goods and activities – sports equipment, foreign holidays, etc.

There are some exceptions to the rule that demand and income are related positively. It appears that the demand for many staple foodstuffs, such as bread and potatoes, falls as a nation becomes richer. Goods for which demand falls as income increases (or for which demand increases as income falls) are known as *inferior goods*.

### 3.311 *The Income Elasticity of Demand*

The response of demand to a change in income is measured by the income elasticity of demand (IED), which is defined as

$$\frac{\text{The percentage change in quantity demanded}}{\text{The percentage change in income}}$$

Although the quantity demanded of most products increases as income increases, i.e. IED is normally positive, there are some products for which, at least over certain time periods, income elasticity appears to have been negative, as noted in the previous section.

The demand for some products may be influenced more by changes in the incomes of certain segments of the population than by a change in the total national income or in the average income per head. In the U.K., for instance, the demand for private education may be particularly sensitive to changes in the incomes of the higher income groups. On the other hand, the demand for cigarettes may be particularly sensitive to changes in the incomes of poorer members of the community.

The different paths that demand may follow as income changes are illustrated in Figure 3.6. Until income reaches A, demand increases faster than income. (Income elasticity of demand is more than one.) Within the range of incomes A–B demand and income increase at the same rate. (Elasticity is one or unity.) Within the income range B–C demand continues to increase, but less quickly than income. (Elasticity is less than one but still positive.) So long as elasticity is positive, the product is said to be a *normal good*.

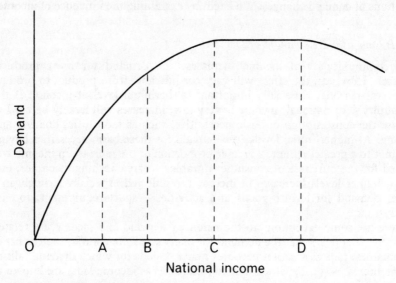

Fig. 3.6 Change of demand with income

Within the income range C–D no change in demand occurs. (Elasticity is zero.) Finally, as income rises above D, demand falls. Elasticity is now negative; the product has become an *inferior good*.

### 3.312 *The Impact of Taxation*

Changes in tax rates and in the structure of taxation affect the level and pattern of demand. An increase in the rate of income tax would reduce disposable income; a reduction in the rate of income tax would increase disposable income. The effect on the demand for particular products will, of course, depend upon their income elasticity of demand.

Changes in tax structure often have marked effects on particular groups of tax payers. For example an increase in personal allowances would affect all taxpayers but would be especially important for any low income earners who would cease to pay tax. Since low income earners usually spend a high proportion of their income on necessities, there would be an increase in the demand for these goods. On the other hand a reduction in the highest rates of taxation would affect only the higher income earners and hence might be expected to cause an increase in demand for luxury products. This might also happen following a reduction in capital gains tax or inheritance tax. A change in corporation tax, levied on the earnings of companies, is likely to affect the demand for investment goods – machines, components etc.

### 3.313 *A Shift of the Demand Curve*

As we said previously, we assume when we draw a demand curve that income is given. A change in income is reflected in a shift of the demand curve. So in **Figure 3.7** we have three demand curves representing different levels of income. If we start with curve M (medium income), we see that a move to a higher level of income would cause the curve to shift to the right (H), indicating that more would be bought at every price than previously. A reduction in income would cause the curve to shift to the left (L).

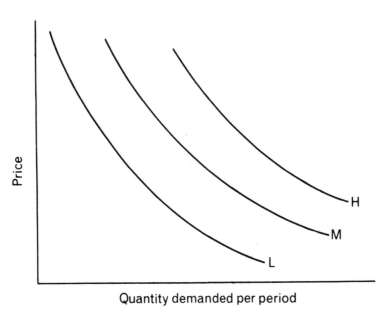

Fig. 3.7 Demand curves for different levels of income

### 3.32 *Other Changes in the Conditions of Demand*

### 3.321 *Changes in Population*

A change in population has two effects on demand. First, it influences the total level of demand, since a change in population will lead to a change in real income. (We are making the reasonable assumption here that changes in population are at least partly reflected in changes in employment, income and output.) Second, a change in population is likely to result in a change in the pattern of demand. An increase in the birth rate will lead to an increase in the demand at first for baby food and clothes and subsequently for educational facilities, transistor radios, etc. Similarly, a fall in the death rate might be expected to lead to an increase in the demand for walking sticks, hearing aids, etc.

### 3.322 *Changes in Tastes*

Changes in demand often follow from changes in tastes, which are themselves often partially the result of various other factors – changes in income, advertising, etc. Changes in tastes have had substantial effects on the demand for certain products, such as clothes (mini-skirt versus maxi), foodstuffs (health foods), etc.

### 3.323 *The Introduction of New Products: Substitution*

The introduction of new products sometimes leads to dramatic shifts in the pattern of demand, as consumers substitute the new for existing products. Examples include the development of synthetic fibres such as nylon and terylene, which has reduced the demand for natural fibres, especially cotton; the introduction of television, which has led to a substantial decline in the number of cinema admissions (against the generally favourable trend in the demand for leisure activities); and the introduction of small motor-cycles and scooters, which has contributed to the decline in the demand for bicycles. The demand for a product will fall if the price of an existing substitute falls, and will rise if the price of a substitute rises. The responsiveness of demand is measured by the cross (price) elasticity of demand (CED).

$$CED = \frac{dQ_A}{Q_A} \div \frac{dP_B}{P_B}$$

where Q and P denote quantity demanded and price, d denotes a small change in these variables, and A and B are two products. When two products are substitutes, CED is positive; the more easily one product can be substituted for another, the higher is the value of CED.

### 3.324 *Complementarity*

Whereas with substitution an increased demand for one product implies a reduction in the demand for another product, complementarity implies that the demand for two products will change in the same direction. So the development of television has contributed to an increased demand for ready-prepared instant meals, for trays on which to eat the meals, and for napkins to use with the meals. (These trends are probably more in evidence in the U.S.A. and various continental countries than in the U.K.) As the demand for cars has increased, so too has the demand for petrol.

Changes in the demand for consumer goods will be reflected in changes in the demand for capital goods, except those rare instances where the new consumer goods are produced on the same machines as the goods for which they are substituted. Incidentally, the same point applies when some capital goods (machines) are used in the manufacture of other capital goods.

The effect on the pattern of demand for capital goods will usually be quite modest, since much of the activity of the capital-goods sector is devoted to the production of machines to replace similar machines that wear out. In some instances, however, the effect may be quite significant. The increasing use of oil led to an upsurge in the orders for oil-tankers, which represented a substantial increase in the total demand for ships. At the other end of the spectrum the fall in the demand for British cotton textiles led to the decline and demise of numerous manufacturers of cotton textile machinery.

The demand for a product will fall if the price of an existing complementary good rises, causing a fall in the quantity of that good demanded. Conversely, a fall in the price of a product will normally lead to an increased demand for complementary products. This relationship can again be measured in terms of the cross elasticity of demand. For complementary products CED is always negative.

### 3.325 *Advertising*

An effective advertising campaign will increase the demand for a product, i.e. cause the demand curve to shift to the right. Conversely an effective advertising campaign for a substitute will cause the demand curve to shift to the left.

## 3.4 Summary and Conclusions

Market demand normally varies inversely to price, i.e. the demand curve slopes down from left to right. However in some instances – where price is seen as an indicator of quality, where products are purchased for conspicuous consumption, or where a negative income effect outweighs the substitution effect (Giffen goods) – the demand curve has a backward sloping portion.

When drawing a demand curve we assume that all factors other than the price of the product are given. Changes in these other factors – income, population, tastes, the price and availability of substitutes and complements, advertising – cause demand to change. An increase in demand is represented by a shift of the demand curve to the right, a decrease in demand by a shift of the demand curve to the left.

The responsiveness of quantity demanded to a change in price is measured by the price elasticity of demand. The responsiveness of demand to a change in income is measured by the income inelasticity of demand.

## Further Reading

Begg, D., Fischer, S. and Dornbusch, R. *Economics* (London: McGraw-Hill, 2nd Edn, 1987), Chs 3 and 4.

Lipsey, R. G. and Harbury, C., *First Principles of Economics* (London: Weidenfeld and Nicolson, 1988), Ch. 5.
Livesey, F., *A Textbook of Economics* (London: Longman, 3rd Edn, 1989), Ch. 4.
Maunder, P., Myers, D., Wall, N. and Miller, R. L., *Economics Explained* (London: Collins, 1987), Ch. 5.

## Revision Exercises

1 Define price elasticity of demand and explain why a knowledge of its numerical value may be very useful.
2 Draw a series of demand curves illustrating (a) a situation of elastic demand; (b) a situation of inelastic demand; (c) a situation of unitary elastic demand; (d) the Giffen effect.
3 Define income elasticity of demand and explain why firms might find it useful to be able to estimate its numerical value for a number of different products.
4 Discuss the major factors that are likely to bring about a change in the demand for (a) any good you wish to choose; (b) any service you wish to choose.
5 In what circumstances might an increase in the price of a product lead to an increase in the quantity demanded?
6 Why do demand curves normally slope downwards from left to right?
7 How would you expect a substantial increase in national income in the U.K. to affect the demand for video recorders, holidays taken in the U.K., passenger railway travel, meals taken in restaurants, cinema seats, fashionable clothes?
8 Why should producers, in planning their activities, take account of substitutability and complementarity?
9 Discuss the likely effects of the discovery of a substitute for tobacco that was not injurious to health.
10 Discuss the effect on demand of the introduction of cheap micro-computers.

## Objective Test Questions: Set No. 1

Each of the following questions has four possible answers. For each question select what you consider to be the best option – A, B, C or D. The correct answers will be found on p. 274.

1 Economic resources are usually defined to include all the following except

A money
B land
C labour
D capital

2 The working population is defined to include

A full-time housewives
B full-time students
C retired people
D the unemployed

3 The size of the working population would be likely to change if a change occurred in

1  the size of the total population
2  the age distribution of the population
3  the sex distribution of the population

A  1, 2 and 3
B  1 and 2 only
C  1 and 3 only
D  2 and 3 only

4 Which of the following statements relating to the immigration of workers is correct?

A  Immigration is beneficial only if the immigrants have special skills
B  Immigration is beneficial if resources other than labour are in excess supply and there is an excess demand for goods
C  Immigration can never be economically beneficial
D  Immigration is always economically beneficial

5 Collective consumption usually indicates that

A  the product concerned is in short supply
B  the government does not wish individual consumers to own the product
C  effective demand for the product from private sources is considered to be too low
D  there is a fully planned economy in operation

6 To which of the following products does collective consumption apply in the U.K.?

1  Roads
2  The fire service
3  Postal services

A  1, 2 and 3
B  1 and 2 only
C  1 and 3 only
D  2 and 3 only

7 If an increase in demand for eggs resulted in a reduction in the demand for bacon we could conclude that

A  bacon was an inferior product
B  bacon and eggs were complementary products
C  bacon and eggs were substitute products
D  bacon was a normal product

8 A demand schedule for a product is constructed on the assumption that all of the following remain constant except

A  consumers' money income
B  consumers' tastes
C  the price of other products
D  the price of the product

9 Which of the following statements applies to the demand curve, Figure 1?

   A  It is of unitary elasticity
   B  It is of constant elasticity
   C  Its elasticity falls as one moves from A to B
   D  Its elasticity falls as one moves from B to A

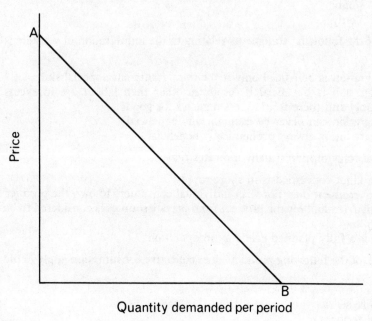

Fig. 1

Questions 10 and 11 are based on the following incomplete quotation:
'Economics is the study of the (1) of scarce resources among (2) ends.'
Taking the two blanks in the order indicated by the numbers in brackets,
indicate which of the words listed below would best fit into the blanks, and
thus complete the quotation.

10 A  Utilization
   B  Organization
   C  Allocation
   D  Pricing

11 A  Limited
   B  Competing
   C  Different
   D  Private

Questions 12 to 14 are based on the four states of price elasticity of demand:

A  perfectly inelastic demand
B  inelastic demand
C  unitary elastic demand
D  elastic demand

Which of the above terms best describes each of the following situations? (Each term may apply once, more than once, or not at all.)

12  After a reduction in price, a greater quantity of the commodity is bought, but total expenditure on the commodity falls.

   A   B   C   D

13  After an increase in price, a smaller quantity of the commodity is bought, but total expenditure on the commodity remains unchanged.

   A   B   C   D

14  After the price of bread falls by 10 per cent, the total expenditure on bread falls by 10 per cent.

   A   B   C   D

15  Consumption of a free good will be carried to the point at which

   A  the total utility derived from the good equals the total utility derived from all other goods
   B  the marginal utility derived from the good equals the marginal utilities derived from all other goods
   C  the total utility derived from the good is at a maximum
   D  the marginal utility derived from the good begins to decline

16  A consumer will maximize his total utility when

   A  the marginal utility derived from each product consumed exceeds its price
   B  the marginal utilities derived from each product consumed are proportional to their prices
   C  the marginal utility derived from each product consumed is equal
   D  the marginal utility derived from each product begins to decline.

17  Question 17 is based on Figure 2, in which $I_1$ and $I_2$ are a consumer's indifference curves and AB is his budget line. Which of the following statements is/are true?

   1  At his present level of income the consumer could not buy the combination of products represented by point Z
   2  At his present level of income the consumer could afford to buy more of both products than the combination represented by point Y
   3  The combination of products represented by point X would yield greater satisfaction than that represented by point Y

A  1 and 2 only
B  2 and 3 only
C  1 only
D  3 only

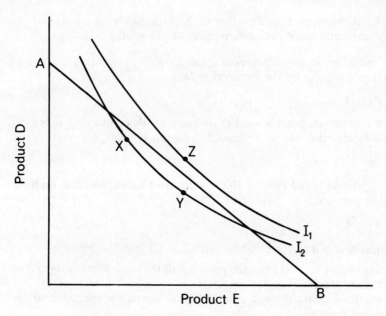

Product D

Product E

$I_1$

$I_2$

A

X

Z

Y

B

Fig. 2

18  A boy with £2 to spend while on a visit to the seaside buys three ice-creams
    at 30p each, keeping £1.10 to spend on other things. Given that he behaves
    rationally, we can conclude that the
    1  total utility from the consumption of ice-cream was at least 90p
    2  utility that he would have obtained from a fourth ice-cream would have
       been less than that derived from the third
    3  total utility derived from four ice-creams would have been less than that
       derived from three ice-creams

    A  1, 2 and 3
    B  1 and 2 only
    C  2 and 3 only
    D  1 and 3 only

19  Three goods have the following income elasticities of demand:

    X: −0.5   Y: 0.0   Z: +0.5

    During a given time period expenditure on each of the three goods was
    identical. If income was then increased by 1 per cent, you would expect that
    in the following time period

1 expenditure on Y would fall by 1 per cent
2 total expenditure on the three goods combined would remain unchanged
3 expenditure on X would fall by 0.5 per cent

A  1, 2 and 3
B  1 and 2 only
C  2 and 3 only
D  1 and 3 only

20  A housewife enters a shop intending to buy twelve oranges at 10p each. She finds that the price has risen to 12p, however, and decides to buy only nine. This situation would be represented graphically by means of

A  a movement along her demand curve
B  a decrease in the elasticity of her demand curve
C  an upward shift of her demand curve
D  a downward shift of her demand curve

# 4. Costs and Production

## 4.1 Introduction

Having examined the various factors influencing consumers' demands, we now consider the factors influencing the willingness and ability of producers to meet these demands.

We pointed out in Chapter 1 that the satisfaction of demand necessitates the transformation of sets of resources, or factors of production, into outputs of goods and services. We have not yet discussed the factors that influence the costs of this transformation process, the costs of production. We begin by considering how costs are affected by changes in the level of output, at a given scale of organization or capacity.

## 4.2 The Behaviour of Costs as Output Changes, at a Given Scale of Organization

### 4.21 *The Scale of Organization*

The scale of organization refers to the effective output of the firm, i.e. the maximum output during a standard or customary length of week (e.g. two 40-hour shifts), with an allowance for normal delays. The maximum output is determined partly by the capital input (in manufacturing, the number of machines installed and the technical capacity of each machine) and partly by the labour input (the number of hours a week for which labour can be found to operate these machines). It is usually less than the maximum output that would be technically feasible if all machines could be operated for a full 168-hour week.

If, in a given period of time, either the capital or the labour input cannot be varied we say that the scale of organization is given, or fixed. For the sake of simplicity we take the capital input to include land, although these two factors were discussed separately in Chapter 1. It is usually more difficult to change the capital than the labour input – for example, it will generally take longer to build a new factory or install new equipment than to recruit and train additional labour. However, this is not always the case. Examples can be found of firms that have spare capacity in machines and buildings but whose effective output is limited by the inability to recruit additional skilled labour.

Many firms choose a scale that is greater than the expected *average* level of output over the planning period. If the demand from regular customers turns out to be higher than expected and the firm does not have sufficient capacity to meet the additional demand, it may lose some customers, perhaps permanently, to rival suppliers.

Conversely, the firm with the capacity to cope with peak demands may expect to gain customers from rival suppliers whose capacity is inadequate at such times. This is especially important in markets where there are no important physical differences between the products of rival suppliers, and where the ability to give a quicker service is a way of increasing market share.

### 4.22 *Fixed Costs*

The average cost of fixed inputs per unit of output will fall as the level of output increases, since the fixed cost is being spread over a greater output (Figure 4.1). Average fixed cost continues to fall beyond E (the expected level of output) to L (the maximum effective output). An increase in output beyond L would require the scale of organization to be increased, by means of an increase in the quantity of the limiting input, here buildings, plant and equipment. This increase in scale would lead to an increase in average fixed costs, as shown by the dotted line.

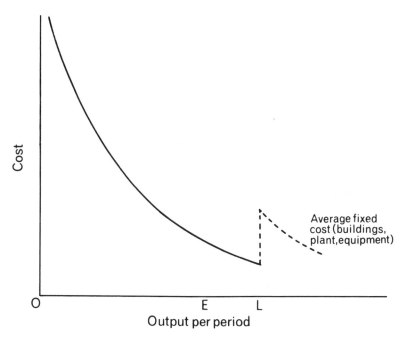

Fig. 4.1 Fixed costs

### 4.23 *Variable Costs*

Variable costs arise from the employment of inputs whose quantities are varied in accordance with the level of output, even when the scale of organization is given. The most important of these inputs are direct materials and direct labour.

### 4.231 *Direct Materials*

The quantity of direct materials used per unit of output is largely determined by technical specifications. It may be that at particularly high levels of output the quantity of materials used per unit of output will increase because of higher scrap rates. On the other hand, a higher level of output may enable the firm to increase its buying quantities and thus obtain more favourable terms. These two factors will therefore tend to cancel each other out, and we can say that as a general rule direct material costs will be constant per unit of output, whatever the level of output (Figure 4.2).

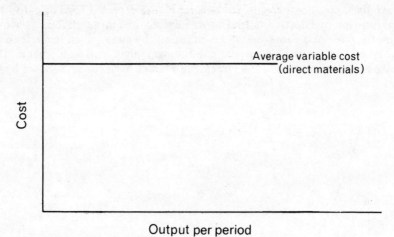

Fig. 4.2 Direct material costs

### 4.232 *Direct Labour*

The amount of direct labour employed will again vary with the level of output. However, the relation will not usually be as close as with direct materials, since it is difficult to hire and fire workers so as to keep employment exactly in step with output.

### 4.24 *Fixed, Variable, and Semi-variable Costs*

In practice there are many semi-variable inputs, e.g. indirect labour, indirect materials, sales expenses, etc., but we shall classify all costs as fixed or variable in order to simplify the analysis. In that way we can demonstrate in a single diagram the behaviour of costs as output changes. As can be seen in Figure 4.3 when output increases, average (total) cost falls until the expected level of output E is achieved. Beyond that point, while average fixed cost (AFC) continues to fall, average variable cost (AVC) has a tendency to rise, so that average (total) cost (ATC) is roughly constant up to L, the point at which the maximum effective output is produced. For ease of presentation the curves in Figure 4.3 have been smoothed. In practice, as we have shown, costs will change less smoothly than this.

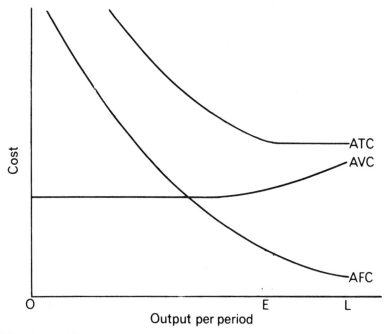

Fig. 4.3 Cost changes with output

## 4.3 The Behaviour of Costs, Changing Scale of Organization

### 4.31 *Economies of Scale*

The various factors that may lead to a fall in average cost as the scale of organization increases are known as economies of scale. These scale economies can be very substantial. For example, it has been estimated that at an annual output of 2 million cars, average cost is only two-thirds of that at an output of 100,000. Scale economies can be grouped into several broad categories.

### 4.311 *Technical Economies*

When cost depends upon area and output on volume, as in gas storage, cost per unit of output falls with increased scale. More efficient technology may become economically feasible when the level of output is sufficiently large. A simple example is the automatic weaving loom, where the recharging of the shuttle, previously performed by hand, is performed by machine. A bigger advance in technology was represented by the introduction of the continuous strip-mill in steel and in plate-glass manufacture.

Firms that keep spare machinery and parts in case of breakdown, and stockpile raw materials, find that the necessary 'reserves' increase less than proportionately to output or capacity.

### 4.312 *Marketing Economies*

We include here economies in both buying and selling, and a feature common to both is that it is often possible to achieve increases in turnover with a less than proportionate increase in staff and in such physical facilities as warehousing and transport. On the buying side substantial purchasing power will often enable large firms to buy materials, components, fuel, etc., at significantly lower prices than are available to smaller firms. The major car assemblers, for instance, are in a position to manufacture many of their own components, and thus are in a very strong bargaining position. On the sales side important scale economies may be enjoyed in advertising costs.

### 4.313 *Financial Economies*

Large firms can usually obtain finance more easily and more cheaply than small firms, mainly because investors feel a greater sense of security when providing finance for large firms, and hence are willing to accept slightly lower returns. In addition, the costs of administration may rise less than proportionately to the amount of finance provided, especially when the general public is asked to subscribe funds.

### 4.314 *Managerial Economies*

This comprises a rather miscellaneous group of economies, the common element being the ability of large firms to employ top-class staff – in research and development, sales, production, personnel, etc. – and to utilize their talents fully.

### 4.32 *Summary: the Behaviour of Costs, Changing Scale of Organization*

The effect of the various economies of scale is summarized in Figure 4.4. This shows the average costs associated with three alternative scales of organization, scale 1 being the smallest and scale 3 the largest. At any output up to M costs are lowest at the smallest scale of organization (giving rise to $AC_1$). For outputs beyond M costs will be lower if the firm reorganizes on a larger scale (giving rise to $AC_2$). Similarly, beyond output N a further reorganization ($AC_3$) becomes desirable. If the firm always adopts the most appropriate scale of organization, its average cost curve will comprise the unbroken parts of the three individual cost curves.

### 4.33 *Economies of Scale in the Motor Industry*

The motor vehicles industry provides a good illustration of the importance of economies of scale. It has been estimated that an annual output of 250,000 vehicles is required to achieve the lowest unit cost in the paint shop and in final assembly, 1 million units in the casting of engine blocks and up to 2 million units in the pressing of various panels. Even larger outputs are required to obtain maximum non-technical economies: 2½ millions in finance and 5 millions in research and development. (This last figure explains why so many vehicle producers have undertaken joint R & D activities.) Estimates prepared by Professor Rhys of the economies of scale in car manufacture are given in Table 4.1

*Table 4.1 Economies of Scale in Car Manufacture*

| Output per year | Index of unit average costs |
| --- | --- |
| 100,000 | 100 |
| 250,000 | 83 |
| 500,000 | 74 |
| 1,000,000 | 70 |
| 2,000,000 | 66 |

*Source*: Rhys, G., 'Economics of the Motor Industry', *Economics*, vol. 24, Winter 1988

Note that despite the disadvantages of small-scale production, a number of small firms have continued to thrive in the motor industry. They produce vehicles which are highly distinctive in one way or another, e.g. in performance, individual craftsmanship or styling, and thus appeal to people who are willing to pay a high price for these advantages.

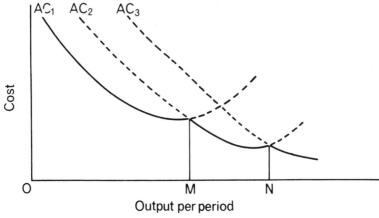

Fig. 4.4 Economies of scale

### 4.34 *Diseconomies of Scale*

A question that has received a great deal of attention among economists is whether costs continue to fall indefinitely as the scale of organization increases. Empirical evidence suggests that this frequently does not happen, probably because after a certain point, economies of scale are balanced by diseconomies. It is not easy to identify these diseconomies, but they are most likely to occur in management, reflecting the difficulty of administrating and controlling very large firms.

In an attempt to prevent these diseconomies from arising, some firms have adopted a decentralized system of management, allowing many decisions to be made at lower levels of the organization. (Sometimes these areas of responsibility are known as profit centres.) The effect is almost like having a number of semi-independent firms under one corporate umbrella. The advent of cheap micro-computers enables many more people to have access to the information required for decision-making.

## 4.4 Forms of Growth

A distinction can be made between internal and external growth. Internal growth occurs when a firm expands its own activities. In external growth the activities of two (or more) firms are combined, following a merger or take-over. (Mergers and take-overs are discussed in greater detail in Chapter 10.) Whether growth is internal or external, it can take one of several forms.

### 4.41 *Horizontal Growth*

In drawing cost curves we make the assumption that output relates to a single type of product, e.g. number of pens or litres of ink. Consequently Figure 4.4, when interpreted strictly, illustrates horizontal growth, i.e. an increase in the output of the firm's existing products. This is, however, by no means the only way in which firms grow.

### 4.42 *Vertical Growth*

Vertical growth or integration implies a move into an additional stage of production or distribution. A distinction can be made between forward and backward integration, as indicated in Figure 4.5.

Vertical growth may give rise to some of the economies of scale associated with the size of the firm, e.g. the full utilization of elaborate data-processing facilities. But in general a more important motive for vertical growth is additional security. Backward integration gives security of supplies, and is most likely to occur when specialist sources of supply are limited. For example in the U.K. there were at the end of the war more car assemblers than firms making car bodies. Gradually these manufacturers of bodies were taken over by the assemblers and there is now no major independent body manufacturer.

Forward integration guarantees outlets for the firm's products and enables the manufacturer to control the conditions under which its products are sold. Considerable capital expenditure is required to establish a distribution network, especially at the retail level, and it is often difficult for a manufacturer to provide the range of products which would justify such an investment. Manufacturers of beer have succeeded in doing so, whereas manufacturers of foodstuffs have not.

If a firm is faced by a dominant supplier or purchaser in the markets in which it deals, vertical expansion may enable it to obtain inputs at a lower cost and sell

### Vertical integration

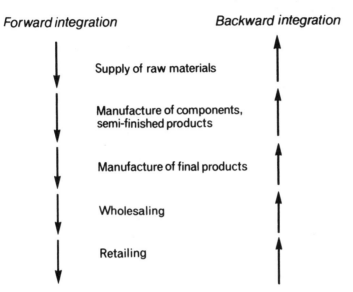

Fig. 4.5 Vertical integration

its output at a higher price. (However, any firm which has the financial resources to expand vertically is usually able to obtain reasonable terms from suppliers or purchasers. This helps to explain why a large retailer such as Marks and Spencer has not felt it necessary to develop its own manufacturing facilities.)

### 4.43 *Diversification*

Sometimes growth demands a movement into other markets, as when Dunlop added to the manufacture of rubber tyres a range of other rubber goods, sports equipment, leisure wear, etc. Diversified growth can often be explained by a lack of suitable opportunities for further growth in the firm's original markets. It may also be due to a desire to spread risks. Many markets are characterized by fluctuations in demand and hence in profits. Since the fluctuations in different markets are seldom completely in phase with each other, diversification should help to reduce the amplitude of the fluctuations in total profits. Similarly, diversification is a safeguard against a loss of sales that might arise from product obsolescence.

Diversified growth is less likely to give rise to economies of scale than other forms of growth. However some cost savings might arise in the use of large-scale data processing facilities and other central services.

### 4.44 *Lateral Growth*

An example of lateral growth would be where a manufacturer of car engines began to produce aero engines. It stands between horizontal and diversified growth, giving rise to fewer economies of scale than the former, but more than the latter.

## 4.5 The Multinationals

A multinational enterprise (M.N.E.) is an organization that owns income-generating assets in more than one country. Most M.N.E.s operate in several countries and together they are estimated to account for over one fifth of the world's output (excluding centrally planned economies). The largest, such as General Motors (one of whose British subsidiaries is Vauxhall Motors) and Exxon (parent of the Esso Oil Company) have annual sales in excess of the national income of many countries, including Denmark and Norway.

In the early stages of growth additional sales are obtained by exporting. This enables full advantage to be taken of economies of scale in production. But once exports have reached a certain level, direct foreign investment becomes attractive. Production economies become exhausted, and the requirements of overseas customers, including the supply of spare parts and the provision of service, can be fulfilled more quickly from local production units. The stage of establishing plants overseas is reached more quickly if overseas governments restrict imports and/or give incentives for the construction of production units.

Further growth of the M.N.E.s may involve setting up a number of subsidiaries. Eventually the responsibility for making a product may be shared among the subsidiaries, perhaps in conjunction with plants in the parent country. This process has been most fully developed in the production of cars. In order to take the fullest possible advantage of economies of scale, production of various parts of the car – engine, gearbox, axles, etc. – is concentrated in different plants located in different countries. The output of one plant may go to any of several countries for use in the final assembly of the vehicle.

## 4.6 De-mergers

In recent years there has been an increasing number of mergers which have been followed by the sale of part of the merged company. In such situations one of the firms usually takes a clear lead in initiating the merger, which may go ahead despite the opposition of the Board of Directors of the other company. (Such a situation is probably better described as a take-over rather than a merger.)

In some instances the initiating company acquires substantial assets which are combined with its own 'core' businesses; assets which do not fit with these businesses are subsequently sold to help to recoup the cost of the acquisition. Hanson Industries is one company whose growth and increased profits owe much to this strategy.

In other instances a company is established primarily to acquire and subsequently dismember another company. The target is frequently a company which has undertaken a series of mergers in a number of unrelated fields (so-called conglomerates); hence the term de-merger is used when parts of the conglomerate are sold. Taking over a conglomerate is often very expensive; in

1988 the American R. J. Nabisco (tobacco, foodstuffs etc.) was acquired for
$25 billions, while in 1989 Hoylake, a consortium formed by Sir James
Goldsmith, Jacob Rothschild and Kerry Packer, bid over £13 billions for BAT
Industries, the U.K.'s third largest industrial concern. Originally a tobacco
manufacturer, BAT had diversified into retailing and financial services.

The initiating company invariably offers shareholders in the other company a
price well in excess of the pre-bid price. Since the intention is to split up the
company, the implication is that the target company is worth less as a single unit
than the sum of its parts. This may suggest that conglomerates suffer substantial
diseconomies of scale. (Other possible explanations are that the existing Board
of Directors of the target company has used the assets under its control
inefficiently, or that the stock market has seriously undervalued the prospects of
the company.)

## 4.7 Other Influences on Cost

Many other factors can influence cost, which explains why different firms may
incur different costs, *even if they are making the same quantity of an identical
product:*

1 Different firms may use different mixes of inputs: for example, it is often
  possible to reduce the amount of labour required by employing more
  capital, and vice versa.
2 Different firms may pay different prices for similar, or even identical,
  inputs: for example, the prices of many raw materials fluctuate substantially
  over time, and one firm may buy at a more favourable time than another
  firm. Again, workers may be paid at different rates in different parts of the
  country. Differences in location may also give rise to differences in transport
  costs.
3 Finally, the efficiency with which firms utilize their resources often varies
  significantly, so that even if the prices paid for inputs are identical, costs per
  unit of output may vary.

## 4.8 Additional Cost Concepts

### 4.81 *Incremental Cost*

Incremental cost is the addition to cost that results from an increase in output. A
small increase may require an increase only in the quantity of direct materials
used, since spare capacity may exist in other inputs. Larger increases in output
may necessitate an increase in the quantity of most inputs, and even perhaps an
enlargement of the scale of organization.

### 4.82 *Marginal Cost*

Marginal cost is a similar concept to incremental cost, in that it denotes the
change in cost that arises as a result of a change in output. But the change is now
specified as a single unit of output. Marginal cost is discussed in detail in
Chapter 8.

## 4.83 *Sunk Cost*

Sunk costs are those costs that have been incurred in the past and do not produce any current cash outflow or liability. A good example would be a machine that had been bought for cash and could be used only by its present owner. Its capital cost would be a sunk cost.

## 4.84 *Escapable Cost*

Escapable cost is the saving in cost that would follow from a contraction of output. As we have just said, the purchase cost of a machine is a sunk cost. The operating cost of that machine would be an escapable cost, since if output was reduced and the machine was taken out of service, the firm would no longer have to meet its operating cost.

## 4.85 *Joint Costs*

Most firms have facilities that are utilized in the supply of more than one type of product. Such facilities may be found in manufacturing processes (e.g. machines), in distribution (e.g. vehicles), in administration (e.g. central planning and design staffs), and so forth. The costs to which these facilities give rise are known as joint or common costs.

## 4.86 *Opportunity Cost*

This is a cost concept of an entirely different nature from any of the others considered above, in that opportunity cost cannot be directly derived from financial data. It refers to the profit that could be obtained if resources (or any part of those resources) were switched from their existing to their most profitable alternative use. For example, for a firm producing rubber mattresses the opportunity cost might be the profit that could be obtained from the production of beach-balls. For the full-time student the opportunity cost of the time he spends studying is the additional income that he could be earning. For a nation the opportunity cost of building a new hospital might be two new schools.

## 4.9 Summary and Conclusions

With a given scale of organization, as output increases average fixed cost falls, while average variable cost is constant at first but rises as the limit to output is approached. Average total cost falls initially and then becomes roughly constant.

With a changing scale of organization economies of scale arise as capacity and output increase. There may come a point at which no further economies arise, and indeed where diseconomies set in. Firms often adopt a decentralized system of management in order to prevent diseconomies arising.

Firms may grow internally or externally, and in both instances growth may be horizontal, vertical, lateral or diversified. Disappointment with diversified growth has recently led to an increase in de-mergers.

## Further Reading

Begg, D., Fischer, S. and Dornbusch, R., *Economics* (London: McGraw-Hill, 2nd Edn, 1987), Chs 6 and 7.
Hardwick, P., Khan, B. and Langmead, J., *An Introduction to Modern Economics* (London: Longman, 2nd Edn, 1986), Ch. 2.
Lipsey, R. G. and Harbury, C., *First Principles of Economics* (London: Weidenfeld and Nicolson, 1988), Ch. 15.
Livesey, F., *A Textbook of Economics* (London: Longman, 3rd Edn, 1989), Ch. 5.
Maunder, P., Myers, D., Wall, N. and Miller, R. L., *Economics Explained* (London: Collins, 1987), Ch. 22.

## Revision Exercises

1 Define the scale of organization and explain why it may sometimes be difficult to effect changes in scale.
2 Explain why firms may choose a scale of organization greater than their expected average level of output, and show the significance of this factor for the behaviour of costs.
3 Explain, with examples, the term 'fixed cost', and show how average fixed cost may vary as changes occur in (a) the level of output and (b) the scale of organization.
4 Draw a diagram showing how fixed, variable and total costs are likely to vary as output varies, the scale of organization being given. Explain briefly the shape of each curve.
5 Discuss the major economies of scale that exist in any two industries with which you are familiar.
6 Explain why, at any given level of output, average cost may differ according to the possibility or not of changing the scale of organization.
7 Show how average cost is likely to behave if the firm is always able to adopt the scale of organization most appropriate to the level of output produced.
8 Explain the statement that different cost concepts are required for different decisions.
9 'Since opportunity cost cannot be measured, it is not a useful concept.' Discuss.
10 What factors should a firm take into account in deciding whether to increase output by working its existing factory more intensively or by building an additional factory?

# 5. *Supply*

## 5.1 Introduction

In this chapter we build on the cost analysis undertaken in the previous chapter, in order to show how supply curves are derived. We begin with the supply curve of the individual firm, and then move on to a discussion of market supply curves.

## 5.2 The Supply Curve of the Firm

The basic determinant of supply is cost, the link between the two being the profit the firm hopes to obtain. In order to obtain the desired profit the firm will add a profit margin to the (estimated) average cost (AC) at the expected level of output, thus arriving at its target price. In Figure 5.1 at output E average cost is EX. Adding to this a profit margin XY gives price EY (= P).

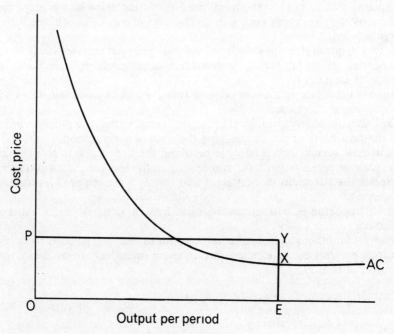

Fig. 5.1 Fixing the target price

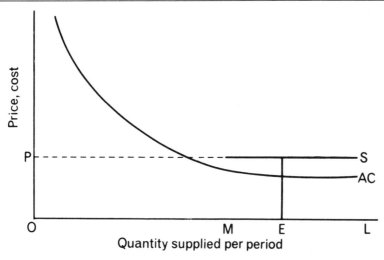

Fig. 5.2 Stable price with changing demand

A supply curve shows what quantities would be offered for sale at various prices in a given time period. As yet we have identified a single point on this curve – point Y. There is strong reason to believe that if output fell short of, or exceeded, the expected level by a modest amount, price would not change, i.e. the supply curve would be horizontal over this range of output (ML in Figure 5.2).

The justification for this belief is as follows. Consider first the situation where demand is higher than expected (output is above E). Since average cost (AC) does not rise at this higher level of output, a maintained price will yield more than adequate profits (remember that output E at price P would yield adequate profits); hence the firm will be happy to maintain its price.

The situation where demand is less than anticipated (output is below E) is less straightforward, since there are two conflicting tendencies at work. On the one hand, average cost is higher at the lower output level, which would provide an incentive to the firm to increase its price. On the other hand, to increase price when demand is low might be very dangerous, since it might drive the remaining customers into the hands of rival suppliers, who will also be short of orders. Taking into account both factors, the firm may well decide to maintain its price, provided that the shortfall in demand is modest.

Although a horizontal supply curve is a highly realistic concept, there are various circumstances in which the curve may not have this shape. The most important of these are the following, in which the references are to Figure 5.3:

1 If a higher than expected output causes average cost to rise significantly, the firm may increase its price to compensate ($S_2$).
2 If demand is sufficiently high, the firm may reorganize on a larger scale. If average cost falls because of economies of scale, the firm may pass on the lower costs in the form of lower prices ($S_3$). Alternatively the firm may take

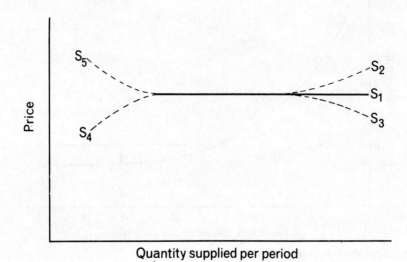

Fig. 5.3 Alternative supply curves

the initiative by cutting its price in the hope that this will generate sufficient sales to justify reorganization.

3  If a substantial fall in demand is experienced, the firm may reduce its price in order to try to regain sales ($S_4$). The price may fall as low as, but not below, average variable cost.

4  The final possibility is that, because of the increase in average cost following a reduction in output, the firm may increase its price ($S_5$). However, as we suggested above, this is a dangerous policy and is unlikely to be followed where rival suppliers are maintaining their prices.

These four possibilities are illustrated in Figure 5.3, where $S_1$ is the original supply curve, as shown in Figure 5.2.

## 5.3 Market Supply Curves

Given that a market supply curve usually comprises the supply curves of more than one firm, its derivation can be quite complex. We can simplify the analysis in the first instance by assuming that all firms are identical in every way – level of costs, scale of organization, etc. Here the market supply curve is derived simply by aggregating the individual supply curves. So in Figure 5.4 each firm would supply 10 units at price $P_1$ and 20 units at $P_2$. If there were five such firms, market supply would be 50 units at $P_1$ and 100 units at $P_2$. (No particular significance should be attached to the shape of this curve. It is simply one of the several curves that appear in Figure 5.3.)

It is important to note that a situation may arise where an individual producer might be able to increase his output without increasing his average cost, but if all producers were to increase their outputs, average costs might rise. The

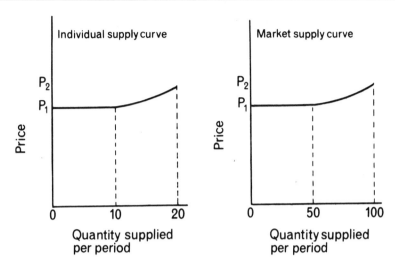

Fig. 5.4 Individual and market supply curves

reason for this is that the increasing demand for resources – labour, materials etc. – might lead to an increase in the cost of these resources.

On the other hand, increased output by several producers can lead to cost reductions that would be unlikely to occur if only one producer increased his output. The sources of these cost reductions are external economies, so-called because they are external to the individual firm. Examples are improvements in transport and communication facilities, and better education and central training facilities. It may not be feasible for a single firm to provide these facilities internally, because they would not be utilized sufficiently to justify the cost.

Returning to the relation between individual and market supply curves, let us consider an alternative situation to the one discussed above. If one large firm dominates the market, perhaps by reason of its size, it may be able to set a price (in the light of its costs) which is accepted by other firms. These other firms will then decide how much to produce at that price. In this situation the supply curves of the different producers will not be identical. Nevertheless, the market supply curve is again derived by aggregating the supply curves of the individual producers. If the dominant firm's supply curve is like that in Figure 5.5, and if there are five smaller firms each willing to supply, at any price, one-fifth as much as the dominant firm, the market supply curve will be as illustrated.

## 5.4 A Shift of the Supply Curve

We have confined our discussion so far to the relation between price and the quantity supplied, i.e. to movements along given supply curves. The shapes (as opposed to the positions) of these curves reflect the effects of changes in output on average costs and/or on profit margins.

As we indicated in the previous chapter, costs and margins may also change,

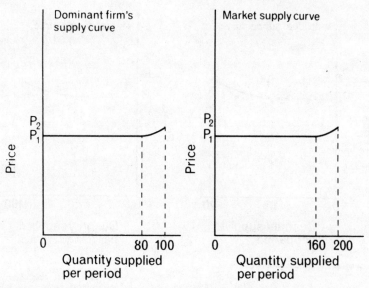

Fig. 5.5 Market supply curve with dominant firm as price-setter

regardless of the level of output. These changes, which we denote as changes in the conditions of supply, cause not as movement along but a shift of the supply curve.

## 5.5 The Response of Supply to an Increase in Cost

In Figure 5.6 $S_1$ represents the initial supply curve and $S_2$ the new supply curve after the increase in cost. The fact that the two curves are parallel indicates that the increase in average cost is the same at all levels of output (although such an

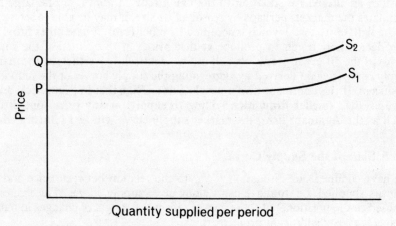

Fig. 5.6 Supply curves indicating cost increase

outcome is not, of course, inevitable). If the extent of the shift of the curve – the distance PQ – equals the increase in average cost, this indicates that the profit margin has been maintained. (Again this may not always happen.)

We can say then that the shift of the supply curve reflects the increase in cost. Alternatively we can say that producers need a higher price than previously in order to supply any given output, the higher price being required to compensate them for the increase in cost.

Average cost may increase for many reasons, most of which can be summarized under the heading of an increase in the cost of factor inputs. Although an increase in factor costs will often be fully reflected in prices (as assumed above) this will not always be so.

### 5.51 *The Significance of Accounting Conventions**

Materials used in production are normally drawn from stock. If the producer values those materials at the price that he will need to pay to replenish his stocks, then a recent price increase in material costs will be reflected in an increase in his costs. On the other hand, if the materials are valued at the price ruling when they were bought, and this could well have been several months previously, a recent price increase will not affect the current cost of production, thus calculated. (The situation is even more complicated than indicated here, since further methods of valuation may be used. Incidentally, note that the argument in this section applies to falls as well as increases in price.)

This distinction between a 'replacement' and 'historical' approach to costs is also important with regard to capital equipment. If machines are bought infrequently – say every five or ten years – an historical system of costing can clearly result in considerable lags between changes in the current cost of inputs and changes in recorded costs.

### 5.52 *Differential Cost Changes*

Different producers may employ different combinations of inputs, so that a given change in the cost of one input will affect different producers to differing degrees. So, for example, a producer with a high ratio of labour to capital will, other things being equal, be affected more by an increase in wages than a producer with a lower labour-capital ratio. If cost increases have a differential effect, for any such reason, there can be no guarantee that the higher costs will be reflected in higher prices, since each producer will be uncertain as to how his competitors are going to react.

### 5.6 The Response of Supply to a Reduction in Cost

A reduction in cost may result either from a reduction in the cost per unit of inputs or from greater efficiency in the utilization of inputs. In the inflationary conditions which appear to characterize modern economies, reductions in the unit cost of inputs are becoming increasingly rare. Examples are now mainly

---

* We are concerned here with the conventions of cost accounting for internal purposes and not with the reporting of profits or assets in 'final accounts'.

restricted to raw materials, whose prices often fluctuate quite violently (see Chapter 7), and to certain situations where rapid technological change allied to economies of scale reduces the cost of production, e.g. micro computers.

Greater efficiency in the utilization of inputs can arise from various sources. Some are fairly mundane, such as improved production planning and a better layout of the factory. Others are more spectacular, making use of such technological developments as the introduction of more efficient machines to reduce the labour requirement, or the development of alternative, cheaper materials.

The effect of a reduction in cost will usually be a downward shift of the supply curve, indicating that producers would be willing to supply more than previously at any given price; or, to put the matter a different way, they would be willing to supply the same amount at a lower price (Figure 5.7).

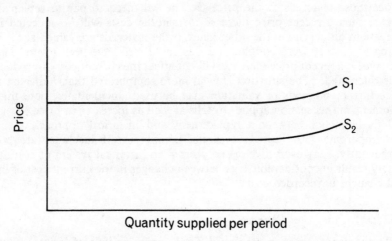

Fig. 5.7 Supply curves indicating cost reduction

## 5.7 The Imposition of An Indirect Tax

The imposition of an indirect tax on a product can be seen as a special case of an increase in cost. If the producers wish to obtain the same revenue per unit as previously, they will pass on the tax increase, as they would any other increase in cost. In that case the new supply curve will lie above the old curve. If the tax is a specific tax, i.e. a constant amount per unit supplied, e.g. 3p per orange or 10p per kilo of apples, the new supply curve ($S_2$) will be parallel to the original one ($S_1$), lying above it by the exact amount of the tax, as in Figure 5.8, where the tax is assumed to be AB. *Ad valorem* taxes, such as Value Added Tax, vary in accordance with the initial (ex-tax) price of the product. As price falls, the tax per unit becomes less. Conversely, as price rises, the tax per unit increases (Figure 5.9). The granting of a subsidy on output will have the same effect as a reduction in cost, and the above analysis applies in reverse.

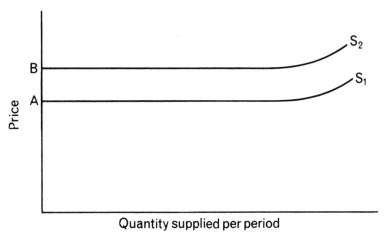

Fig. 5.8 Effect of specific tax on supply curve

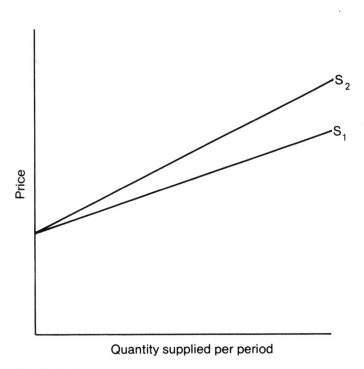

Fig. 5.9 Effect of *ad valorem* tax on supply curve

## 5.8 A Change in Profit Margins

It will probably be clear by now what would be the effect on the supply curve of a change in the target profit margins that producers add to their costs. An increase in margins will shift the supply curve upward, and a fall in margins will shift the curve downward.

## 5.9 Taxes, Subsidies, Price and Output

Figure 5.10 shows the effect on price and output of the imposition of an indirect tax. With demand D and the initial supply $S_1$, $Q_1$ is sold at price $P_1$. The imposition of the tax causes the supply curve to shift to $S_2$. The equilibrium price rises from $P_1$ to $P_2$, and equilibrium output falls from $Q_1$ to $Q_2$.

Figure' 5.10 can also be used to illustrate the impact of a subsidy. We take $S_2$ as indicating supply before the subsidy and $S_1$ supply after the subsidy. The effect of the subsidy is a fall in the equilibrium price and an increase in the equilibrium output.

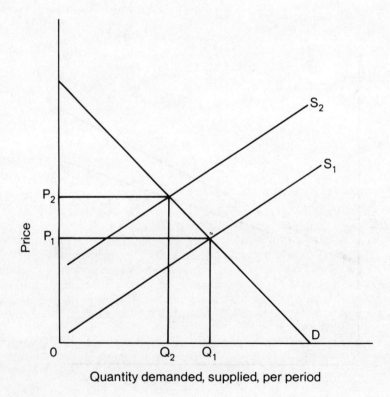

Fig. 5.10 The impact of an indirect tax

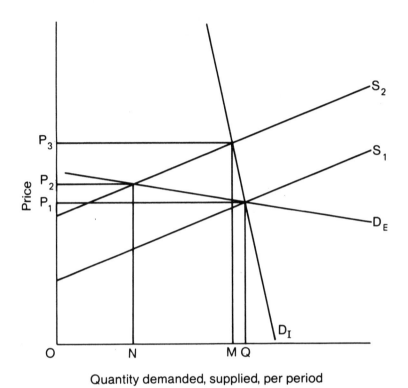

Quantity demanded, supplied, per period

Fig. 5.11 An indirect tax and differing demand elasticities

## 5.91 *Taxes and the Elasticity of Demand*

The revenue received from an indirect tax varies in accordance with the elasticity of demand for the product. In Figure 5.11 the initial point of equilibrium is given by the intersection of the supply curve $S_1$ with the demand curves $D_I$ and $D_E$; Q is sold at price $P_1$. Following the imposition of the tax the supply curve shifts to $S_2$. With an elastic demand $D_E$, price rises to $P_2$ and the quantity sold falls by around 60 per cent to N. With an inelastic demand $D_I$, price rises to $P_3$ but demand falls by only some 7 per cent to M. Since the tax revenue per unit sold is constant, it is clear that the total revenue is much higher with the inelastic than the elastic demand.

If the main motive for the imposition of an indirect tax is to raise revenue, the government will choose products with an inelastic demand. On the other hand if the main motive is to reduce consumption, for example because the product is felt to be injurious to health, the greatest degree of success will be achieved if the demand for the product is elastic.

## 5.10 Summary and Conclusions

Cost is the most important factor determining the amount of a product that is supplied at a given price. However there are other important influences, including the objectives of the producer (especially in terms of his target profit), the structure of the market (especially the extent to which it is dominated by a small number of firms), and the accounting conventions adopted by producers (which are of particular significance when a change in costs occurs).

## Further Reading

Begg, D., Fischer, S. and Dornbusch, R., *Economics* (London: McGraw-Hill, 2nd Edn, 1987), Ch. 3.

Hardwick, P., Khan, B. and Langmead, J., *An Introduction to Modern Economics* (London: Longman, 2nd Edn, 1987), Ch. 5.

Lipsey, R. G. and Harbury, C., *First Principles of Economics* (London: Weidenfeld and Nicolson, 1988), Ch. 6.

Livesey, F., *A Textbook of Economics* (London: Longman, 3rd Edn, 1989), Ch. 5.

## Revision Exercises

1 Explain the statement that the basic determinant of supply is cost.
2 What is the justification for the belief that the supply curve of an individual firm will be horizontal over a certain range of output?
3 In what circumstances is a market supply curve least likely to be horizontal?
4 What are external economies? Discuss their significance in relation to (a) the supply curve of individual firms and (b) market supply curves.
5 Discuss the possible relationships between the supply curves of individual firms and market supply curves.
6 Outline the factors that affect (a) the shape and (b) the position of supply curves.
7 Discuss the ways in which supply may change in response to a change in cost.
8 Explain, with the use of diagrams, how supply is likely to be affected by (a) an increase in the rate of Value Added Tax and (b) the granting of a subsidy on output.
9 What factors may make supply relatively inelastic?
10 Explain why the government should take the elasticity of demand into account when placing a tax on a product.

# 6. Cost-based Pricing

## 6.1 Introduction: a Simple Model

We have seen that both demand and supply curves can take alternative shapes and positions, so that the analysis of price determination is clearly a complex matter. However, we start with a simple model (Figure 6.1), utilizing demand and supply curves of shapes which the analysis above suggested were typical of many markets.

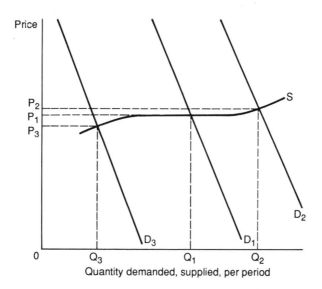

Fig. 6.1 Changes in demand, price and quantity

The demand curve slopes down from left to right. The supply curve has a horizontal segment over the expected range of output, reflecting constant average costs over this range. When output is above this level, the supply curve rises, reflecting increasing average cost. Below this level the supply curve falls, indicating that producers are willing to accept lower profit margins in order to try to maintain their volume of sales.

Figure 6.1 shows that with the initial demand and supply curves, $D_1$ and $S$, the equilibrium price is $P_1$, the quantity sold being $Q_1$. A modest increase or decrease in demand would leave the price unchanged (although the quantity sold would, of course, change). However, a substantial increase in demand to $D_2$ results in an increase in price to $P_2$ and in the quantity sold to $Q_2$. A substantial fall in demand to $D_3$ results in a fall in price to $P_3$ and in the quantity sold to $Q_3$.

The results of a change in supply are shown in Figure 6.2, where the initial demand and supply curves are D and $S_1$. An increase in supply to $S_2$, reflecting a fall in cost, results in a fall in price to $P_2$ and an increase in the quantity sold to $Q_2$. A decrease in supply to $S_3$, reflecting an increase in cost, results in an increase in price to $P_3$ and a fall in the quantity sold to $Q_3$.

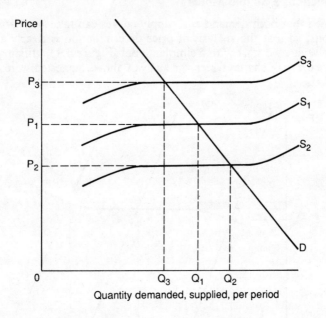

Fig. 6.2 Changes in supply, price and quantity

## 6.2 The Structure of the Market

### 6.21 *The Number of Suppliers and the Co-ordination of Activities*

The relation between demand and cost is sometimes such that the possibility of earning more than adequate (supernormal) profits clearly exists. However, these profits are not earned automatically. An appropriate 'mechanism' must be devised.

This can probably be seen most clearly if we consider the situation from the point of view of an individual producer. In Figure 6.3 the producer initially sells Q at price P. He believes demand to be such that if all producers were to raise their price to $P_1$, he would sell $Q_1$. (The demand curve $D_1$ is drawn on the assumption that all producers set identical prices.) But if he were to raise his price to $P_1$, and some other producers failed to raise their prices, he might sell much less than $Q_1$. The demand curve $D_2$, which is drawn on the assumption that all other producers continue to charge P, indicates that he would sell only $Q_2$. Profits would then actually be less than they were initially. In the face of this uncertainty he may maintain price P.

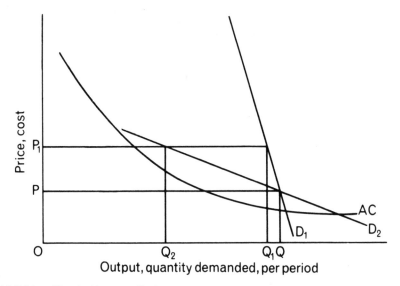

Fig. 6.3 Pricing with and without co-ordination

If all other producers react in a similar manner to the uncertainty, there is no reason why price should rise above P, no reason why they should achieve supernormal profits. These profits will be attainable, however, if a mechanism can be devised whereby all producers raise their price to $P_1$.

The most obvious way of bringing this about may appear to be that producers should simply agree to raise their prices. However, price agreements among rival suppliers are illegal in many countries. In the absence of a formal agreement an 'understanding' may arise that price competition is undesirable. Then, if one producer raises his price, competitors will follow. (Sometimes one firm may become accepted as the *price-leader* – as the firm that always initiates price changes.)

The chances of one or other of these mechanisms emerging will tend to be greater, with fewer suppliers in the market. As far as short-run profit maximization is concerned, it is the number and behaviour of *existing* suppliers that is important. But the firm aiming to maximize long-run profits will also take into account the possibility of new entry. Very high profits this year may encourage new suppliers to enter the market and hence reduce the profits of existing suppliers in subsequent years.

### 6.22 A Fall in Demand

A fall in demand will cause firms to consider whether to maintain or reduce price. Prices are most likely to be maintained when the fall in demand is modest and likely to be short-lived. Another important factor is the ability of producers to co-ordinate their activities. We can again explore the significance of this factor by considering the viewpoint of a single producer.

In Figure 6.4, with demand initially at $D_1$, the producer sells Q at price $P_1$. Demand then falls, and the producer has to decide whether to maintain or to reduce price. $D_2$ indicates his demand if all producers charge identical prices. If producers can agree on the price they should charge, they will clearly earn higher profits by charging $P_1$ than $P_2$, since $D_2$ is inelastic within that price range.

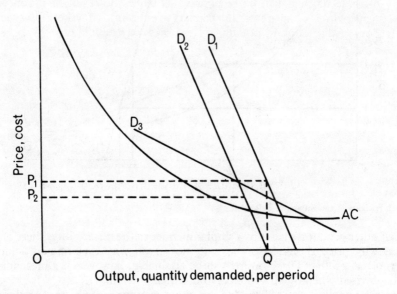

Fig. 6.4 Pricing with a fall in demand

However, in the absence of co-ordination, our producer will be strongly tempted to reduce his price. He may be afraid that other producers will reduce their prices and thus, by undercutting him, eat into his sales. Alternatively he may believe that all other producers will maintain their prices and that he will be able to undercut them and increase his sales. (This belief gives rise to demand curve $D_3$, which represents this producer's demand when all other producers maintain price $P_1$, Q being sold at price $P_2$).

Clearly, then, prices are more likely to be maintained if producers co-ordinate their activities. This assumes that the combined profits of all producers will benefit from maintained prices. This need not always be so, of course. If aggregate demand is elastic, a higher revenue, and perhaps also higher profits, will follow from a price reduction. But even here the ability of producers to co-ordinate their activities remains advantageous to them.

### 6.23 *Barriers to Entry*

We noted above that existing suppliers take account of the fact that high profits may attract potential new suppliers. The intensity of the threat of new entry will largely depend upon whether serious barriers to entry exist. Large amounts of capital may be required before production can get under way. Smaller but still substantial sums may be required in order to advertise the product adequately (and this without any guarantees that consumers will be persuaded by the advertising). A process or a product may be protected by a patent. Even in the absence of legal protection, potential entrants may lack technical expertise, skilled manpower or access to raw materials. At the other end of the chain they may find it difficult to persuade established distributors to handle their goods. (Many of these barriers will be recognized as being the result of producers' marketing activities.) The greater the barriers to entry into a market, the greater the freedom or discretion in pricing enjoyed by existing suppliers.

### 6.24 *Product Differentiation*

As we have seen, product differentiation, including that resulting from advertising (often known as branding), can inhibit the entry into a market of potential new suppliers. It may also have the effect of reducing the possibility of substitution between the products of existing suppliers, i.e. it creates market imperfections. This in turn implies a decline in the price elasticity of demand of each product. The extreme example of an imperfect market is where a producer supplies a product for which there is no good substitute. This sole supplier is known as a monopolist (see Chapter 8).

When demand is relatively inelastic one consequence is, of course, that relatively few sales are lost when price is increased. In this situation a producer may be able, via higher prices, to earn supernormal profits.

## 6.3 Price Discrimination

Different prices may be charged for identical goods or services in different markets because of the differences in the cost incurred in supplying these different markets. Price discrimination exists when differences in prices do *not* reflect differences in costs. If a producer is to increase his profits by means of a policy of price discrimination, the following conditions must be fulfilled:

1 The two (or more) markets must have different elasticities of demand.
2 There should be no 'leakage' between the two markets: customers must be unable to benefit by buying in one market and reselling in another, or, alternatively, a redistribution of demand between the two markets must be accompanied by a reduction in total costs (see Section 6.313).

The fact that, given these conditions, price discrimination can increase profits can be demonstrated by reference to Figure 6.5. We start from a position where the firm sets the same price, P, in both markets. In order to simplify the analysis we assume that at this price the same quantity, Q, is sold in both markets.

The firm now introduces a price differential, raising the price in the less elastic market, B, and reducing the price in the more elastic market, A. The total amount sold is unchanged, i.e. $Q_B + Q_A = 2Q$. Total cost will therfore also

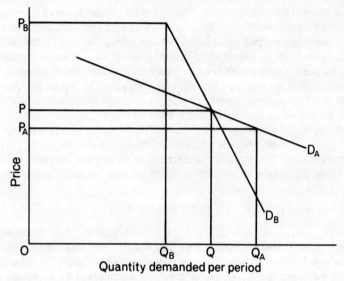

Fig. 6.5 Price discrimination in different markets

be unchanged. However, it can clearly be seen that total revenue, and therefore total profit, has increased:

$$(P_B \times Q_B) + (P_A \times Q_A) > 2(P \times Q)$$

When they have excess capacity, producers may adopt a policy of price discrimination in order to increase the volume of sales as well as revenue. This

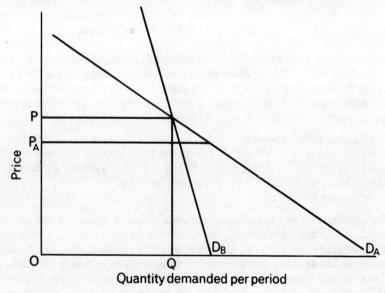

Fig. 6.6 Price discrimination to increase sales

situation is illustrated in Figure 6.6. We again start from a position where price, P, and the quantity sold, Q, are the same in the two markets. At price P demand is elastic in market A but inelastic in market B. Therefore, although a reduction in price will increase the volume of sales in both markets, it will increase revenue only in market A. Again the producer's objective will be met by a policy of price discrimination, with price P being charged in market B, and price $P_A$ in market A.

### 6.31 *Different Markets: Market Segmentation*

On what basis might the producer distinguish between one market and another, or, as the marketing man would put it, how might the overall market be segmented? There are several possibilities.

### 6.311 *Segmentation by Space*

Perhaps the most obvious basis is geographical. Demand elasticities in two different countries might differ because of differences in national income, in the distribution of that income, in the degree of competition, etc.

### 6.312 *Segmentation by Type of Customer*

A second basis for discrimination is by the type of customer. Some manufacturers sell to other manufacturers, to wholesalers and to retailers. A good example is the manufacturer of car components, who sells to assemblers for incorporation into new vehicles, and to distributors of various types, either for their own use in repair work or for resale to the general public. Again, many food manufacturers sell both to wholesalers (who in turn supply small retailers) and to large retailers.

It is known that many manufacturers, anxious to obtain additional sales, offer to supply 'own label' or 'private label' goods at prices well below those for the corresponding manufacturer's brand. In some instances the products supplied are, apart from the labels, identical. Even in those instances where there are additional differences, the differences in costs to which these give rise are far less than the differences in selling price.

### 6.313 *Segmentation by Time*

There are many examples of markets that are subdivided on the basis of the time at which the products are supplied or bought. Many of these examples relate to the supply of services, e.g. telephone calls, which are cheaper in the evenings and at weekends, and railway travel, which is cheaper at off-peak times. A similar pattern is found in the supply of electricity.

It is believed that the demand for railway travel by commuters who travel at peak times is less price-elastic than the demand by people who use the train for shopping or leisure activities and travel off-peak. Again, business telephone calls, believed to be relatively price-inelastic, account for a greater proportion of calls during peak than off-peak hours.

As we noted above, one of the conditions for successful price discrimination is that there should be no 'leakage' between the markets. One of the dangers in charging different prices at different times is that it may encourage leakage. For example, some telephone calls (especially of a non-business nature) may be deferred until off-peak hours. If leakage is substantial, price discrimination could result in a fall in revenue. However, even here the policy might still lead to an increase in profits, since the change in the distribution of demand over time might enable the cost of supply to be reduced.

An appreciable part of the costs of the industries that we have been considering in this section is accounted for by the cost of capital equipment – railway rolling stock, telephone exchanges, electricity generation plant, etc. The amount of this equipment installed depends upon not the average but the peak demand. Thus if some of the peak demand is redistributed to off-peak periods, capital requirements will be reduced.

### 6.32 *Quantity Discounts*

Quantity discounts are price reductions given in respect of large orders. They are mainly intended to (a) increase the volume of orders or (b) influence the pattern of orders so that a given volume can be met at minimum cost. There is therefore a parallel with the objectives of time/price differentials, discussed above.

As far as increasing volume is concerned, if the discount is related to the size of the order, it can be seen merely as a special form of price reduction designed to increase sales. If, on the other hand, the discount is related to the total orders received in a given period (often a year), it may well be intended as a means of 'tieing' the purchaser to the supplier. Once a purchase has been made, there is an incentive to make additional purchases from the same supplier, since a higher rate of discount will thereby be applied to both the previous and the additional orders.

On the cost side, if purchasers can be persuaded to order in large quantities (especially likely under a system that relates the discount to the size of the individual order), savings may arise both in manufacturing costs, especially via longer production runs, and in order-processing costs – packing, documentation, etc.

## 6.4 Pricing with Cost Differentials

In general we assumed in the previous chapter that competing suppliers had similar cost structures. Very often, of course, this is not so. In Figure 6.7 firm A is more efficient than firm B, and has a lower average cost ($AC_A$) at every level of output. In this situation it is highly likely that the price in the market will be determined by firm A.

Basically A's choice is as follows. It can set a price, $P_1$, which is high enough to allow B to stay in the market. Hence the market will be shared between the two firms. (For the sake of simplicity we assume equal market shares, so that each firm, with demand at D, sells Q.)

Since, at price $P_1$, B is earning adequate profits, we can reasonably assume that A is earning supernormal profits. However, A might do even better by

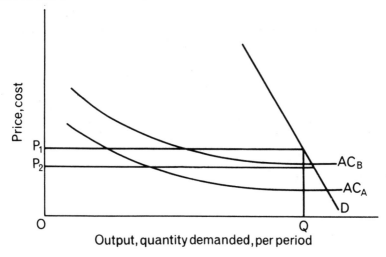

Fig. 6.7 A price leader's strategy

following the second alternative, namely charging a price, $P_2$, which will force B out of the market. A would hope to attract B's former customers and might be able to supply them at a lower average cost than at present. This is especially likely if producing on a much larger scale gives rise to substantial economies of scale.

Incidentally, setting price $P_2$ might not cause B to leave the market immediately. Although this is below B's average total cost, it might be above average variable cost. Consequently B could survive until more costs become variable e.g. because machines required replacing, and variable cost exceeded price. Moreover, if B is a multi-product firm, it might subsidize this product, at least for a time, from the profits derived from other products.

## 6.41 *Price Followers*

If, in the above situation, we consider firm A as the price leader, then firm B (and other similar firms) may be considered as price followers. A price follower's demand curve will be as shown in Figure 6.8. P is the price set by A. This may or may not yield B adequate profits, but even if it does not, B would not improve his position by charging more than P, since his demand within that range of prices is highly elastic.

On the other hand, if, in desperation, he were to start a price war, charging less than P, his sales would increase relatively little, since A, having the benefit of lower costs, would almost certainly match the price reduction. The fact that A reacts differently to an increase and a decrease in price by B explains why B's demand curve is 'kinked' at the existing price. (The kinked demand curve is also discussed during our examination of oligopoly in Section 8.51.)

### 6.42 *Price-minus Costing*

If B wishes to remain in this market, he may try to improve his profitability in one of two ways. First, he can attempt to differentiate his product, and then set a price above P, hoping that consumers will choose between products on grounds other than price, i.e. hoping that demand will be less elastic than indicated in Figure 6.8. For example, a manufacturer may offer a wider range of colours or sizes than his competitors, or he may seek to create a distinctive image for his brand. A small retailer may attempt to combat the lower prices of multiple retailers by offering more personal service and by opening longer hours. Alternatively, he may try to increase his efficiency and thus reduce his costs. This may mean (slight) changes in the product, due, for example, to the use of alternative raw materials, or it may reflect a pure increase in efficiency.

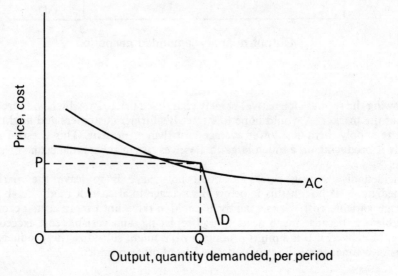

Fig. 6.8 A price follower's strategy

There is widespread evidence that considerable scope exists for cost reduction, which is often undertaken only when profits prove to be inadequate. This process, whereby costs are adjusted in the light of the prevailing market price, is known as price-minus costing.

### 6.5 Break-even Analysis

In this chapter we have usually expressed the relation between revenue and cost in terms of average-revenue and average-cost curves. Businesses frequently present the same information in a somewhat different form, namely a break-even chart, using total revenue and cost curves. To end the chapter we show the relation between these alternative forms of presentation.

Figure 6.9 is based on the data contained in Table 6.1. The left-hand diagram shows that with a price of 30 the firm would break even at an output of 25 units, both total cost and revenue equalling 750. This break-even point can be equally easily derived from the conventional right-hand diagram. It is the point at which the average-revenue curve (AR) cuts the average-total-cost curve (ATC), at an output of 25 units.

Table 6.1 A Hypothetical Cost Schedule

| | Total cost | | | | Average cost | | |
| Output | Fixed | Variable | Total | | Fixed | Variable | Total |
|---|---|---|---|---|---|---|---|
| 10 | 500 | 100 | 600 | | 50 | 10 | 60 |
| 20 | 500 | 200 | 700 | | 25 | 10 | 35 |
| 50 | 500 | 500 | 1,000 | | 10 | 10 | 20 |

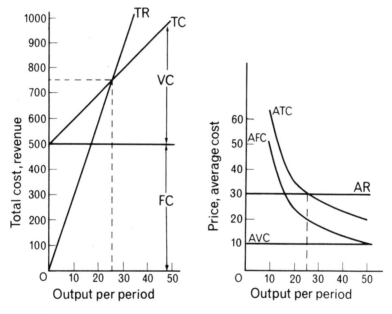

Fig. 6.9 Break-even (left) and cost-curve charts

## Further Reading

Devine, P. J., Jones, R. M., Lee, N. and Tyson, W. J., *An Introduction to Industrial Economics* (London: Allen and Unwin, 3rd Edn, 1983), Chs 7–9.

Griffiths, A. and Wall, S., *Applied Economics* (London: Longman, 2nd Edn, 1986), Ch. 9.

Livesey, F., *A Textbook of Economics* (London: Longman, 3rd Edn, 1989), Chs 5 and 7.

Turvey, R., *Demand and Supply* (London: Allen and Unwin, 2nd Edn, 1980), Ch. 6.

## Revision Exercises

1 Define price discrimination and state the conditions that are required if price discrimination is to yield higher profits than a policy of uniform prices.
2 Discuss the ways in which a producer who wished to adopt a policy of price discrimination might segment his market.
3 Distinguish between cost-based pricing and price-minus costing, and outline the circumstances in which each policy is most likely to be adopted.
4 Outline the main barriers to the entry of new firms into a market, and discuss their significance.
5 Explain why railway passenger travel is cheaper at off-peak than at peak periods.
6 'The charging of cheap fares for bus journeys taken by retired people can be justified on social but not on economic grounds.' Discuss.
7 The owner of a local cinema is considering introducing a scheme, either for some or all performances, whereby a party of four would be admitted for the price of three individual tickets. What factors should he take into account in his decision?
8 A study of the pricing policies of British engineering firms found that firms were more willing to charge less than the target price for export than for domestic orders. What might explain this policy?
9 Define equilibrium price, and show how this price may be affected by changes in (a) demand, (b) supply.
10 Show how market structure may influence pricing decisions.

## Objective Test Questions: Set No. 2

For answers see p. 274.

1 Which of the following factors will tend to make supply inelastic?

  A  A mobile labour force
  B  Good transport facilities
  C  A shortage of highly specialized capital equipment
  D  An absence of barriers to entry into markets.

2 Which of the following factors might help to explain why a supply curve slopes downward as output increases?

  A  Diseconomies of scale arise
  B  Workers work overtime at premium rates
  C  The quantity of a fixed factor of production cannot be increased
  D  Purchasing economies arise as a result of quantity discounts.

3 Which of the following statements is correct?

  A  An increase in sales revenue necessarily implies an increase in profitability
  B  An increase in sales revenue necessarily implies an increase in profitability in the short-run but not in the long-run

C An increase in sales revenue necessarily implies an increase in profitability in the long-run but not in the short-run
D An increase in sales revenue may be accompanied by either an increase or a fall in profitability.

4 A demand curve may have a backward sloping position because

1 a positive income effect outweighs a negative substitution effect
2 consumers see the price of the product as an indicator of its quality
3 the product is bought for the purpose of conspicuous consumption

A 1 and 2 only
B 2 and 3 only
C 1 only
D 3 only

5 If a car assembler took over a firm making car components this would be an example of

A diversification
B backward integration
C forward integration
D horizontal integration

6 An inferior good is one for which

A the quantity demanded decreases as price falls
B the income effect of a price change outweigh the substitution effect
C the quantity demanded changes less than proportionately to the change in price
D the quantity demanded rises as income falls

7 Which of the following may constitute a barrier to entry into a market or industry?

1 Labour is highly mobile
2 A large amount of capital is required to start production
3 Existing suppliers spend heavily on advertising

A 1 and 2 only
B 2 and 3 only
C 1 only
D 3 only

8 Which of the following is/are necessary for profitable price discrimination?

1 Leakage between markets
2 Identical costs of supplying different markets
3 Different markets have different elasticities of demand

A 1 and 2 only
B 2 and 3 only
C 1 only
D 3 only

9 Quantity discounts may relate to the total orders received in a given period or to a single order. Which of the following relates to the former but not the latter?

A Savings may arise in manufacturing costs
B Savings may arise in order-processing costs
C Once a purchase has been made, there is an incentive to make additional purchases from the same supplier
D The discount can influence the pattern of orders

10 Which of the following helps to explain why a supplier's demand curve is kinked?

1 If the supplier were to reduce its price, other suppliers would reduce their prices
2 If the supplier were to raise its price other suppliers would not raise their prices
3 The supplier is a price leader

A 1 and 2 only
B 2 and 3 only
C 1 only
D 3 only

11 Question 11 is based on Figure 1, in which $S_1$ is the initial supply curve and $S_2$ the new supply curve. The shift from $S_1$ to $S_2$ could have been caused by any of the following except

A the imposition of a tax on the product
B a fall in the price of labour
C an increase in labour productivity
D technological progress

Fig. 1

Questions 12 and 13 are based on Figure 2, in which TR denotes total revenue and TC total cost.

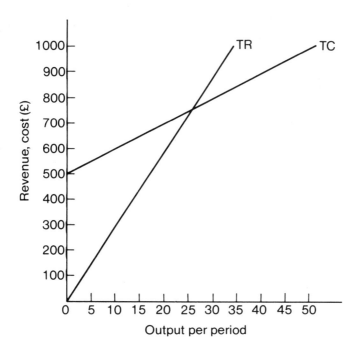

Fig. 2

12 Which of the following statements is/are correct?

    1 At output 25 price is £30
    2 Fixed cost equals £500
    3 Variable cost equals £6 per unit

    A 1 and 2 only
    B 2 and 3 only
    C 1 only
    D 3 only

13 Which of the following statements is/are correct?
    1 Profits are zero at an output of 25
    2 Price is constant at all levels of output
    3 Average total cost is constant at all levels of output

    A 1 and 2 only
    B 2 and 3 only
    C 1 only
    D 3 only

14 At a price of 50p, 1,000 units of a product are supplied. If elasticity of supply is 1·5, the quantity supplied at a price of 51p will be

A  1,005 units
B  1,010 units
C  1,015 units
D  1,030 units

15 Which of the following is least likely to lead to a shift in the supply curve for leather footballs? An increase in the

A  wages paid in the tanning industry
B  standard rate of Value Added Tax
C  price of hides
D  popularity of soccer

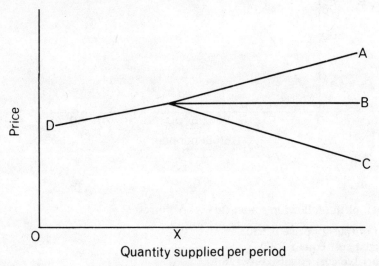

Fig. 3

Items 16 to 19 are based on Figure 3, which shows parts of four alternative supply curves. Assuming that the original equilibrium, at which output was X, is disturbed by a change in demand, indicate which supply curve will apply in each of the situations specified below. (Each curve may apply once, more than once, or not at all.)

16 As output increases average and marginal costs rise.

A  B  C  D

17 As a result of a fall in demand firms accept lower profit margins.

A  B  C  D

18 As a result of an increase in demand firms enjoy greater economies of scale.

A   B   C   D

19 Average cost is constant at all levels of output.

A   B   C   D

20 The best definition of a supply schedule is that it shows the quantities which

A  were offered for sale at various prices at various points in time
B  would be offered for sale at various prices
C  would be offered for sale in a given time period
D  would be offered for sale at various prices in a given time period.

# 7. *Price Determination in Open Markets*

## 7.1 Introduction

We define an open market as one in which price is determined by the interaction of aggregate demand and supply, the individual supplier having no control over price. Examples of open markets include auction sales and exchanges of various kinds, the commodities dealt in often being primary products – foodstuffs, raw materials, etc.

## 7.2 The Determination of Prices

Let us consider the operation of a fish auction. In Figure 7.1 the total catch of a particular type of fish on a given day is Q. If we assume for the moment that any fish not sold on that day will be useless (i.e. opportunity cost is zero), then the owners will sell their catch for the best price they can obtain, so that the supply curve will be vertical. If demand turns out to be high ($D_1$) the equilibrium price, i.e. the price at which purchasers are willing to buy Q, is $P_1$. If demand is lower ($D_2$), the fishermen will obtain the lower price, $P_2$. Although this may not cover the cost of supplying the fish, a supplier will accept this price in preference to receiving nothing. This implies that the costs that have been incurred are irrelevant to the price that is obtained on this day. In this sense prices in open markets are said to be demand-determined.

Costs are, however, relevant to the longer-term decision as to whether or not the trawler owners should remain in the industry. If over a prolonged period of time, prices fail to yield an adequate profit, some resources will leave the industry and the average quantity of fish landed will fall. For a given level of demand, this implies that prices will rise. In the long run, then, costs do influence prices in open markets, though indirectly.

In some open markets a producer may have a third alternative to accepting the going price or scrapping the product. If the product is not perishable, he may withdraw from the market and re-enter when demand conditions are judged to be more favourable. It is not unusual for expensive items such as works of art to be withdrawn from auction if the reserve price is not achieved.

Even if the product is perishable, there may be an alternative open to the supplier. For example, trawler owners might take the precaution of arranging a fixed-price contract with a manufacturer of animal food. If all the owners enter into such an arrangement, the price agreed with the animal-food manufacturer will provide a floor to the auction price. This is indicated by $P_F$ in Figure 7.2.

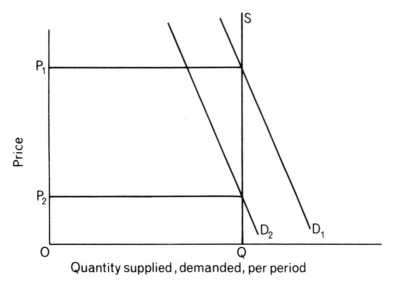

Fig. 7.1 Determining price in open market

With demand at $D_1$, the floor price does not function. However, with demand at $D_2$, since only bids at least equal to $P_F$ will be accepted, the quantity sold at action will be F, FQ being sold at price $P_F$ to the animal-food manufacturer.

We can apply Figure 7.2 to other markets, such as those for vegetables. At very low prices it may not be worth the farmer's expense and trouble to harvest and transport his crops to market. The costs incurred in these activities will constitute the floor below which price will not fall.

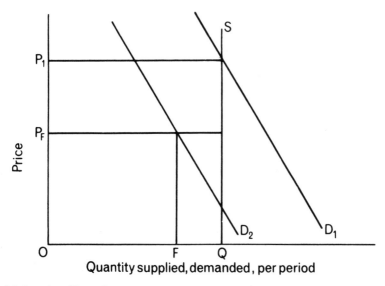

Fig. 7.2 Operation of floor price

## 7.3 Price Fluctuations

One of the chief characteristics of prices in open markets is that they are subject to frequent fluctuations, often of considerable amplitude. The basic reason for these fluctuations is the inability of producers to control supply. When there are a large number of producers, it is difficult to reach agreement on the amount to be supplied by each producer. In addition, the situation in agricultural products is often made worse by the inability to control the processes of nature. If demand is price-inelastic, as is often the case for foodstuffs, we reach the paradoxical situation where bigger harvests due to favourable weather can mean lower profits for the farmers. This situation is illustrated in Figure 7.3. Revenue, and hence profits, are greater with output $Q_1$ than $Q_2$.

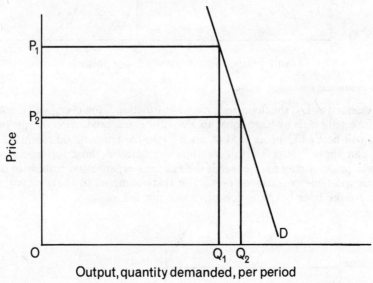

Fig. 7.3 Revenue inversely related to output

Once a crop is harvested, the individual farmer may have no better alternative than to sell the crop for the best price he can. But in the longer term he can respond to price by changing the use to which he puts his land.

This longer-term response may not, however, have the effect that was anticipated. In Figure 7.4 we assume for the sake of simplicity that demand does not change from one year to another. In year 1 there is a large supply, $S_1$, and consequently a price, $P_1$, that is considered to be unsatisfactory by some farmers. In view of the low price, some farmers switch their land to an alternative crop, with the result that in year 2 supply is only $S_2$. Ironically, price $P_2$ is now such as to yield profits that are considered to be more than adequate. Encouraged by the high prices, farmers move back into this crop in year 3. Supply increases to $S_3$, and prices slump once more to $P_3$.

There is no reason to think that the fluctuations in price will eventually cease.

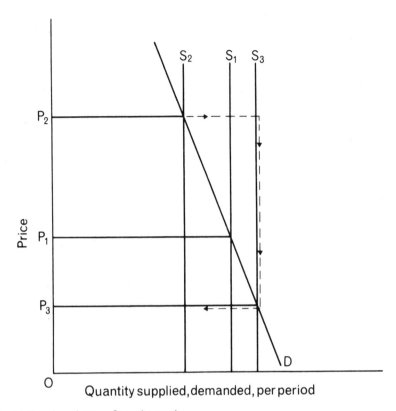

Fig. 7.4 Price dependence on fluctuating supply

Although each farmer may recognize the consequences of changes in supply, he will have to make a decision about the allocation of his land without knowing what decisions the hundreds or thousands of other farmers have made.

Indeed the absence of co-ordination among producers can lead to fluctuations in supply, and hence in price, quite apart from such natural causes as unduly good or poor harvests. The 'cobweb theorem' of price fluctuations, a simplified version of which has been presented here, was in fact first used to explain fluctuations in the prices of pigs in the U.S.A. Farmers decided how many pigs to rear in the light of the price ruling in the previous year. Consequently a high price in one year was followed by a high supply, and therefore a low price. This in turn led to a reduction in supply in subsequent years, and therefore a high price. The broken lines in Figure 7.4 trace the beginnings of the 'cobweb' pattern.

In some open markets price fluctuations result from substantial changes in demand rather than in supply. Raw-material markets such as metals are especially prone to disturbances from this source. This is partly due to the fact that a substantial part of the demand for such materials is accounted for by the capital-goods industries, where demand is often less stable than in consumer goods. In addition, the initial change in demand by the final customer is often magnified by the building up and running down of stocks at the various stages of the production and distribution process. Ironically, many raw-material industries comprise a large number of small producers, not competent to organize effective controls on supply. Consequently the fluctuations in demand result in substantial fluctuations in price.

## 7.4 The Control of Prices in Open Markets

Various schemes have been introduced in order to reduce price fluctuations. The most common scheme is the operation of a buffer stock by a central agency, on either a national or an international scale. This scheme can be illustrated by reference to Figure 7.5. $D_1$ represents the consumers' demand curve, and P the target price. If supply is Q, the target price is achieved. If supply is greater than Q e.g. M, the price is below the target. Conversely, if supply is less than Q e.g. N, price is above the target. The central agency might perhaps try to stabilize price by taking QM off the market or releasing NQ on to the market, as required.

The danger of this policy is that the agency might accumulate stocks it could

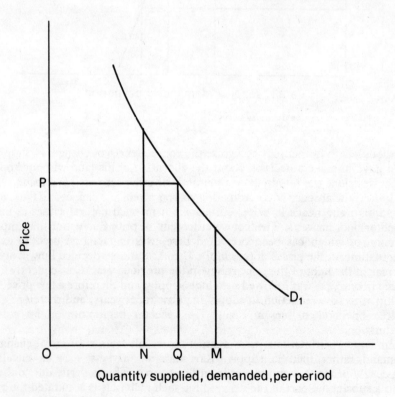

Fig. 7.5 The stabilization of price by means of buffer stocks

not subsequently sell at the target price. The 'butter mountain' accumulated by the E.E.C. was created in this way. In order to 'solve' this problem the E.E.C. had to sell the butter at very cheap prices in outside markets, thus making a substantial loss on the operation.

A less drastic version of the scheme would be to take off the market, and subsequently release, a proportion of the 'excess' supply. This would minimize but not prevent price fluctuations. We could again illustrate this process with reference to Figure 7.5, but a more elegant formulation is presented in Figure 7.6.

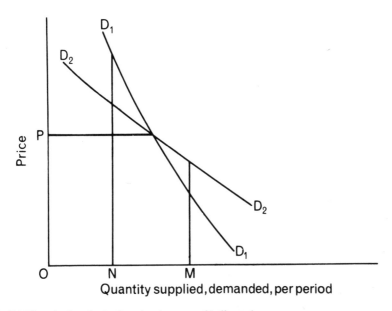

Fig. 7.6 The reduction of price fluctations by means of buffer stocks

As before, P indicates the target price and $D_1$ the consumers' demand. $D_2$ is the demand curve after intervention by the central agency, and indicates the demand to be met by producers from current production. At any price above P consumers' demand is met partly by stocks released by the central agency. At any price below P the central agency enters the market as a purchaser. The reduction in price fluctuations following intervention can easily be seen by comparing the prices, with and without intervention, at supply N and M.

The operation of a buffer-stock scheme when price fluctuations are due to fluctuations in demand rather than supply is illustrated in Figure 7.7. P is again the target price, and in order clearly to identify the effect of demand we assume that supply, Q, does not vary from one year to another. Given this supply, demand $D_T$ would yield the target price. If demand from consumers falls below $D_T$ ($D_1$), the central agency will buy YX. If demand is greater than $D_T$ ($D_2$), ZX will be supplied from the agency's stocks. (For the reasons given

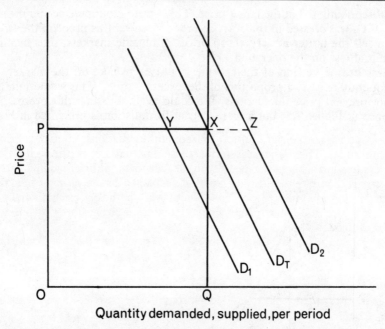

Fig. 7.7 Buffer-stock scheme when prices fluctuate with demand

above, the agency may not take the risks associated with attempting to maintain complete stability of prices; it may, in fact, buy and sell less than indicated here.)

An alternative method of reducing price fluctuations is the allocation, either by agreement or by central direction, of production quotas. This method is used more frequently with non-agricultural products, whose output can be more easily controlled, than with agricultural. If the quotas are changed in line with changes in demand, both upward and downward price fluctuations will be reduced; the application of fixed quotas will permanently reduce supply and therefore limit downward movements only.

Downward price movements are also reduced by the payment of compensation to producers who reduce their capacity. This sort of payment may be illustrated by the 'land bank' schemes in the U.S.A. and the European Community, under which farmers are compensated on the basis of the acreage that is not utilized.

Currently the best known organization for increasing producers' revenues by cutting back production and raising prices is the Organization of Petroleum Exporting Countries. Encouraged by the example of OPEC, producers of wool, bauxite, bananas, iron ore, copper, tungsten, quicksilver and phosphates have agreed to limit production. But all of these agreements, including that made by OPEC members, have had only limited success. Most agreements break down after a few years because of disputes about members' shares of the target output.

## 7.5 Summary and Conclusions

In open markets price is determined by the interaction of aggregate demand and supply, the individual supplier having no control over price. Since in the short run suppliers are often unable to alter the quantity supplied significantly, prices in open markets can be said to be demand-determined. However, the longer the time-period, the greater is the scope for altering the quantity supplied. Consequently, in the longer term, prices reflect the influence of both demand and (via costs) supply.

Prices in open markets are subject to frequent fluctuations, often of considerable amplitude. The basic reason for these fluctuations is the inability of producers to control supply, especially in the short run. Substantial fluctuations in the prices of agricultural products often occur because of changes in supply through particular climatic conditions. Fluctuations in the prices of minerals and metals often occur because producers are unable to alter supply in line with changes in demand.

Since frequent price fluctuations are often considered to be undesirable from the viewpoint of both producers and consumers, many open markets have been subject to central intervention designed to reduce the frequency and the amplitude of the fluctuations. Several forms of intervention were examined, and we shall return to this topic in our discussion of international economic institutions in Chapter 20.

### Further Reading

Johnson, P. Ed., *The Structure of British Industry* (London: Granada, 1980), Ch. 2.

Lipsey, R. G., *An Introduction to Positive Economics* (London: Weidenfeld and Nicolson, 6th Edn, 1983), Ch. 10.

Livesey, F., *A Textbook of Economics* (London: Longman, 3rd Edn, 1989), Ch. 7.

### Revision Exercises

1  Explain why price is likely to be more responsive to changes in demand in open than in other markets.
2  'Prices in open markets are demand-determined, costs being irrelevant.' Discuss.
3  What factors, if any, may set a floor to price in an open market?
4  'The revenue of producers of goods sold in open markets is often found to vary inversely to the quantity of goods produced. An individual producer would therefore be able to increase his revenue by reducing his output.' Comment.
5  Explain why price fluctuations may be very pronounced in open markets, making particular reference to (a) agricultural products, (b) metals.
6  Freedom of entry into a market is often said to be a guarantee against excessive price rises, and yet very substantial price rises have been found to occur in many agricultural markets, to which entry is very easy. How do you explain this apparent paradox?

7 Explain why frequent attempts have been made to control the behaviour of prices in open markets, and outline the methods that have been adopted.

8 'If buffer stocks benefit producers, this must be at the expense of consumers.' Discuss.

9 Show how the operation of a buffer stock could, while allowing fluctuations in price, prevent fluctuations in producers' incomes.

10 What factors might influence the degree of success attaching to attempts by producers to increase revenue by limiting supply?

# 8. An Alternative Approach to Price Determination

## 8.1 Introduction

In Chapters 6 and 7 we examined price determination in two types of markets, those in which individual producers have a considerable degree of direct influence on price, and those in which price is set by the interaction of aggregate demand and supply, the influence of the individual producer being negligible.

In this chapter we adopt an alternative approach to price determination. This approach assumes that firms attempt to maximize short-run profits; to achieve this objective they adopt the decision-rule that output should be set at the level at which marginal cost equals marginal revenue.

It is not claimed that firms behave this way in practice. The purpose of the models presented in this chapter is to show what would be the consequences if firms did attempt to maximize short-run profits. We shall see that the consequences differ depending upon the structure of the market.

## 8.2 Perfect Competition

A perfectly competitive market comprises a large number of producers who supply identical products. Since consumers have no reason to prefer the products of one supplier rather than another, any supplier who set a price above that of other suppliers would not sell anything. Consequently each producer accepts the price set by the interaction of aggregate (market) supply and demand.

### 8.21 Marginal Revenue

Marginal revenue is defined as the change in revenue that results from a change in output (or sales) of one unit. Since price, or average revenue, is the same whatever the quantity sold by the individual supplier, marginal revenue also equals price. This relationship between price (average revenue) and marginal revenue is demonstrated in Table 8.1 and Figure 8.1.

### 8.22 Marginal Cost

Marginal cost was defined in Chapter 4 as the change in cost that results from a change in output of one unit. The relationship between total, average and marginal cost, as output increases, is shown in Table 8.2.

*Table 8.1  The Firm's Revenue in Perfect Competition*

| Price (= Average revenue)<br>(£) | Output<br>(Units) | Total revenue<br>(£) | Marginal revenue<br>(£) |
|:---:|:---:|:---:|:---:|
| 10 | 1 | 10 | 10 |
| 10 | 2 | 20 | 10 |
| 10 | 3 | 30 | 10 |
| 10 | 4 | 40 | 10 |

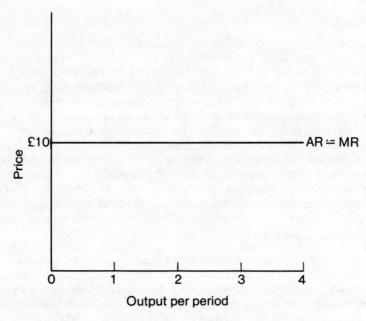

Fig. 8.1 Revenue in perfect competition

*Table 8.2  A Hypothetical Cost Schedule*

| Output<br>(units) | Total cost<br>(£) | Average cost<br>(£ per unit) | Marginal cost<br>(£) |
|:---:|:---:|:---:|:---:|
| 1 | 100 | 100 | 100 |
| 2 | 180 | 90 | 80 |
| 3 | 240 | 80 | 60 |
| 4 | 360 | 90 | 120 |
| 5 | 500 | 100 | 140 |

Figure 8.2 presents a more comprehensive view of these relations. This diagram assumes that output can be varied continuously, i.e. that the percentage changes in output are not as large as in Table 8.2.

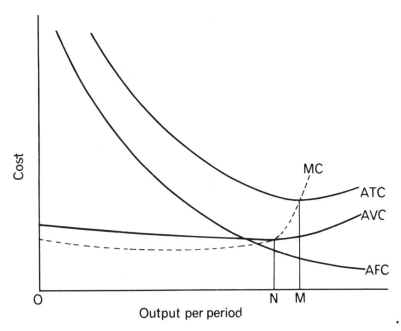

Fig. 8.2 Average and marginal costs

If we consider an increase in output, we see that marginal cost (MC) is below average total cost (ATC) when the latter is falling, and above average total cost when the latter is rising. It follows that marginal cost must cut the average total cost curve at the latter's lowest point, at output M. Since, by definition, marginal cost relates to variable (but not fixed) cost, the same relationship holds between marginal and average variable cost (AVC). The marginal cost curve cuts the average variable cost curve at the latter's minimum point, at output N. (Note that if average variable cost had been constant – as it often is in practice – AVC and MC would have been equal.)

### 8.23 *Profit Maximization*

As noted in the introduction, suppliers maximize profits by producing that output at which marginal cost equals marginal revenue; putting the matter more precisely, profits are maximized at the point where the marginal cost curve cuts the marginal revenue curve from below, at output Q in Figure 8.3. Q is known as the equilibrium output, and the corresponding price, P, as the equilibrium price. If output were to increase beyond Q, the additional revenue (marginal revenue) would be exceeded by the additional cost (marginal cost), and profits would decline. Conversely if output were less than Q, the chance of additional profits would be foregone, since in this range of output marginal revenue exceeds marginal cost.

In the models presented in this chapter, cost is defined to include normal profit. This is the minimum profit required if a firm is to remain in a given

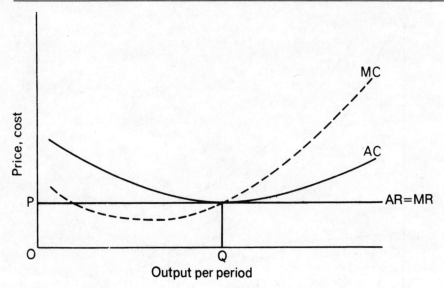

Fig. 8.3 Price determination in a perfectly competitive market

market. With output Q average revenue equals average cost, i.e. at the equilibrium output, normal profit is earned. (In order to simplify the analysis, it is sometimes assumed that normal profit is akin to the average profit rate earned by all firms. But more advanced analysis recognizes that normal profit may vary from firm to firm.)

### 8.24 *The Supply Curve in Perfect Competition*

As noted above, the supply curve indicates the amount of a product that a producer is willing to supply in a given time period at various prices. In the left-hand diagram in Figure 8.4, the producer would supply Q units at price P, implying that X is a point on the producer's supply curve. The right-hand diagram refers to the market. Given demand D, M units are sold at price P. (If there are n firms each producing Q units, M = nQ.) Here Y is a point on the market supply curve.

To identify other points on the supply curve we must consider output at other prices. In Figure 8.5 demand increases from $D_1$ to $D_2$. It will pay each producer to increase output provided the marginal (additional) revenue covers the marginal (additional) cost. The marginal cost curve indicates the expansion path of output; at price $P_2$ output is $Q_2$. In other words XT is a segment of the firm's supply curve. Market output is $M_2$ (= $nQ_2$), and YZ is a segment of the market supply curve.

A similar process applies, but in reverse, following a fall in demand. The firm's output falls along the path of the marginal cost curve, and there is a corresponding fall in market supply. Even though price is below average total cost producers continue to supply, since they are still covering the variable costs

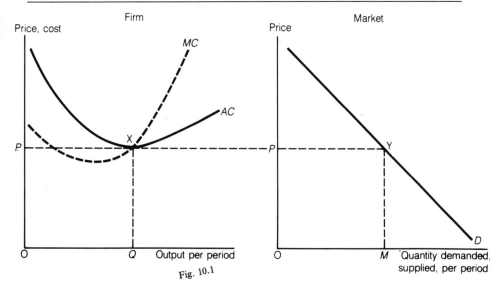

Fig. 10.1

Fig. 8.4 Output of firm and market

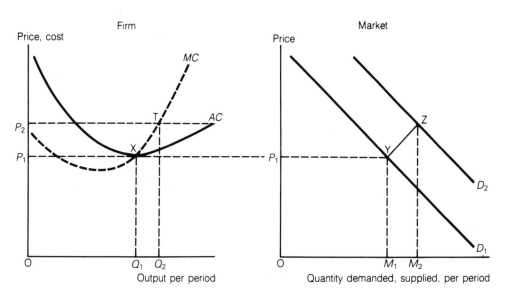

Fig. 8.5 Firm and market supply curves

incurred in producing the current output. The process will end, however, if price falls below average variable cost, since revenue would no longer cover costs currently incurred.

We can, therefore, define the supply curve of the firm in perfect competition as that segment of the marginal cost curve that lies on and above the average variable cost curve. The market supply curve is, of course, the summation of the individual producers' supply curves.

### 8.241 *Time and the Supply Curve*

In the above section we assumed that when demand increased there was sufficient time to enable existing producers to increase output, but not to allow the entry of new firms. If the time period under consideration is shorter than that assumed above, output may increase less, i.e. supply may be less elastic. Indeed in some instances it may be impossible to increase output at all, as when only a fixed amount of fresh food is supplied to a certain wholesale market on a given day. In such a situation the supply curve is vertical, and supply is said to be absolutely or infinitely inelastic.

On the other hand the time period may be longer than assumed above, allowing other producers to enter the market. Output will therefore increase more than assumed above, i.e. supply will be more elastic. Indeed if the new entrants are as efficient as existing producers, the additional output required to meet the higher demand will be supplied at the initial price; i.e. the supply curve will be horizontal, and supply is said to be infinitely elastic.

These three situations are illustrated in Figure 8.6, where $S_{vs}$ denotes supply in the very short period, $S_s$ supply in the short period and $S_L$ supply in the long period.

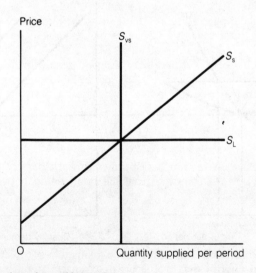

Fig. 8.6 Supply in very short, short and long period

Note that in the very short and short period, existing suppliers earn supernormal profits. In Figure 8.5 average revenue exceeds average cost as output increases from $Q_1$ to $Q_2$. But in the long run new suppliers enter the market and price falls again; only normal profits are earned.

## 8.3 Monopoly

We now consider a market at the opposite end of the spectrum from perfect competition. Monopoly denotes a market in which there is a single supplier.

### 8.31 *Marginal Revenue*

Since there is only one supplier in a monopoly market, the market demand curve is also the demand curve for that supplier. We saw in Chapter 3 that in most markets the quantity demanded varies inversely to the price, (the demand curve slopes down from left to right). This relationship is illustrated in Table 8.3.

*Table 8.3 Revenue in a Monopoly Market*

| Price (= Average revenue) (£) | Quantity sold (units) | Total revenue (£) | Marginal revenue (£) |
|---|---|---|---|
| 10 | 5 | 50 | – |
| 9 | 6 | 54 | 4 |
| 8 | 7 | 56 | 2 |
| 7 | 8 | 56 | 0 |
| 6 | 9 | 54 | −2 |
| 5 | 10 | 50 | −4 |

Within the price range £10 to £8, demand is elastic. A price reduction results in an increase in total revenue, i.e. marginal revenue is positive. Within the price range £8 to £7, demand is of unitary elasticity. A price reduction leaves total revenue unchanged, i.e. marginal revenue is zero. Finally, within the price range £7 to £5, demand is inelastic. A price reduction results in a fall in total revenue, i.e. marginal revenue is negative. The relationship between average and marginal revenue is shown in Figure 8.7.

### 8.32 *Marginal Cost*

The analysis of cost in section 8.22 applies to both perfect competition and monopoly and Figure 8.7 shows the usual relationship between average and marginal cost.

### 8.33 *Profit Maximization*

The decision rule for profit maximization, explained in section 8.23, applies also in monopoly. In Figure 8.7 profits are maximized at output Q, where the marginal cost curve cuts the marginal revenue curve from below. Since average revenue exceeds average cost (which includes normal profit) supernormal or monopoly profit of RX per unit is earned. Total monopoly profit is Q(RX).

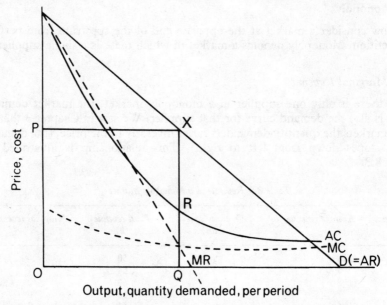

Fig. 8.7 Price determination in monopoly

## 8.34 *The Supply Curve in Monopoly*

In Section 8.24 we showed how a supply curve is derived in perfect competition. In view of that analysis and since in Figure 8.7 Q is sold at price P, it might be thought that X is a point on the firm's supply curve. Unfortunately this is not so. In fact a supply curve for an imperfect market cannot be derived from a model based on marginal analysis.

To see why this is so consider Figure 8.8 (the average cost curve has been omitted to simplify the diagram). With demand $D_1$ and marginal revenue $MR_1$, Q units would be sold at price P. If the demand curve shifted from $D_1$ to $D_2$, T units would be sold at price P, implying a horizontal supply curve (XY). On the other hand, if demand shifted from $D_1$ to $D_3$, T units would be sold at price R, implying an upward-sloping supply curve (XZ).

We arrive, therefore, at the conclusion that the shape of the supply curve is influenced by the shape of the demand curve. But this conclusion is incompatible with the assumption underlying models incorporating marginal analysis, that supply and demand are determined independently.

## 8.4 Monopolistic Competition

In monopolistic competition a large number of producers supply products that are similar but not identical, i.e. the products are differentiated. Product differentiation may be due to differences in the physical characteristics of the products – quality, styling, colour etc. – to the images created by advertising

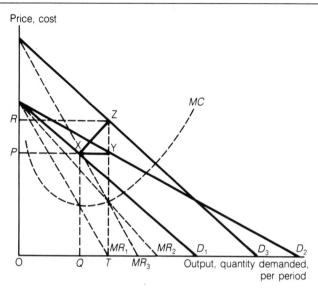

Fig. 8.8 Alternative supply curves in monopoly

(branding), or to other aspects such as the level of after-sales service offered by the various suppliers.

Because of these differences each supplier's demand or average revenue curve slopes down from left to right. If he raised his price he would lose some customers but would retain those who placed most value on the features that distinguished his product from those of his competitors.

### 8.41 *Profit Maximization*

In Figure 8.9 demand is initially $D_1$. Profits are maximized where the marginal cost curve cuts the corresponding marginal revenue curve, $MR_1$, from below i.e. at output $Q_1$. It can be seen that at this output average revenue exceeds average cost, i.e. supernormal profits are earned.

This is a similar situation to that in Figure 8.7. There is, however, a very important difference. The monopolist shown in Figure 8.7, is able to protect his position against potential competitors. Barriers to entry against new competitors may take the form of a patent on the product, control of a vital raw material, control of suitable production sites, and so forth. The existence of barriers to entry means that the monopolist is able to earn supernormal profits in the long run.

In monopolistic competition, on the other hand, there is nothing to prevent competitors from entering the market with similar products. As new suppliers enter the market, demand for the products of existing suppliers falls; the demand and marginal revenue curves shift to the left. This process continues until the supernormal profits have been competed away. In Figure 8.9, when demand falls to $D_2$, output is $Q_2$, where MC cuts $MR_2$. At this output average cost equals average revenue, i.e. normal profits only are earned.

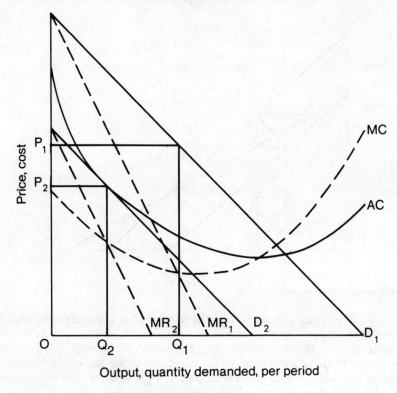

Fig. 8.9 Price determination in monopolistic competition

It will be noticed that at equilibrium output $Q_2$, average cost is above the minimum. This has given rise to the argument that product differentiation, a major feature of monopolistic competition, is wasteful. It is true that a higher output would result in a fall in the firm's average cost which would be beneficial. On the other hand, product differentiation widens consumer choice, and it is impossible to say in principle where the balance of advantage lies.

For example, given the existence of so many brands of toothpaste it may seem obvious that the benefit of an additional brand would be very small, and that the consumer would prefer a lower price. But if the new brand led children to brush their teeth more often or more thoroughly, e.g. because of the taste or the design of the tube, the benefit, in terms of less dental decay, might be enormous.

## 8.5 Oligopoly

Oligopoly denotes a market in which a high proportion of sales is accounted for by a relatively few suppliers. (This is sometimes the result of product differentiation which causes a market to be split into smaller, distinct markets.) Such *highly concentrated* markets are extremely common in modern industrialized societies. In making decisions on price each supplier has to carefully consider what the reactions of his rivals might be.

### 8.51 *Uncertainty and the Kinked Demand Curve*

In fact there is often a great deal of uncertainty surrounding the reactions of rivals. The assumption is made that each supplier believes or fears that if he were to raise his price rivals would *not* follow suit, with the result that he would suffer a substantial fall in sales, i.e. demand would be elastic.

On the other hand he believes that if he were to lower his price his rivals *would* follow suit, so that sales would not increase very much, i.e. demand would be inelastic. These different reactions expected to an increase and a fall in price give rise to the kinked demand curve shown in Figure 8.10, in which P is the going price.

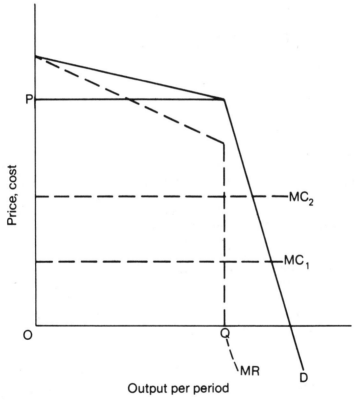

Fig. 8.10 Price determination in

### 8.52 *Sticky Prices*

Associated with the kinked demand curve is a marginal revenue curve with a vertical segment. This means that if marginal cost changes, e.g. from $MC_1$ to

$MC_2$ in Figure 8.10, no change in output is required since both marginal cost curves cut the marginal revenue curve at the same output, Q. This is said to be another reason why prices tend to be more sticky or stable in oligopoly than in other types of market.

The main deficiency of the oligopoly model is that it does not explain how the going price, P, arises in the first place. This deficiency is very serious given the widespread existence of oligopolistic markets, noted above.

### 8.53 *Non-price Competition*

If a firm believes that cutting prices would lead to lower profits, it may try to increase sales in other ways: by advertising its products, by introducing new product features giving better performance, by changing the product's styling, by offering better service, and so forth. We have met these various forms of non-price competition in earlier sections, indicating that they are by no means confined to oligopoly.

Non-price competition may shift the firm's demand curve to the right, enabling more to be sold at any price. It may also cause the demand curve to become less elastic, enabling the firm to increase its price without losing as many sales as it would otherwise have done.

### 8.6 Summary and Conclusions

In this chapter we have examined price determination in several types of market. In all these markets firms maximize profits by setting output at the point at which marginal cost equals marginal revenue. (This decision rule cannot however be applied satisfactorily to oligopoly.)

Markets may differ in terms of the number of suppliers, the degree of product differentiation and the existence or absence of barriers to entry, and these differences give rise to differences in profitability. The usual situation is that in perfect competition normal profits are earned, in monopoly supernormal profits are earned, and in monopolistic competition supernormal profits may be earned in the short run, but these are competed away in the long run.

Differences in profitability are one reason why governments have sought to influence price determination. However, the higher profits earned in monopoly do not necessarily mean higher prices. Since monopolists enjoy economies of scale, costs and prices may be lower than they would be in perfect competition.

### Further Reading

Begg, D., Fischer, S., Dornbusch, R., *Economics* (London: McGraw-Hill, 2nd Edn, 1987), Chs 8 and 9.

Hardwick, P., Khan, B. and Langmead, J., *An Introduction to Modern Economics* (London: Longman, 2nd Edn, 1986), Chs 9 and 10.

Lipsey, R. G. and Harbury, C., *First Principles of Economics* (London: Weidenfeld and Nicolson, 1988), Chs 16–18.

Livesey, F., *A Textbook of Economics* (London: Longman, 3rd Edn, 1989), Ch. 6.

Maunder, P., Myers, D., Wall, N. and Miller, R. L., *Economics Explained* (London: Collins, 1987), Chs 23, 24 and 25.

## Revision Exercises

1 Explain why short-run profit maximization requires that output should be at the level at which marginal cost equals marginal revenue.
2 In what ways does monopolistic competition differ from (a) perfect competition, (b) monopoly?
3 Define equilibrium price and show how this price is likely to respond to changes in costs.
4 Define equilibrium price and show how this price is likely to respond to changes in demand.
5 Why is the kinked demand curve said to be characteristic of oligopolistic markets?
6 Explain the conditions under which a firm's marginal cost curve is also its supply curve.
7 Explain the process of profit maximization in monopolistic competition.
8 Discuss the significance of branding for (a) producers, (b) consumers.
9 Evaluate the argument that product differentiation is wasteful.
10 Compare price, output and resource allocation in monopoly with that in perfect competition.

# 9. *Labour*

## 9.1 Introduction

In this chapter we discuss the factors which influence wage rates. We then examine the structure of wages. Finally we consider government labour market policies.

## 9.2 Demand, Supply and the Equilibrium Wage Rate

We showed in Chapters 6 to 8 that the prices of products are determined by the interaction of demand and supply. Demand and supply analysis is also used to explain the determination of the price of labour, i.e. the wage rate. In Figure 9.1 D and S represent the demand for, and supply of, labour in a particular occupation, say shop assistants or car mechanics. The equilibrium wage rate is W, at which Q workers are employed.

## 9.3 The Demand for Labour

If a firm wishes to maximize its profits it will continue to recruit workers provided that they add at least as much (and preferably more) to the value of output than they add to the firm's costs. Putting this more technically, labour will be employed up to the point at which its marginal cost equals its marginal revenue product. In order to explain the behaviour of marginal revenue product we need to examine the law of diminishing returns (sometimes known as the law of variable proportions).

### 9.31 *The Law of Diminishing Returns*

The law of diminishing returns states that if increasing quantities of a variable factor are applied to a given quantity of a fixed factor, the marginal and average product of the variable factor will eventually decrease. The operation of this law is illustrated in Table 9.1 and the associated Figure 9.2, which relates to a clothing factory and in which capital is the fixed, and labour the variable, factor.

If one worker looks after 10 machines the daily output is 50 metres of cloth. If a second worker is employed average and marginal product increase because there are certain jobs which can be performed far more efficiently with two workers. However if a third worker is employed average and marginal product fall. The same applies to the fourth and fifth workers; indeed the employment of a fifth worker would leave total output unchanged. This means that four

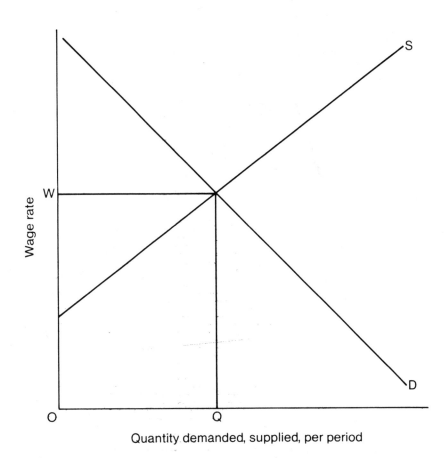

Fig. 9.1 The determination of wage rates

workers are fully capable of performing all the necessary tasks: feeding raw material into the machines, controlling the operation of machines, etc.

Table 9.1 Average and Marginal Product

| Number of machines | Number of workers | Total product (metres) | Average product (metres) | Marginal product (metres) |
|---|---|---|---|---|
| 10 | 1 | 50 | 50 | 50 |
| 10 | 2 | 120 | 60 | 70 |
| 10 | 3 | 150 | 50 | 30 |
| 10 | 4 | 160 | 40 | 10 |
| 10 | 5 | 160 | 32 | 0 |

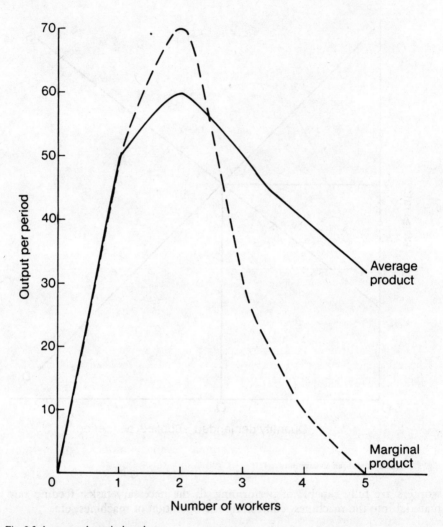

Fig. 9.2 Average and marginal product

### 9.311 *Marginal Revenue Productivity*

Table 9.1 refers to average and marginal *physical* productivity. To convert physical product to revenue product, it has to be multiplied by the price of the product. If price remains the same at all levels of output – as in perfect competition – physical and revenue productivity change at the same rate. But if price falls as output increases – as in monopoly and monopolistic competition – revenue productivity falls more rapidly (or rises less rapidly) than physical productivity.

Fig. 9.3 Marginal revenue productivity

The effect of price on marginal revenue product is shown in Figure 9.3. $MRP_1$ is the marginal revenue product curve when price is the same at all outputs. $MRP_2$ is the marginal revenue product curve when price falls as output increases.

### 9.312 *The Demand Curve*

As noted earlier, the profit maximizing firm employs labour to the point at which its marginal cost equals its marginal revenue product. The marginal revenue product curve is the firm's demand curve for labour.

## 9.4 The Supply of Labour

We discussed in Chapter 1 the factors that influence the size of the working population. Given the working population, the number of people wishing to enter a particular occupation is determined by the financial and other benefits offered by that occupation as compared to other occupations. (Of course some of the people who wish to enter an occupation may not be able to do so. The implications of this are discussed below.) We can illustrate this by reference to the supply of electricians.

### 9.41 *Transfer Earnings and Economic Rent*

In Figure 9.4 S indicates the supply of electricians at various wage rates. It will be seen that supply is zero at any wage rate below W. This is because at these

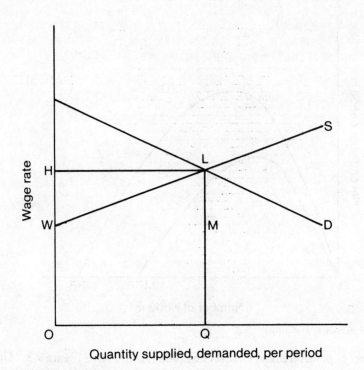

Fig. 9.4 Transfer earnings and economic rent

wage rates all workers would prefer to work in other occupations. W, the minimum wage rate required to prevent workers transferring to other occupations, is known as their transfer earnings.

The demand for electricians is such that the equilibrium wage rate is H, at which Q electricians are employed. The last worker employed has to be paid H to persuade him to work as an electrician; his transfer earnings are H. But the other workers would have been willing to work as electricians at lower wage rates. The part of the income of these workers that is above what would be necessary to persuade them to work as electricians is known as economic rent. The total amount of economic rent in Figure 9.4 is WHL.

The two concepts, transfer earnings and economic rent, can be used to analyse the income of any factor of production. It is therefore appropriate to discuss them in a little more detail. But remember that in all situations the income of a factor equals transfer earnings plus economic rent. In Figure 9.4 OHLQ = OWLQ plus WHL.

### 9.411 *The Elasticity of Supply and Economic Rent*

Given the demand for labour, the division of income between transfer earnings and economic rent depends upon the elasticity of supply. Figure 9.5 illustrates the situation when the supply of labour is perfectly elastic at wage rate W. This might apply to an occupation such as labouring where few skills or abilities, apart from strength, are required. It can be seen that whatever the demand for labourers, the wage rate would be W, and that income would entirely comprise transfer earnings. Economic rent is zero.

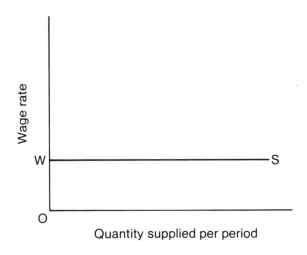

Fig. 9.5 Transfer earnings with perfectly elastic supply

Figure 9.6 illustrates the situation at the other end of the spectrum. The supply of labour is fixed at Q. This could apply if we defined occupation extremely narrowly, e.g. opera singers or pop groups of a certain 'quality'. With demand $D_1$ the wage rate is $W_1$. If demand increased to $D_2$ the equilibrium wage rate would rise to $W_2$. In both instances income would entirely comprise economic rent. Transfer earnings would be zero.

In fact the idea of a supply curve that is completely inelastic at all wage rates is scarcely realistic. Even artists or other workers with unique abilities, may have positive transfer earnings. There may be a wage rate, a fee, below which they would refuse to perform, or at least would perform less often. Nevertheless Figure 9.6 does illustrate an extremely important fact, namely that income, and' hence economic rent, is very sensitive to changes in demand when supply is inelastic.

### 9.5 Other Factors Influencing the Supply of Labour

We have seen that the supply of labour to an occupation depends upon the rewards currently offered by that occupation by comparison with other occupations. It follows that supply will be influenced by any change in conditions in other occupations. In Figure 9.7 the shift in the supply curve from $S_1$ to $S_2$ indicates a fall in the amount of labour supplied at any wage rate. The rise in transfer earnings from $W_1$ to $W_2$ could have been brought about by

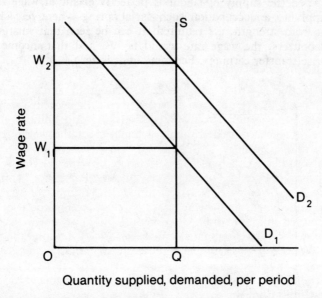

Fig. 9.6 Economic rent with perfectly inelastic supply

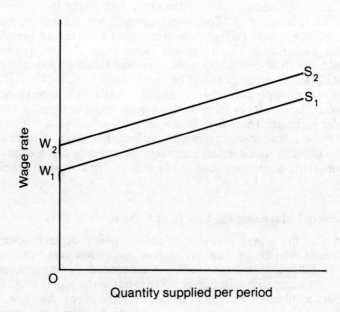

Fig. 9.7 A change in transfer earnings

an increase in wage rates in other occupations, or by an improvement in non-financial rewards such as the introduction of cleaner or less noisy machines, in these occupations.

### 9.51 *Barriers to Entry into Occupations*

We noted in section 9.4 that some people wishing to enter a particular occupation might not be able to do so. Barriers to entry into occupations are of two types. First, the occupation may require skills and abilities that are possessed, or could be acquired, by only a minority of the workforce, e.g. doctors, airline pilots, jewellers.

Second, entry to the occupation may be restricted by the activities of trade unions, professional associations or employers. In some occupations unions and employers have negotiated agreements concerning the number of apprentices employed per skilled man and the length of apprenticeship (both of which influence the future supply of trained workers). The government, usually in consultation with the relevant professional association, determines or at least influences the number of places available for educating and training people for certain professions, e.g. doctors, teachers, lawyers. The smaller the number of places, the lower the supply of labour and hence, given the demand for labour, the higher the equilibrium wage rate.

In some occupations government influences both supply and demand, and there is no guarantee that the wage rate will be consistent with the price in the product market. In Figure 9.8 S is the supply of doctors and D the demand for

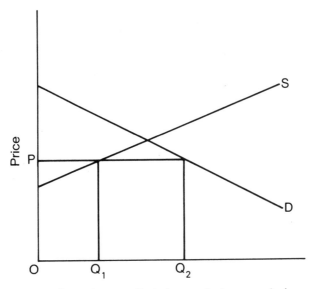

Fig. 9.8 Excess demand for labour

their services. If the government sets a price in the product market, i.e. a price for operations and other forms of treatment, of P, the quantity demanded is $Q_2$. But if this price is reflected in the wage rate of doctors, only $Q_1$ will be supplied. The excess demand, $Q_1 Q_2$, will be manifested in long waiting lists. One way of meeting the excess demand in the long run would be to increase the number of places in medical school and hence the supply of doctors.

## 9.6 Wage Determination under Different Market Conditions

Having discussed the demand for and supply of labour we now analyse the determination of wage rates under different market conditions.

### 9.61 *A Perfectly Competitive Labour Market*

The simplest situation, from an analytical viewpoint, is where both sides of the market are competitive. On the supply side each worker decides how much labour to offer at each wage rate. On the demand side each firm decides how much labour to employ at each wage rate; since there are a large number of employers the wage rate is not affected by the action of any one firm. The equilibrium wage rate is that at which the aggregate supply and demand curves intersect. This is the situation illustrated in Figure 9.1.

### 9.611 *Labour Supplied Competitively but Demanded Monopolistically*

We now consider the situation where the suppliers of labour continue to make their decisions independently as above, but where employers can influence the wage rate by varying the amount of labour they employ. The extreme situation is where there is a single employer of the type of labour in question (or where all the employers are represented by an employers' association). Such an employer is known as a monopsonist, just as the single supplier of a product is known as a monopolist.

We have the usual upward sloping supply curve which, as before, indicates the average price of labour paid by the employer. However there is a very important difference between this and the previous situation. As noted above, the wage rate varies according to the number of workers employed by the (single) employer. Consequently the marginal cost of labour differs from the average cost.

Table 9.2 shows that the firm could attract one worker by paying a weekly

*Table 9.2 Average and Marginal Cost of Labour*

| Number of workers | Average wage rate (£ per week) | Total wage bill (£ per week) | Marginal wage cost (£ per week) |
|---|---|---|---|
| 1 | 40 | 40 | 40 |
| 2 | 42 | 84 | 44 |
| 3 | 44 | 132 | 48 |
| 4 | 46 | 184 | 52 |
| 5 | 48 | 240 | 56 |

wage of £40. But if it wished to attract a second worker it would have to pay both workers £42. The marginal cost of employing the second worker is therefore £44, comprising the £42 paid to the second worker and the additional £2 paid to the first worker. (This analysis assumes that the firm is unable to discriminate between workers in accordance with their transfer earnings.) At every level of employment the marginal cost of labour exceeds average cost.

The monopolistic firm employs labour up to the point where its marginal cost equals its marginal revenue productivity. In Figure 9.9 AC denotes the average cost of employing differing numbers of workers; putting it the other way round it indicates how many workers would be willing to work at various wage rates, i.e. the supply of labour. MC denotes the associated marginal cost. The firm employs Q workers since at that point marginal cost equals marginal revenue product. To employ fewer workers would be to forego the opportunity of additional profits. To employ additional workers would be to add more to cost than to revenue. We can see from the average cost curve that the wage rate is W.

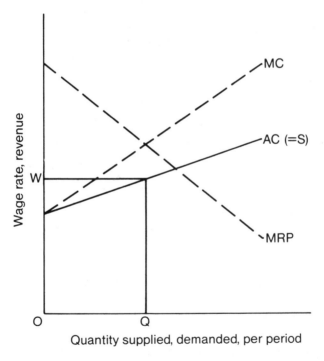

Fig. 9.9 Marginal cost equals marginal revenue productivity

### 9.62 *Trade Unions and Wage Determination* .

We have already noted that trade unions can influence the supply of labour through restrictions on recruitment, training, etc. In this section we are concerned with the involvement of unions in the negotiation of wage rates. If the employer negotiates only with the union, the union in effect acts as a monopoly supplier of labour.

### 9.621 *Labour Supplied Monopolistically but Purchased Competitively*

In Figure 9.10 S and D denote the supply and demand for labour under competitive conditions, as in Figure 9.1. Under these conditions the equilibrium wage rate would be $W_1$, at which $Q_1$ workers would be employed. If the union, acting as a monopoly supplier of labour, negotiated a higher wage rate, $W_2$, employment would fall to $Q_2$.

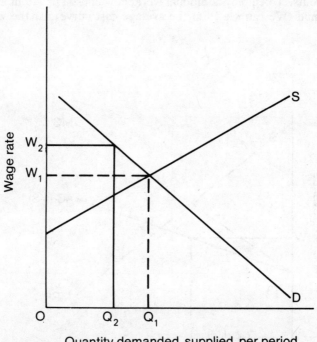

Fig. 9.10 An increase in the wage rate and a fall in employment

It might seem unrealistic to suggest that a trade union would negotiate a wage rate that would lead to a loss of employment among its members. But the suggestion becomes more realistic when it is recognized that the labour force is not static, but constantly changes as older members retire and younger replacements are recruited. The reduction in employment $Q_2Q_1$, shown in Figure 9.10, may occur not because workers are dismissed, but because new workers are not hired to replace workers who leave voluntarily.

### 9.622 *Labour Supplied and Purchased Monopolistically*

In Figure 9.11 $AC_1$ and $MC_1$ denote the cost of labour supplied competitively to a monopolistic purchaser whose marginal revenue productivity and demand curve is MRP. At wage rate $W_1$, $Q_1$ workers would be employed. If the union acts as a monopoly supplier of labour, the average and marginal cost of labour will coincide, as we showed above. In this situation the union could use its monopoly power to increase both the wage rate and employment. When average and marginal cost are constant at wage rate $W_2$, employment is $Q_2$.

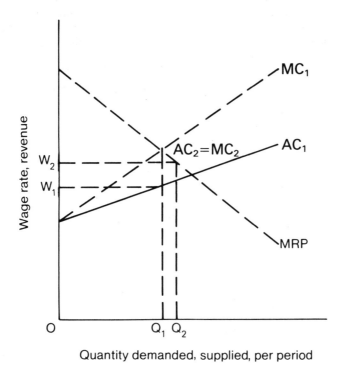

Fig. 9.11 An increase in the wage rate and in employment

### 9.623 *The Impact of Trade Unions on Relative Wages*

It is difficult to measure the effect of trade unions on relative wages because wage rates are affected by many factors in addition to union activity. But it has been estimated that British unions have been able to raise wages on average about 10 per cent above what they would otherwise have been. Insofar as this has led to fewer jobs in the occupations concerned, the effect is an increased supply of labour – and hence lower wages – in other, non-unionized occupations, and/or increased unemployment.

## 9.7 Changes in Relative Factor Prices and Substitution

It is doubtful whether factor markets operate in precisely the way suggested by the marginal productivity theory. To measure marginal productivity it is necessary to hold constant the quantity employed of every factor except one. But in practice it is usual to vary the employment of more than one factor. For example if more labour is employed, more materials will probably be used.

Nevertheless the theory draws attention to a very important fact, namely that as the price of a factor increases the quantity employed falls. This can happen for two reasons. First, if the increase in the price of the factor causes an increase in the prices of those products in which that factor is used, less of those products will be bought, and consequently less of the factor will be employed. (If, at the higher price, the same amount of the product is purchased because all prices and incomes are rising to the same extent, the real price of the factor is unchanged.)

Second, if the price of one factor increases, firms will substitute another factor in order to minimize the increase in their costs. As labour becomes more expensive relative to capital, firms install labour saving machinery. As land becomes more expensive, for example when city centres become highly developed, high-rise offices are constructed.

## 9.8 Productivity

A changing factor mix often leads to change in productivity. For example the installation of labour saving machines will lead to an increase in the productivity of the smaller labour force. For much of the post-war period it was believed that the U.K.'s relatively slow growth in labour productivity was due to a lack of capital investment. But the volume of investment may be less important than its effectiveness. This can be influenced by many of the policies and practices of both management and unions.

From the firm's point of view the productivity of any one factor is less important than the efficiency with which it uses all its factors, its total resources. It is overall efficiency that has an impact on profitability.

## 9.9 Occupational Wage Structures

Table 9.3 gives details of average male earnings in a number of occupations. It can be seen that weekly earnings are almost a half higher in non-manual than in manual occupations. This reflects the fact that overall non-manual occupations require more education and training, which reduces the supply of labour to these occupations.

Of the individual occupations listed, medical practitioners had by far the highest earnings, well ahead of two other groups in the same industry, nurses and hospital porters. (Even after taking account of the higher expenses incurred by doctors, their net earnings remain well above other groups.) These differentials reflect differences in education and training, as well as in aptitude. In some instances education acts as a screening or signalling device. It helps to identify people who are likely to be capable of undertaking demanding tasks; for example students obtain good grades in examinations partly because they can

Table 9.3 Average Gross Weekly and Hourly Earnings

| | Males on adult rates, 1988 | |
| --- | --- | --- |
| | £ per week | pence per hour |
| Medical practitioners | 512 | – |
| Mechanical engineers | 341 | – |
| Scientists and mathematicians | 334 | – |
| Teachers in establishments for further education | 321 | – |
| Primary teachers | 283 | – |
| Managers–department store, supermarket etc. | 260 | – |
| Toolmakers, tool fitters etc. | 229 | 510 |
| Plumbers, pipe fitters | 220 | 492 |
| Laboratory technicians | 208 | – |
| Motor vehicle mechanics (skilled) | 192 | 433 |
| Registered and enrolled nurses, midwives | 191 | 497 |
| Carpenters and joiners (builders and maintenance) | 189 | 428 |
| Painters and decorators | 171 | 402 |
| Refuse collectors, dustmen | 170 | 403 |
| Caretakers | 151 | 347 |
| Salesmen, shop assistants, shelf fillers | 149 | 361 |
| General farm workers | 146 | 308 |
| Hospital porters | 145 | 322 |
| All non-manual occupations | 294 | 749 |
| All manual occupations | 201 | 446 |
| All occupations | 246 | 574 |

– not available
*Source*: Department of Employment: New Earnings Survey

absorb large amounts of information and work well under pressure. In addition education may impart specific skills and knowledge which are useful in the student's future profession. This is clearly true of the education of medical students.

Other professional groups with high earnings include mechanical engineers and scientists and mathematicians. Note the lower earnings of laboratory technicians who are usually educated to a lower level, and who often support the work of engineers and scientists.

Of the two groups of teachers listed in the table, those working in establishments of further education usually have higher qualifications, frequently including a research degree, than primary teachers.

The premium paid for managerial abilities is illustrated by the difference between the earnings of department store and supermarket managers on the one hand and salesmen, shop assistants and shelf fillers on the other.

In the manual occupations the earnings of craftsmen are considerably greater than those of non-craftsmen. Moreover, there are subtantial differences within each of these two groups. For example, compare the earnings of toolmakers and toolfitters, who in many factories are the elite of craftsmen, undertaking a very long training period, with those of motor vehicle mechanics, carpenters and joiners, and painters and decorators.

Within the non-craftsmen group, refuse collectors and dustmen earn more than caretakers and general farm workers. This differential is due partly to the unpleasant nature of the job and partly to the fact that most dustmen benefit from payment-by-results schemes; payments under these schemes accounted for about a quarter of their total earnings.

In general, the differentials in weekly earnings are reflected in hourly earnings. But fewer hours are usually worked in service industries than in manufacturing. This explains why a relatively higher place is occupied in the hourly earnings 'league table' by nurses, shop workers and hospital porters.

## 9.10 Government Labour Market Policies

Labour market policies have four main objectives, whose relative importance varies over time. These are: to reduce the rate of inflation, to influence the distribution of income, to increase the efficiency with which resources are utilized, to reduce the level of unemployment. We discuss these objectives in turn, although one set of policies may contribute to more than one objective. We begin by discussing prices and incomes policies, which are designed mainly to reduce the rate of inflation.

## 9.11 A Reduction in the Rate of Inflation

We show in Chapter 16 that prices and incomes policies might be introduced in an attempt to improve the trade-off between inflation and unemployment. Their advocates believe that these policies enable aggregate expenditure to be sustained at the level necessary to keep unemployment at an acceptable level without causing an unacceptably high rate of inflation.

If only prices *or* incomes are controlled, this is likely to lead to a feeling that the policy is unfair. If wages are held down while prices rise, the real incomes of wage-earners will fall. (Incidentally this does not imply that profits must rise. The increase in prices may be due to higher prices of imported goods, either raw materials and components or finished products.) Conversely, if prices are held down while costs, including wage costs, rise, profits will fall. This is likely to cause the real incomes of shareholders to fall, and lead to a redistribution of purchasing power in favour of wage-earners. In addition, it may lead to a reduction in firms' investment expenditure.

A widespread feeling of unfairness may reduce people's willingness to co-operate with the government in a *voluntary* incomes policy. In the absence of this co-operation the government may be obliged to introduce a *statutory* policy, i.e. a policy backed by law. The difficulties of implementing a voluntary policy, and the interference with individual liberties inherent in a statutory policy, have led some economists to oppose prices and incomes policies.

The post-war years, particularly in the 1960s and 1970s, saw many varieties of prices and incomes policies in the U.K. In the periods of severest restraint wages and prices rose less rapidly than would have been expected in the absence of restraint, given the economic conditions. But when the restraints were subsequently relaxed, much of the ground 'lost' was regained as wages rose more rapidly than the economic conditions suggested they should. This process of catching up has also occurred in other countries that have operated an incomes policy.

Studies have suggested that the effect of an incomes policy on inflation has been modest, the rate of price increase having been reduced by no more than perhaps one per cent. Indeed a report by the Department of Employment suggested that the net impact of the incomes policies during the period 1965–69 was nil.

Although in this sense incomes policies have not been successful, it can be argued that their long-term effects are less important than their short-term contribution to the solving of economic crises.

One of the dangers to which the U.K. is especially prone is that inflation may lead to a loss of confidence in sterling and a consequent outflow of money, causing balance of payments problems.

Even many of its opponents might admit that an incomes policy, if applied for only a short period of time (a few months), could be a useful weapon in the government's economic armoury. Their criticisms apply rather to the long-term consequences of the policies. If prices are being controlled more strictly than wages, the squeeze on company profits and the adverse effects on investment will be emphasized. If wages are being strictly controlled, attention will be drawn to the lack of incentive to workers to work harder, to the difficulties facing employers who wish to increase wages in order to attract additional workers, and to the dangers of confrontations with the unions, which are potentially damaging to the economy.

In more general terms incomes policies are criticized as inhibiting the operation of the price mechanism in product and labour markets, and therefore interfering with the efficient allocation of resources. It is also argued that the conclusion that, in the absence of an incomes policy the government would be forced to restrict demand to such an extent that an unacceptably high rate of unemployment would result, follows only if there has previously been mismanagement by the government. This mismanagement might take the form of too high a level of public expenditure, too rapid an increase in the money supply, or the granting of too strong (monopoly) powers to the trade unions.

### 9.12 Policies Intended to Influence the Distribution of Income

We have seen that the distribution of income can be affected, albeit slightly, by prices and income policies. A more sustained attempt to protect the incomes of the lower paid was the establishment of wages councils, which set wage rates in various occupations. However, the Conservative governments that held office in the 1980s argued that if wages were held above the level that would be established in a free market, employment in these occupations would fall, thus working against one of the other objectives of labour market policies. Consequently the number of Councils was reduced from 40 to 26, covering two and a half million workers. Moreover, the scope of these councils was restricted, in that workers under 21 are no longer covered, and minimum and overtime rates are the only ones set for other workers.

### 9.121 *A National Minimum Wage*

The Labour party opposed the lessening of the influence of the Wages Councils. Indeed some sections of the Party have advocated the introduction of a national minimum wage, as in some other countries. However, there is evidence that a minimum wage seldom achieves its aim of reducing wage differentials.

One possible outcome is that higher-paid workers negotiate pay rises which restore the differentials vis-à-vis the lower paid. If producers pass on the increased costs in the form of higher prices, the real incomes of the lower-paid will not have been improved.

Alternatively, if the lower paid do obtain an increase in real incomes this may be at the expense of the number of such workers employed. This is most likely to happen if the wage differentials are due to differences in productivity. If the wages of the lower-paid workers are increased, and there is not a corresponding increase in productivity, employers will dismiss workers, preferring to use more skilled workers or to substitute capital for labour. Therefore, the overall wages of workers who were formerly low paid may actually fall.

Moreover, this response may occur even when there is a 'non-economic' reason for the differential. For example, if employers have a prejudice against ethnic minority workers they will employ such workers only if they are allowed to pay them lower wages than white workers. Legislation which prevents this may lead to employers substituting white for ethnic minority labour. In 1959 the minimum hourly wage in the U.S.A. was raised from 75 cents to $1. Subsequently a Department of Labour survey of twelve industries affected by the new minimum found that employment had decreased in all but one. The workers whose employment prospects were most affected by the legislation were black teenagers. A survey of thirty studies of the U.S. economy arrived at the conclusion that a 10 per cent increase in the minimum wage would reduce teenage employment by 1–3 per cent.

The operation of a minimum wage can be illustrated by reference to Figure 9.10, already used to show the effect of union monopoly power, and now related to workers affected by the national minimum wage. In the absence of legislation $Q_1$ workers are employed at wage $W_1$. After the introduction of the minimum wage $W_2$, the number of workers employed falls to $Q_2$.

## 9.13 Policies to Increase Efficiency: Training

Governments have sought to increase efficiency by bringing about an increase in the total amount of training, and by trying to ensure that training is directed towards the acquisition of skills for which demand seems likely to exceed supply. Efficiency implies not only that the skills of individual workers are enhanced, but also that, overall, the workforce has the skills required by employers.

### 9.131 *The Industrial Training Act*

These objectives led to the passing in 1964 of the Industrial Training Act, under which a number of Industrial Training Boards were established, each having the responsibility of increasing the quantity and quality of training undertaken in a particular industry. In order to carry out this responsibility, each I.T.B. was empowered to operate a levy and grant system. Each employer above a certain size paid a levy based on its payroll, and in turn received a grant whose value depended upon the Board's assessment of its training performance. Grants of up to 150 per cent of the levy were payable, but in total a surplus of levy over grant was required in order to pay the administrative costs incurred by the Boards.

### 9.132 *The Employment and Training Acts*

Although the levy-grant system had the worthy aim of a fairer distribution of the costs of training, it was a rather cumbersome and costly mechanism and under the Employment and Training Act 1973 employers (except in the construction industry) were allowed to opt out of the scheme, provided they could prove that their training was satisfactory.

There were in 1981 twenty-four I.T.B.s covering 63 per cent of Britain's industrial workforce, plus a number of non-industrial Boards. Despite this extensive coverage, there is little firm evidence concerning their impact on training. For example, although the proportion of boy school-leavers starting apprenticeships rose from 36 per cent in 1963 to 43 per cent in 1968, it had fallen back to 39 per cent by 1972, and shortages of skilled workers continued to occur – shortages which may limit the ability of the economy to expand in line with future increases in demand.

It appeared that the money spent by the I.T.B.s was not producing a satisfactory return and the Employment and Training Act 1981 allowed the Secretary of State for Employment to change the number and scope of the I.T.B.s. It was subsequently announced that the number of Boards was to be reduced to seven (plus the Agricultural Training Board which comes under the Ministry of Agriculture). Moreover these Boards were henceforth to be financed by the industries concerned, under another provision of the 1981 Act.

### 9.133 *Government-sponsored Training Schemes*

A wide range of training opportunities is now sponsored by the government. *The Youth Training Scheme* provides a two-year training programme for 16-year-old school leavers, and a one-year programme for 17-year-old leavers. The two-year programme involves at least twenty weeks off-the-job training, e.g. at a local technical college, in addition to on-the-job training and planned work experience. The second year provides specific skill training leading, wherever possible, to vocational qualifications.

Trainees receive a tax-free allowance, and the total cost to the government in 1987–8, when the number of trainees was 376,000, was over £1 billion. The number of trainees expected in 1988/9 was 423,000 and the eventual target is 500,000 trainees a year.

The *Employment Training* programme, launched by the Training Agency in 1988, is a comprehensive training programme which incorporated all other training programmes for unemployed adults, such as the Community Programme and the Job Training Scheme. The programme is aimed primarily at adults who have been unemployed for at least 6 months. The target is to provide training for 600,000 people at an estimated cost of £1.4 billion a year.

Everyone on the programme is entitled to spend at least 40 per cent of their time on 'off-the-job' learning, provided by colleges, employers etc. People who do not find employment after completing their training, are able to join a Jobclub where they receive advice on finding employment, or they may start up their own business with assistance from the Enterprise Allowance Scheme.

In total the government planned to spend £3.5 billion in 1988–9 and almost £3.8 billion in 1989–90 on employment, training and related measures.

In 1989 the government announced plans for a country-wide network of *Training and Enterprise Councils*. The directors of the Councils will be local industrialists, trade union officials etc. They will have the responsibility for assessing training needs in their area and for ensuring that these needs are met. It is envisaged that eventually the Councils will take over the running of existing government-sponsored programmes such as YTS and ET.

## 9.14 Industrial Relations Legislation

An improvement in efficiency is one of the objectives of industrial relations legislation. Especially important is legislation intended to reduce the incidence of strikes. The Employment Act 1982 made trade unions liable in the same way as their individual officials if they are found to be responsible for unlawful industrial action. It also restricted lawful trade disputes to disputes between workers and their own employer. The Trade Union Act 1984 provided for secret ballots by union members on proposals for strikes or other industrial action. The Employment Act 1988 protected workers against dismissal for non-union membership, and against unjustifiable discipline by their union (e.g. if imposed for working during a dispute).

## 9.15 A Reduction in Unemployment

We begin our discussion of this objective by examining the main types of unemployment.

### 9.151 *Demand-deficient Unemployment*

This term denotes unemployment arising from a general deficiency in demand affecting almost all industries.

### 9.152 *Cyclical Unemployment*

A number of economists have claimed to have found evidence of fairly regular cycles in economic activity, one aspect of which has been the rate of unemployment. Some economists have suggested that the high unemployment of the 1980s was part of a 50-year Kondratieff cycle, previous peaks being in the 1880s and the 1930s. Other economists claim to have identified cycles lasting from six to eleven years, and from two to four years.

Many economists suggest that demand deficient and cyclical unemployment can be most appropriately countered by general demand-management policies, and in particular by fiscal and monetary policy (see Chapters 16–18). However, there has been an increasing awareness of the need to supplement such policies by other measures, including those discussed in Section 9.13.

### 9.153 *Frictional Unemployment*

This type of unemployment arises when workers change jobs, either voluntarily or because of redundancy, and do not *immediately* find another job. Frictional unemployment is essentially short-term and can be reduced by improving information about vacancies, e.g. through Jobcentres.

### 9.154 *Structural Unemployment*

Structural unemployment arises when there is a long-term decline in the demand for the products of an industry, and other industries are unable to absorb the redundant workers. This inadequacy of alternative employment is clearly most likely to occur when the declining industry accounts for a high proportion of the total employment in a given area. Examples of industries that have suffered from structural unemployment in twentieth-century Britain have included cotton textiles, coalmining, slate-quarrying and shipbuilding.

One method of tackling structural unemployment is to induce firms in other industries to move into the area that is suffering from heavy unemployment. The various forms of inducement that may be used are outlined in Chapter 21 during our discussion of regional economic policy. Another approach, often used in conjunction with the first, is to re-train the workers in skills required by employers in other industries.

### 9.155 *Technological Unemployment*

The demand for workers in a particular industry may fall because of the introduction of machines that can perform the same operations more quickly and/or accurately. Unemployment due to this cause (which may not be confined to specific industries) is sometimes known as technological unemployment. The policies adopted to deal with structural unemployment are also appropriate here especially those designed to increase the amount of training undertaken.

### 9.156 *Seasonal Unemployment*

As the term suggests, seasonal unemployment arises when the demand for workers' services is seasonal, e.g. tourism, agriculture, catering. Although not very important numerically, seasonal unemployment gives rise to a situation of conflict. On the one hand, the incomes of the workers affected would rise if permanent employment in other industries were provided. On the other hand, this provision of alternative employment would make it difficult for the 'seasonal employers' to attract and retain labour. This dilemma is especially acute when the local economy is highly dependent on the prosperity of the seasonal industries.

## 9.16 Summary and Conclusions

Wage rates and employment are determined by the supply and demand for labour, both of which are influenced by a wide range of factors. The interaction of supply and demand may not always produce a satisfactory outcome, and governments have introduced many measures intended to affect the rate of change of wages, to influence the distribution of income, to improve the efficiency of the labour force and to reduce unemployment.

Structural, frictional, technological and seasonal unemployment could all exist, even though the level of demand was sufficient for full employment. The failure to attain full employment is then due to a mismatch in the labour market: workers remain unemployed because they do not have adequate information about vacancies, because they do not possess the skills required by employers, or because they do not live in (and will not move to) areas in which jobs are available.

Demand deficient unemployment, on the other hand, affects all sectors of the economy (although not equally) and is due to a general deficiency of demand. This deficiency in demand may arise in (irregular) cycles.

## Further Reading

Artis, M. J., Ed., *The U.K. Economy* (London: Weidenfeld and Nicolson, 11th Edn, 1986), Ch. 5.

Begg, D., Fischer, S. and Dornbusch, R., *Economics* (London: McGraw-Hill, 2nd Edn, 1987), Chs 10 and 11.

Griffiths, A. and Walls, S., *Applied Economics* (London: Longman, 2nd Edn, 1986), Ch. 20.

Hardwick, P., Khan, B. and Langmead, J., *An Introduction to Modern Economics* (London: Longman, 2nd Edn, 1986), Ch. 15.

Lipsey, R. G. and Harbury, C., *First Principles of Economics* (London: Weidenfeld and Nicolson, 1988), Chs 20 and 21.

Livesey, F., *A Textbook of Economics* (London: Longman, 3rd Edn, 1989), Ch. 8.

Maunder, P., Myers, D., Wall, N. and Miller, R. L., *Economics Explained* (London: Collins, 1987), Ch. 26.

## Revision Exercises

1 Discuss the factors that influence the equilibrium wage rate and employment.
2 Define 'transfer earnings' and 'economic rent' and explain their significance.
3 Why are doctors paid more than nurses?
4 Under what circumstances do trade unions have the greatest influence on the incomes of their members?
5 Discuss the proposition that a trade union can increase the incomes of its members only at the cost of reducing the number of jobs.
6 State the law of diminishing returns (variable proportions) and explain its significance.

7 Explain, with examples, how changes in the relative prices of factors of production give rise to substitution.
8 Discuss the main objectives of government labour market policies.
9 Explain why it is important to distinguish between the various forms of unemployment.
10 'Government policies sometimes conflict; this is especially true of labour market policies.' Discuss.

# 10. *Competition Policy*

## 10.1 Introduction

In Chapters 6 to 9 we have discussed the ways in which prices are determined in various types of market. We have also shown that the higher the price in any market the less will be the quantity produced and sold.

Governments frequently intervene in the operation of the price mechanism in such a way as to affect the price set and the resources employed in particular markets.

We have already discussed three forms of intervention. In Chapter 5 we showed how equilibrium price and output are affected by the imposition of indirect taxes or the granting of subsidies. In Chapter 7 we examined the effect on price of land banks and buffer stock schemes. In Chapter 9 we showed that prices may be controlled as part of a prices and incomes policy. Competition policy, the theme of this chapter, seeks to influence the structure of markets and the behaviour of firms including pricing behaviour.

## 10.2 Market Structure, Conduct and Performance

The three aspects of a market, or industry, that are of most concern to competition policy are structure, conduct and performance. Examples of each aspect are given in Figure 10.1. This figure also suggests that the structure of a market affects the conduct (or behaviour) of the firms in that market, which in turn affects their performance.

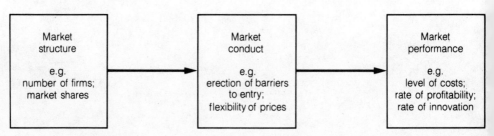

### 10.21 *Market Structure*

Competition policy is most concerned with the number of suppliers and with their market shares. In Chapters 6 and 7 we distinguished between concentrated markets, in which a few firms, each with a substantial market share, adopt cost-based pricing, and less concentrated, open markets where price is determined by the interplay of aggregate demand and supply. In the models presented in Chapter 8, there are a large number of suppliers (each with a small market share) in perfect and monopolistic competition, a few suppliers in oligopoly and only one supplier in monopoly.

## 10.22 *Market Conduct*

Pricing is a very important aspect of market conduct, and we have already indicated how market structure may affect pricing policies. Briefly, the more concentrated the market, the greater the degree of influence over price exerted by the individual supplier. One consequence is that prices tend to be less flexible in concentrated than in unconcentrated markets.

It is further suggested that although price competition is relatively unimportant in concentrated markets, the firms adopt various forms of non-price competition, e.g. advertising, research and development aimed at creating new products and/or new processes. One consequence of non-price competition may be that it is more difficult for new suppliers to enter the market. (But barriers to entry do not necessarily arise directly from the activities of existing suppliers. For example, in some markets huge capital expenditure may be required prior to production.)

## 10.23 *Market Performance*

A very important aspect of performance is the rate of profitability. If the firms in concentrated markets take advantage of their greater freedom to set prices that are high in relation to costs, this may enable them to earn above-average profits. This is one example of the relationship shown in Figure 10.1, where market structure affects conduct and performance. (However, note that there could be an alternative explanation of the relationship between concentration and profitability. If some firms in an industry are very efficient they may well earn above-average profits and also increase their market share, i.e. performance (superior efficiency) affects structure rather than the other way round.)

We have shown in earlier chapters that large firms (in concentrated markets) are likely to benefit from economies of scale and hence to enjoy lower costs. If this occurs it means that even if these firms earn higher than average profits, their prices might still be below what they would have been if the industry had been less concentrated.

The final aspect of market performance identified in Figure 10.1 is the rate of innovation (the introduction of new products and/or processes). The higher spending on R and D, an aspect of conduct noted above, is likely to result in a higher rate of innovation in concentrated than in less concentrated markets. (However, it should be noted that there is some evidence that when the level of concentration reaches a very high level, as in monopoly, the rate of innovation tends to decline. Moreover, many important innovations have been made by small firms, as shown in Section 10.10.)

## 10.3 Implications for Competition Policy

The main implication of the above analysis is that economic theory provides very few clear principles on which to base competition policy. This is partly because a particular market structure may give rise to performance which is desirable in some respects but undesirable in others. (As we show below, one of the consequences of this is that policy in the U.K. has proceeded on a pragmatic basis, with each situation being considered on its merits.) Moreover, as noted above, it may be difficult to decide whether market structure affects conduct and performance as indicated in Figure 10.1, or whether structure is influenced by conduct and performance. Finally, it should be noted that monopoly and perfect competition are theoretical models that often appear in examination questions but seldom in the real world. Consequently any conclusions drawn on the basis of these models are of very limited use for policy makers.

However, economic theory does lead to the conclusion that, in general, more stringent control should be exercised over collective restrictive practices, i.e. situations in which several firms co-ordinate their policies, than over the policies of firms acting independently. The reasoning leading to this conclusion is as follows. While a collective agreement may have the adverse effects associated with monopoly, especially above-average profits, it is less likely to give rise to the beneficial effects of monopoly; in particular, since each firm remains separate, economies of scale are less likely to be achieved.

## 10.4 The Scope of Competition Policy in the United Kingdom

The main areas of legislation examined in this chapter are those relating to monopolies, mergers, collective restrictive practices, and resale price maintenance. We also look briefly at official policy towards small firms.

## 10.5 Legislation Relating to Monopolies

Under the *Monopolies and Restrictive Practices Act 1948* a monopoly was said to exist when one-third of the supply of a good was in the hands of one firm or group of companies. Monopolies could be referred by a government minister (the Secretary of State) for investigation by the Monopolies and Restrictive Practices Commission, now the Monopolies and Mergers Commission (MMC). The 1965 *Monopolies and Mergers Act* made it possible for the supply of services to be referred to the MMC, thus doing away with the distinction between goods and services that never made economic sense. Under the *Fair Trading Act 1973* the Director General of Fair Trading (DGFT) was also given the right, subject to the Minister's agreement, to refer monopolies to the MMC. This Act also reduced the market share definition of a monopoly from one-third to one-quarter, and added 'maintaining and promoting competition' to the list of criteria by which a monopoly was to be evaluated by the Commission.

In an attempt to make policy more flexible and less cumbersome the *Competition Act 1980* made it possible for specific practices by named individual firms to be investigated without the need for a full investigation of all major suppliers in the market. Examples of anti-competitive practices are: arrangements under which a distributor agrees to sell the products of only one manufacturer; the refusal to supply one product unless the distributor buys other products from the same manufacturer; selling below cost in order to force competitors out of business.

### 10.6 Legislation Relating to Mergers

Mergers were first brought within the scope of legislation under the *Monopolies and Mergers Act 1965*. Since then proposed mergers have, like monopolies, been referred to the MMC. The Minister may refer a merger either on the market-share criterion or because the assets of the merged companies would exceed a certain size (currently £30 million). If the MMC finds that the merger would be against the public interest, the Minister can (and usually does) forbid it.

One of the problems in implementing the legislation is that because of its size and composition – most members serve in a part-time capacity – the MMC cannot investigate more than a fraction (about 3 per cent) of 'eligible' mergers. Since only about one-third of the referred proposed mergers actually go ahead the decision as to which mergers are referred is crucial.

### 10.7 Legislation Relating to Collective Restrictive Practices

The investigations conducted by the Monopolies and Restrictive Practices Commission under the 1948 Act, revealed that collective restrictive practices, e.g. agreements on price, output, forms of supply, were widespread in British industry. To counteract these practices, the *Restrictive Trade Practices Act* was passed in 1956.

The Act laid down that all restrictive agreements should be registered with the Registrar of Restrictive Trading Agreements. Restrictive agreements were defined as agreements between two or more persons carrying on business in the production or supply of goods, under which restrictions are accepted by the parties in respect of the prices to be charged, the terms or conditions of sale, quantities or types to be produced, the process of manufacture, the persons or areas from which goods are to be acquired. The Act did not apply to agreements between one manufacturer and one distributor.

The Registrar was given the responsibility of selecting agreements for consideration by the Restrictive Practices Court, and also of presenting the case against the agreement to the Court. Under the Fair Trading Act 1973, discussed below, these responsibilities were taken over by the Director-General of Fair Trading.

The Court has to determine whether an agreement operates in or against the public interest, and whether it should be allowed to continue in existence. This case-by-case approach demonstrates the pragmatic attitude adopted in the U.K. However, the Act provides specific guidance to aid the Court in its deliberations. There is a presumption underlying the Act that restrictions on competition operate against the public interest, and the parties to the agreement can attempt to justify it before the Court only on certain specified grounds. These 'gateways' are the following:

1 That the restriction is reasonably necessary to protect the public against injury.
2 That the removal of the restriction would deny to the public, as purchasers, consumers or users of any goods, specific and substantial benefits.
3 That the restriction is reasonably necessary to counteract measures taken by a person, not party to the agreement, with a view to restricting competition.
4 That the restriction is reasonably necessary to enable fair terms to be negotiated with a larger supplier or purchaser.
5 That the removal of the restriction would be likely to have a serious and persistent adverse effect on unemployment in areas in which the industry is concentrated.
6 That the removal of the restriction would be likely to cause a substantial reduction in export business.
7 That the restriction is reasonably required for the purpose of supporting other restrictions in the agreement which are in the public interest.
8 That the restriction does not directly or indirectly restrict or discourage competition to any material degree in any relevant trade or industry and is not likely to do so.

This last 'gateway' (8) was added by the Restrictive Trade Practices Act 1968, which also introduced more flexibility into the policy by empowering the Department of Trade and Industry to negotiate with firms about a modification of an agreement that would otherwise have gone to the Court. In addition to successfully negotiating one or other of the eight gateways, the parties to the agreement have to satisfy the Court that the benefit they have demonstrated is sufficient to outweigh any disadvantages, or any detriment to the public, found to arise from the agreement.

It proved difficult to convince the Court that a restrictive agreement should be allowed to continue, particularly in the early hearings. Of the first forty-one cases referred to the Court only seven were defended. Of these seven, only one was defended successfully. Although the success rate has subsequently improved, it has remained below 30 per cent.

The small chance of success in the Court, together with the not inconsiderable cost in time and money of fighting a case, led to the abandonment of the vast majority of agreements.

Some of the abandoned agreements were replaced by agreements to exchange information about such matters as changes in costs and prices. Since these *information agreements* can have a similar effect to the abandoned agreements, they were brought within the scrutiny of the Registrar (subsequently the D.G.F.T.) by the *Restrictive Trade Practices Act 1968*.

Under the 1973 Fair Trading Act the coverage of the restrictive practices legislation was extended to commercial (as distinct from professional) services, e.g. estate agents, hairdressers. The Act covered agreements in four broad fields:

1 Any arrangement between two or more companies to fix prices or charge a standard rate of commission.
2 Agreements between companies to standardize terms on which they will deal with their customers.
3 Agreements between competitors to take only orders of a certain size.

4 Arrangements whereby companies agree only to deal with certain sectors of the population or specific geographical areas.

## 10.8 Policies Relating to Resale Price Maintenance

Under the *Resale Prices Act 1964* a manufacturer is allowed to enforce resale prices only if he can convince the Restrictive Practices Court that this would be in the public interest.

As with collective agreements, specific grounds are laid down for the justification of r.p.m. These are that, in its absence, the public would suffer in one of the following ways:

1 The quality and variety of goods available for sale would be substantially reduced.
2 The number of retail establishments in which the goods were sold would be substantially reduced.
3 The retail prices of the goods would increase.
4 Goods would be sold under conditions likely to cause danger to health in consequence of their misuse by the public.
5 Any necessary services provided in connection with the sale of the goods would cease to be provided, or would be substantially reduced.

Moreover the Act is based upon the presumption that distributors, especially retailers, who wish to try to increase their sales by reducing prices, should not normally be prevented by manufacturers from doing so. Consequently, even if a manufacturer succeeds in justifying r.p.m. on one of the above grounds, he then has to show that this advantage of r.p.m. outweighs the disadvantage of restricting the freedom of distributors. This has proved to be a very difficult task, and only the manufacturers of books, maps and certain medicaments have succeeded in proving their case.

## 10.9 Changes in Policy

Since the first legislation was passed in 1948, competition policy has steadily become wider in its application. However, many economists believe that a tougher policy is required, and there is no doubt that further changes in policy will be made in the near future.

### 10.91 *Policy Concerning Monopoly and Mergers*

We have already noted one of the main criticisms of the way in which policy is implemented at present, namely the very small proportion of proposed mergers considered by the M.M.C. The low referral rate means, of course, that the vast majority of proposed mergers have gone ahead. This has resulted in a marked increase in concentration in many industries.

Most investigations of the performance of merged firms have found that relatively few of the benefits claimed at the time of the merger had actually arisen. Given the potential disadvantages of concentration, discussed above, it is argued that the rate of merger activity should be slowed. One way of doing this, suggested by the D.G.F.T. and others, would be that for mergers above a certain size, the burden of proof should be changed. Instead of the M.M.C. having to demonstrate that a merger would be against the public interest in order for it to be blocked, the merging companies would have to demonstrate that the merger would be in the public interest for it to proceed.

However, this proposal has not been accepted by the present government. Indeed the government's view, as stated in *Mergers Policy*, a paper issued by the Department of Trade and Industry in 1988, is that the present policy is satisfactory. The proposals for change contained in that document were concerned solely with procedures, the aim being to speed up the vetting process.

### 10.911 *Policy in the European Community*

Policy concerning monopolies is based on Article 86 of the Treaty of Rome, which states that any abuse of a dominant position within the Common Market or in a substantial part of it shall be prohibited. This is tougher than the corresponding U.K. legislation. Practices deemed to constitute abuse include: imposing unfair purchase or selling prices; limiting production, markets or technical development to the prejudice of consumers; applying dissimilar conditions to equivalent transactions with other trading parties.

As an example of a practice that would be allowed under U.K. but not E.C. legislation, consider 'dual pricing'. British producers selling abroad have sometimes found it desirable to allow their overseas distributors higher margins because, for example, tougher competition from domestic products requires the overseas distributors to undertake more promotional activities than their counterparts in the U.K. The higher margins to distributors would imply higher consumer prices abroad than at home. For example, the Distillers Company sold whisky at a higher price in France than in the U.K. and to support the higher price tried to restrict 'parallel imports' via unofficial distributors at lower prices. This was, however, ruled to be illegal by the E.C. on the grounds that it distorted competition.

With the move towards the single European market in 1992 we can expect the E.C. to exert a greater influence over the activities of monopolies so that, despite the government's current attitude, U.K. monopolies may experience more curbs on their activities when they engage in trade with other E.C. countries.

The European Community is also likely to exert more influence over proposed mergers. The member countries have agreed that the E.C. should vet cross-border mergers involving companies with a combined turnover of 5 billion Ecus (approximately £3.6 billion) This means that about thirty or forty mergers a year require E.C. approval.

### 10.92 *Policy Relating to Collective Restrictive Practices*

In contrast to its views on monopoly and mergers policy, the U.K. government has suggested major changes in restrictive practices legislation. The D.T.I. paper, *Review of Restrictive Trade Practices Policy*, issued in 1988, proposed that the system followed since 1956 should be replaced by a system based on Article 85 of the Treaty of Rome.

Under Article 85 'Agreements between undertakings, decisions by associations of undertakings and concerted practices which may affect trade between member states and which have as their objectives the prevention, restriction or distortion of competition within the Common Market shall be prohibited as incompatible with the Common Market.' An agreement may be exempted from this prohibition if it contributes to improving the production or distribution of goods, or to promoting technical or economic progress, while allowing consumers a fair share of the resulting benefits.

This article is similar to U.K. restrictive practices legislation in its emphasis on conduct and performance, and the requirement to weigh possible benefits and detriments. But on paper the E.C. policy is tougher: it covers a wider range of agreements, imposes heavier penalties (fines up to 10 per cent of the company's turnover in the previous year as well as the annulment of the agreement) and has more limited conditions for exemption (gateways).

The D.T.I. paper also promised that the authorities would be given greatly enhanced powers to command information, e.g. by inspecting company files without giving prior notice. This is sure to be welcomed by the Director General of Fair Trading who complained in a speech given in 1986 about his limited powers: 'My powers to investigate suspected unregistered agreements . . . are only exercisable when I already have reasonable grounds for believing that an unregistered and therefore unlawful agreement exists – a catch 22 situation if ever there was one.' We noted earlier that the vast majority of registered agreements have been abandoned. However, unregistered agreements on market sharing and collusive tendering have subsequently been discovered in industries as diverse as telephone cables, concrete pipes, copying equipment, gas boilers, bread manufacturing and ferry services. This is clear evidence of the inadequacy of the existing policy.

## 10.10 Small Firms and Economic Efficiency

In the earlier discussion about the size of firm, we gave most attention to legislation designed to limit the size of firm and control the activities of large firms. There are also good reasons for government action to promote the interests of small firms, because of the contribution to economic efficiency made by small firms.

### 10.101 *Small Firms and Economic Growth*

A study of U.K. experience by Professor Gallagher of Newcastle University concluded that of the new jobs created between 1971 and 1981 31 per cent came from businesses employing less than 20 people, even though this sector accounted for only 13 per cent of the workforce at the beginning of the period. A further 21 per cent of new jobs were created in firms with between 20 and 99 workers, a sector which had only 16 per cent of the workforce at the beginning of the period.

## 10.102 *Small Firms and Consumer Welfare*

Innovation – the introduction of new products and processes – contributes to consumer welfare. Although their superior financial and technical resources often give large firms an advantage here, many important innovations have been made by small firms. Some of those listed by the Committee of Inquiry into Small Firms (the Bolton Committee) included the tufting of carpets, the ultrasonic detector, solid state laser machining and the use of lasers for drilling, printed circuit boards, glass reinforced plastic lifeboats, four-wheel drive for private cars, and polyurethane coatings for leathers. More recently small firms have been responsible for many innovations in micro-processors and other aspects of information technology.

Another aspect of consumer welfare is the provision of variety, in terms of style, colour, etc. Flexibility of supply in response to changes in demand is also beneficial to consumers. It has been claimed that in these latter two respects, small firms play an especially important role. The physical facilities of large firms are often geared to the production of standardized products. Also, in so far as large firms have elaborate procedures for taking decisions, they may lack the flexibility to compete successfully in markets where demand constantly fluctuates and where fashions frequently change. This contention was supported by some of the evidence presented to the Bolton Committee. A large London department store indicated that virtually all its turnover of women's fashions and half of its sales of top-quality clothing were supplied by small firms, defined as firms with less than 200 employees. A large diversified manufacturing company had 950 suppliers, of which 40 per cent were small firms. A tractor manufacturer reported that 60 per cent of the parts and components entering its main plant came from small firms.

## 10.103 *Government Support for Small Firms*

Measures adopted to support small firms include certain forms of regional assistance not available to large firms, a concessionary rate of corporation tax on small profits, the introduction of specialist sources of finance (see below), and granting exemption from certain obligations placed on larger firms e.g. with respect to workers' rights.

Several official enquiries have revealed that the expansion of small firms is frequently hindered by an inability to raise sufficient finance, and several government-sponsored schemes have been introduced in order to counteract this problem.

The *Business Expansion Scheme* (BES) grew out of the Business Start Up Scheme, which was introduced in 1981. The BES permits investors to offset the cost of buying shares against their marginal rate of tax. They can also sell their shares free of capital gains tax. To qualify for relief investors must invest at least £500 and may not invest more than £40,000 in any tax year. They must also retain the shares for at least five years. Investment can be made directly in the company concerned or via a fund. Finance has been provided for established businesses, start-up businesses and management buy-outs. The average investment made by BES funds has been estimated at £150,000, and about a third of BES companies are thought to raise less than £50,000.

The tax incentives offered to investors are intended to compensate for the high risks attached to this form of investment; it was estimated that one-fifth of the BES companies financed in 1983–4 went bankrupt within the next two years.

The *Loan Guarantee Scheme* (LGS) was also introduced in 1981, initially for three years and subsequently renewed. By January 1989 the LGS had helped 20,000 small firms to raise £680 million.

The rationale of the LGS is that some worthwhile projects might fail to find adequate finance because of the absence of a 'track record'. Under the scheme the government provides to the lender a guarantee of up to 70 per cent of the loan. A premium of 2.5 per cent over normal business lending rates is charged on loans, intended to compensate for possible losses. The need for a premium can be seen from the fact that 40 per cent of the companies that used the LGS in the year to May 1982 foundered within the next three years. By April 1987 business failures had cost the government more than £100 million.

The main objective of *Local Enterprise Boards* is to preserve and create jobs, and it is therefore not surprising that they are most active in the more depressed parts of the country. They are funded by local authorities, but use this funding as a lever to attract private capital to finance projects. Most of this finance is used to support smaller businesses: funding between £10,000 and £100,000 is typical.

### 10.11 Consumer Protection

Since all the policies discussed in this chapter are intended to increase economic efficiency, and to prevent firms from abusing their market power, they can all be seen as helping to protect consumers. But in the U.K. (as in many other countries) governments have also introduced legislation to provide more immediate protection for consumers. When formulating their production and marketing policies, firms have to take account of this legislation.

Various Acts, consolidated in the Weights and Measures Act 1985, established a uniform system of weights and measures. They also provided for the control of weighing and measuring equipment used for trade purposes and for protection against short weight and short measure in commodities, and laid down that certain prepacked items should display the quantity of their contents.

Three Acts were designed to protect the consumer against dangers, short- or long-term, to health and life. The Food Act 1984 and its forerunner, the Food and Drugs Act 1955, empowered the government to make regulations concerning the composition and nutritional quality of food, and its labelling and advertising. The Medicines Act 1968 gives the government similar powers in respect of medicinal products. The Consumer Safety Act 1978 empowered the government, in order to prevent risk of death or personal injury, to make regulations about the composition, design and construction of goods.

The Sale of Goods Act 1893 set out the implications for both parties in any contract of sale of goods. The Supply of Goods (Implied Terms) Act 1973 ensured that consumers could no longer lose the rights they have under the 1893 Act. This meant, for example, that these rights were not negated by notices exhibited in a shop or on the back of a receipt. These rights entitle the buyer, among other things, to goods corresponding to the description and fit for the purpose for which they were sold. These two Acts were subsequently replaced by the Unfair Contract Terms Act 1977 and the Sale of Goods Act 1979.

The Trade Descriptions Act 1968 made it an offence to describe goods incorrectly and to give misleading indications as to their price. In addition, the government can require the provision of specified information in advertisements.

These Acts constitute a substantial body of legislation designed to protect the consumer. Nevertheless the Fair Trading Act represented an important step forward in that it established an Office, that of the Director-General of Fair Trading, with the responsibility of keeping a close and continuous watch over the effect upon consumers' interests of trading practices and commercial activities of all kinds.

If the Director-General identifies a practice he considers to be against the public interest, he may propose that an order be made to regulate or prohibit the practice. This proposal is first considered by the Consumer Protection Advisory Committee, which is composed of people who are experienced in all aspects of consumer protection. If the Committee approves the proposal, the Minister (Secretary of State) may place an order before Parliament and, if Parliament approves, it acquires the force of law.

In practice the Director-General has preferred wherever possible to obtain a *voluntary* undertaking that a practice he considers to be unsatisfactory will be changed. For example, he has initiated discussions that have led to the drawing up of improved codes of conduct by several groups, including travel operators, the manufacturers of domestic electrical appliances, the advertising industry, area electricity boards, motor traders and shoe retailers. A common feature of these codes is that the industry should set certain minimum standards of conduct and establish an independent arbitration service for complaints.

The voluntary self-regulating approach, however, is not always practicable, for various reasons. It may be, for example, that so many trade interests are interwoven that it is impossible for an 'industry' view to be obtained or for industry representatives to police any agreement that might be reached. This was an important factor in the decision of the Director-General that the regulation of 'bargain offers' would necessitate a Parliamentary order. The intention of the regulations would be to ensure that the consumer was given a more precise definition of such an offer. So if, for example, petrol is advertised at '4p off the usual price', the advertisement has to state what the garage's usual price is, thus justifying the claim. In addition certain claims such as 'worth half as much again' or '30 per cent saving on big city prices', are forbidden. The Fair Trading Act also provided powers to control pyramid selling and similar schemes.

The Consumer Credit Act 1974 increased the protection afforded to the consumer across the whole spectrum of credit transactions, including hire purchase, personal loans, credit cards and trading checks. An especially important provision of the Act requires the disclosure of the full cost of credit.

Finally, orders under the Prices Act 1974 require that information should be provided not only on the selling price of an article but also on the equivalent price for a standard quantity. For example, if the standard quantity for a product was a kilogram, and a tin containing 2.25 kilograms sold at 67.5p, then the unit price of 30p per kilogram would also be stated.

## 10.12 Summary and Conclusions

Competition policy has several aims: to influence market structure, especially by preventing mergers which would result in high levels of concentration; to control firms' activities judged to be anti-competitive or against the public interest in other ways; these activities might refer to one firm e.g. if a manufacturer attempted to enforce the price at which distributors sold his products, or to two or more firms acting together e.g. when several suppliers agree what price each will set.

Governments have sought to exercise stricter control over the activities of firms acting together than over monopolists. But in view of increasing evidence that many collective restrictive practices exist, the government has announced its intention to move to a system nearer to that adopted in the European Community. This system has a wider scope and gives the authorities more power to command information and to fine firms found guilty of breaking the law.

Although the present government is broadly satisfied with the existing legislation relating to monopolies and mergers, critics of the policy have advocated strengthening the policy e.g. by requiring firms to show that a proposed merger would benefit the public before being allowed to proceed.

The government has introduced a number of measures to benefit small firms, especially by making it easier to acquire the capital required to finance expansion. A thriving small firms sector is believed to be an important contributor to economic growth and consumer welfare.

## Further Reading

Artis, M. J., *The U.K. Economy* (London: Weidenfeld and Nicolson, 11th Edn, 1986), Ch. 4.

Begg, D., Fischer, S. and Dornbusch, R., *Economics* (London: McGraw-Hill, 2nd Edn, 1987), Ch. 16.

Griffiths, A. and Wall, S., *Applied Economics* (London: Longman, 2nd Edn, 1986), Chs 4 and 5.

Livesey, F., *A Textbook of Economics* (London: Longman, 3rd Edn, 1989), Ch. 10.

Turvey, R., *Demand and Supply* (London: Allen and Unwin, 2nd Edn, 1980), Ch. 5.

## Revision Exercises

1 'Economic analysis provides no firm conclusion on which government can base policies relating to competition.' Discuss.

2 'Policies designed to increase the level of competition will increase economic efficiency only in the long run, if at all.' Discuss.

3  Discuss the advantages and disadvantages of different forms of growth.
4  Why is it sometimes said that collective restrictive agreements give rise to the disadvantages associated with monopoly without any of the latter's advantages?
5  Discuss the case for a policy that would reduce the number of mergers, and outline the main features of such a policy.
6  Discuss the relationship between market structure and consumer welfare.
7  Discuss the advantages and disadvantages of a policy which prevents manufacturers from enforcing the prices at which their products are sold by distributors.
8  'The introduction of a large body of legislation designed to protect the consumer provides a sad commentary on the nature of business ethics.' Discuss.
9  In view of the many advantages enjoyed by large firms, why do so many small firms exist?
10  Discuss the contribution of small firms to economic efficiency and consumer welfare.

# 11. *Public Sector Producers*

## 11.1 Introduction

Of the various types of public-sector producers the most important are the nationalized industries – British Rail, the Post Office, British Coal etc. The nationalized industries account for around 5 per cent of U.K. output and almost 4 per cent of employment. Other public-sector producers include central government trading bodies, e.g. Her Majesty's Stationery Office, local authority trading bodies operating, for example, markets or leisure centres, and public corporations which do not derive most of their revenue from the sale of goods and services, e.g. the British Broadcasting Corporation, whose main source of revenue is licence fees.

The existence of public-sector producers may seem to imply that the production of these goods and services would be undertaken less satisfactorily by private-sector producers. It is therefore appropriate to begin this chapter by considering the *potential* advantages of public ownership. (We stress potential since experience suggests that these advantages frequently fail to occur in practice.)

## 11.2 The Economic Case for Public Enterprise

### 11.21 *Greater Efficiency*

In some instances, although under private ownership each individual producer may be highly efficient, the efficiency of the industry as a whole may be less than if production is concentrated in the hands of a single publicly owned enterprise.

### 11.22 *Economies of Scale*

One reason for public ownership is that it may be possible to take advantage of economies of scale. The various types of economies of scale were discussed in Chapter 4. Their combined effect in any industry can be summarized as follows: the greater the capacity, or scale, of the producer, the faster average cost falls as output increases.

In Figure 11.1 firm A operates on a larger scale than firm B. This does not confer any advantage if output is equal to or less than M. Indeed at any output below M firm B has the lower cost. However, if an output greater than M is produced, firm A has the advantage of lower costs. For example, if output N was required, costs would be substantially lower if this output were supplied

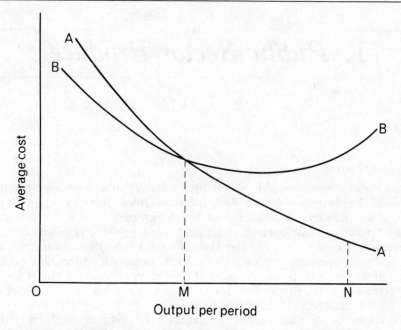

Fig. 11.1 Economies of scale

entirely by one producer operating at the scale of A than by two producers operating at the scale of B and each producing M.

### 11.23 *Greater Integration of Operations*

Figure 11.1 refers to the cost of supplying a given product, whereas by definition integration covers more than one type of product. For example, in the steel industry the siting in close proximity of plants producing ingots and plants rolling these ingots allows savings in transport costs, fuel costs, etc. Thus integration results in lower costs for the operations as a whole.

Following a merger of two producers A and B, each previously producing two products X and Y, production may be rearranged so that firm A specializes in product X and firm B in product Y. Through the economies of long production runs, and the specialized buying of raw materials, the costs of producing both products may fall. If it is felt that there are serious obstacles to such mergers among private firms, public enterprise may be justified.

If integration reduces costs and these reductions are passed on in the form of lower prices, then the consumer will certainly benefit. Integration may also provide the consumer with the benefit of greater convenience. For example if two transport companies, perhaps bus or rail, were competing in a given area, each might try to win a greater share of the passenger traffic by running immediately ahead of the other, whereas the convenience of passengers would require that services should be provided at regular intervals, each company 'supplying' in turn.

## 11.24 *A Reduction in External Costs*

In the early development of what have now come to be known as public utilities, e.g. gas, electricity and water, competing producers often supplied one area. One result of this was that an area might have, for example, three sets of gas pipes. In this situation, the costs of production would probably be higher than with only one supplier who could benefit from economies of scale.

In addition, some production costs are not borne by the producer (these are known as external costs). An example of external costs is the inconvenience caused to traffic and pedestrians by the digging up of the road in order to lay pipes or cables. To some extent such costs are, of course, inevitable, but they are likely to be fewer when there are fewer producers. Since public enterprise invariably implies a reduction in the number of producers, we would expect it to result in lower external costs of the type considered here.

## 11.25 *Cost Reduction and Consumer Welfare: Summary*

As we have indicated, public enterprise *may* benefit consumers by means of lower prices and added convenience. It does not follow that consumers will necessarily obtain these benefits. It may be that the absence of direct competition will reduce the incentive to efficiency so that the potential savings are not achieved. (In terms of Figure 11.1 the average cost curve for firm A would lie above the curve shown, *at all levels of output.*) Moreover, in a situation where there is only one producer, there must, of course, be a restriction on consumer choice, a disadvantage that should be balanced against the potential advantages discussed above.

## 11.26 *The Provision of an Adequate Supply of Goods and Services*

We now turn to a situation where the balance of advantage may seem to lie more clearly with public enterprise. This is where the economics of the market, the relation between revenue and cost, is so unfavourable that private producers are unwilling to supply the quantity of goods or services considered by the government to be adequate. There are several reasons why this might occur.

## 11.261 *Capital Requirements*

The capital requirements of the industry may be so great that it is very difficult to raise sufficient private capital. Even when the private market may technically be able to provide such capital, it may be unwilling to do so because of the risk. There is, however, little evidence that this factor is important in modern, industrialized economies. Vast amounts of money have been raised to finance take-overs, and shares in de-nationalized (privatized) companies have usually found ready buyers.

## 11.262 *Preventing Bottlenecks*

A large number of 'bottlenecks' occuring in the supply of vital materials could have a significant long-term effect on the level of economic growth in the country.

This is especially likely to happen if purchasers, unable to obtain adequate supplies from domestic producers, buy from foreign suppliers. If production is in public hands, it may be easier for the government to ensure that such bottlenecks do not arise.

### 11.263 *Unprofitable Market Segments*

For some products, the cost and revenue conditions may differ considerably from one part of the market to another, and it may not be profitable to supply some parts of the market, e.g. sparsely populated areas distant from the source of supply. Whereas commercially motivated private-sector producers might refuse to supply these areas, public sector producers normally do accept this obligation, (although they are often compensated by the government out of general tax revenue).

### 11.264 *The Maintenance of Employment*

In Britain numerous examples can be provided of employment levels in the nationalized industries that are higher than they would have been had purely commercial criteria been applied. This is even more true of public sector employment in less developed countries.

### 11.27 *Balance of Payments Considerations*

Production of goods and services that are important in international trade may be maintained at a higher level than indicated by commercial criteria. This may occur in order that exports can be increased or imports decreased. In the U.K. one of the justifications advanced for continuing to produce coal from high-cost pits was that it reduced our dependence on imported oil.

### 11.28 *Security*

Most countries rely on the public sector for the supply of manpower and, less heavily, materials for defence and internal-security purposes. However, the public control of these industries is a political as much as an economic matter.

### 11.29 *The Reallocation of Profits*

If firms in a certain industry are earning unduly high profits, this may be taken as an indication of a lack of competitiveness in that industry. One way of trying to increase the degree of competitiveness would be to split the firms into a larger number of smaller units. An alternative solution is for the state to take over production. In this way it is hoped that the advantages of large-scale production will be maintained, and more of the benefits passed on to consumers in the form of lower prices.

Another motive for nationalization, which has been especially important in some developing countries in recent years, has been to ensure that the profits earned are retained within the country.

## 11.3 The Pricing Policies of the Nationalized Industries

Guidelines for pricing policies were laid down in a White Paper issued in 1967. The major guidelines were as follows:

(a) '. . . nationalized industries' revenues should normally cover their accounting costs in full';
(b) '. . . pricing policies should be devised with reference to the costs of the particular goods and services provided. Unless this is done, there is a risk of undesirable cross-subsidization and consequent misallocation of resources';
(c) '. . . In the long run, the main consideration is . . . long run marginal costs.' (This guideline was emphasized in a later White Paper, published in 1978.)

Guidelines (a) and (c) may be compatible in principle, but are frequently incompatible in practice. Figure 11.2 refers to an industry whose average cost continues to fall as output increases. In this situation, at price $P_1$ and output $Q_2$ revenue covers average cost but the price exceeds marginal cost. Conversely, although at output $Q_2$ price $P_2$ equals marginal cost, revenue does not cover average cost. In other words it is impossible in this situation (whatever the demand conditions) to set a price which meets both guidelines (a) and (c). (If price is set equal to marginal cost the result is, of course, that the industry makes a loss and requires a government subsidy.)

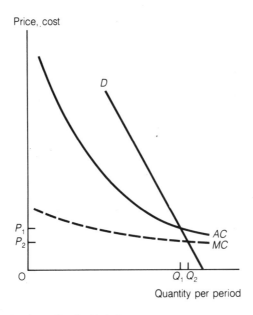

Fig. 11.2 Alternative prices in a nationalized industry

It may be possible to reconcile these objectives by means of a two-part tariff, comprising a charge per unit consumed and a standing charge (to meet the organization's fixed costs). In Figure 11.3 D indicates the number of units that would be purchased at various unit charges. At price $P_1$ Q is bought and price

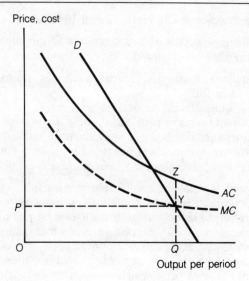

Fig. 11.3

equals marginal cost. In order to meet fixed costs a standing charge has to be levied to yield revenue Q(YZ). Two-part tariffs are used in the once nationalized gas, electricity and telecommunications industries, although the standing charge is sufficient to cover only part of the organization's fixed costs.

## 11.4 Investment Decisions in the Nationalized Industries

The investment programmes of the nationalized industries are influenced by three sets of measures.

### 11.41 *Target Rates of Return*

The industries have been expected to invest only in projects which promise to yield more than the test discount rate (TDR) (set at 10 per cent in 1969). The TDR is intended to approximate to the average rate of return achieved on low-risk projects in the private sector, and in principle is a sound guideline to the allocation of resources. It is, however, a guideline that has often been difficult to follow in practice, since many individual projects must be undertaken because they form part of a much bigger investment programme determined by prior strategic decisions, for example to instal sufficient generating capacity to meet the peak demand for electricity.

In order to overcome this problem the government specified a required rate of return (RRR) on investment which was intended to give more weight to investment programmes as a whole rather than to individual projects. The RRR is 5 per cent in real terms before tax, a good approximation to the average rate of return earned by private sector firms.

## 11.42 *Financial Targets*

When the RRR was introduced, it was suggested that it could be translated into a financial target by which the industry's performance as a whole could be judged. In specifying these financial targets the government takes account of the industries' economic circumstances. Since these differ, the financial targets also differ. It is not unknown for the target of an industry facing very difficult circumstances to be expressed in terms of a maximum loss.

## 11.43 *External Finance Limits*

Each year the government specifies the maximum amount of external finance that can be raised by each industry. Any industry that is in danger of exceeding the limit is expected to seek to improve its efficiency rather than to gain additional revenue via higher prices.

## 11.5 The State as Customer

We have already noted that the state's responsibility for security is reflected in the scope of the public sector's 'production' activities. There are many other goods and services provided by the government for individual users, e.g. educational and medical services. Although the state acts as the customer, this does not necessarily imply that 'production' must be the responsibility of the public sector. Indeed there are in the U.K. some private-sector suppliers of both educational and medical services. Moreover, although most hospitals in the U.K. are publicly owned, it has not been thought appropriate for the state to take over the production of the equipment and the drugs that are used in those hospitals. Nevertheless there is clearly a tendency for an extension of the state's role as customer to be accompanied by an extension of public-sector production.

## 11.6 Some Alternative Solutions

### 11.61 *The Licensing of Private Producers*

Two major forms of control can be exercised via a system of licensing. First, restrictions can be placed on the number of suppliers, so that the duplication and underemployment of resources, especially fixed assets, are avoided. One of the most extensive licensing exercises undertaken in the U.K. in recent years was concerned with the North Sea oil exploration; here the rights to explore specific blocks of the ocean bed were granted to a single company or group of companies.

Second, conditions may be laid down concerning the operations of the licensees. These conditions may take many forms and may be designed to achieve different objectives. For example, the timetables of private passenger-transport operators might have to be approved in order to ensure that, where there were competing suppliers, their services were complementary rather than competitive. The suppliers might also be obliged to provide a service in areas where routes were unprofitable, as a condition of obtaining a licence to operate the more profitable services.

## 11.62 *The Provision of Subsidies*

If it was felt that private producers, adopting normal commercial criteria, would supply less of a product than was considered desirable by the government or the community, subsidies might be offered to producers in order to increase the attractiveness of supplying that product (known as a *merit good*).

## 11.63 *Price and Profit Controls*

We noted above that one reason for establishing public-sector producers might be to avoid the possibility of excessive profits being earned by private-sector producers. An alternative solution would be to control the price charged by these producers. There are four situations in which price controls on particular producers or products might be advocated.

The first is where the supplier has been granted a monopoly or dominant position through the operation of a licensing system. In such instances, if prices were uncontrolled, high profits might result, not from high efficiency but merely from the absence of competition. Second, high profits might be earned by a supplier who was the first to enter a market that was not big enough to support more than one supplier, e.g. in many towns the population is sufficient to support only one evening newspaper. Third, high profits might be earned by a supplier whose efficiency was greater than its competitors, actual or potential. The argument for price and profit control is weaker in this than in the other situations. Finally, high profits may be earned by a group of firms who co-ordinate their activities, especially their pricing policies. This situation was discussed in detail in Chapter 10.

## 11.7 Privatization

In the Introduction we noted that experience has shown that many of the potential advantages of public sector production fail to occur in practice. Furthermore, the advantages that do occur may be outweighed by disadvantages. It is, therefore, not surprising that the move towards public sector production has in recent years been reversed, with public enterprises being returned to the private sector.

The 1980s saw privatization programmes undertaken in countries of widely differing political complexions including France, Spain, Brazil, Bangladesh and even, on a very limited scale, Cuba and China. It seems highly likely that following the recent political changes in Eastern Europe the 1990s will see privatization in more countries.

In the U.K. around thirty enterprises were returned to the private sector during the first ten years of the privatization programme, beginning in 1979. The enterprises sold during this period included British Telecom (for almost £3.7 billion), British Gas (around £5.5 billion), B.P. (the government's remaining stake being sold for over £6.6 billion), and the regional water authorities in England and Wales (£5.3 billion). Another massive transaction, the sale of the assets owned by the Central Electricity Generating Board, was planned for 1990.

## 11.71 *The Objectives of Privatization*

The objectives of privatization have included to:

(a) increase producers' exposure to competition and hence provide an incentive to greater efficiency;
(b) raise revenue for the government;
(c) widen share ownership;
(d) free producers from detailed government intervention;
(e) allow enterprises to compete more freely for funds in the capital market;
(f) ease problems of public sector pay determination;
(g) redistribute income and wealth.

### 11.711 *Conflicts between Objectives*

Conflicts inevitably arise between objectives. For example, in order to increase competition an industry might be split into several separate enterprises. However, the prospect of greater competition could make the industry less attractive to potential shareholders and so reduce the revenue raised by the government from the issue of shares, i.e. it would militate against the second and third objectives listed above.

The government decided that the National Bus Company should be split into seventy-one enterprises, (including engineering companies) even though it was predicted (wrongly in the event) that this would reduce the value of the issue by as much as a half. But considering the privatization programme as a whole, most economists would probably say that the government has given too little weight to the aim of increasing competition and too much weight to other factors. It could, for example, have split B.T. and British Gas into a number of regionally-based competing units. Additional competitors to B.T., other than Mercury, could have been licensed.

### 11.72 *The Regulation of Privatized Industries*

The decision to confirm B.T.'s monopoly status (except for the limited competition offered by Mercury), was accompanied by the establishment of a regulatory agency, the Office of Telecommunications, responsible for preventing anti-competitive behaviour. Moreover, a pricing formula was introduced whereby the maximum price increase allowed on about half of B.T.'s output (those services where little or no competition exists) is 4½ per cent below the annual change in the retail price index. In addition, B.T. is required to provide a number of 'public service' facilities, including public phone boxes and emergency services.

Agencies have also been established to regulate the activities of the gas and water industries and one is planned to oversee the electricity generating industry.

### 11.73 *The Consequences of Privatization*

Evidence from a number of countries suggests that on the whole private sector producers are more efficient than their public sector counterparts. However, the difference in efficiency is mainly found in industries where there is competition. It seems that government intervention often prevents public sector producers from responding to competition as quickly and effectively as private sector producers.

## 11.8 Summary and Conclusions

The state, especially by means of the nationalized industries, is an important producer of goods and services. We examined the arguments that are advanced for public-sector production, and also the counter-arguments. We showed why pricing and investment decisions in nationalized industries might differ from those in the private sector.

In recent years the disadvantages of public-sector production, especially the lack of competition which can lead to a loss of efficiency, have become increasingly recognized, and this has led to the adoption of privatization programmes in many countries.

## Further Reading

Begg, D., Fischer, S. and Dornbusch, R., *Economics* (London: McGraw-Hill, 2nd Edn, 1987), Ch. 17.

Griffiths, A. and Wall, S., *Applied Economics* (London: Longman, 2nd Edn, 1986), Ch. 8.

Livesey, F., *A Textbook of Economics* (London: Longman, 3rd Edn, 1989), Ch. 11.

Maunder, P., Myers, D., Wall, N. and Miller, R. L., *Economics Explained* (London: Collins, 1987), Ch. 29.

## Revision Exercises

1 Evaluate the economic case for public enterprise.
2 Discuss the concept of efficiency with particular reference to (a) individual industries, (b) the economic system.
3 'If private producers are unwilling to supply any goods or services, we can deduce that this is because consumers are unwilling to pay a price that would cover the cost of production. There is therefore no justification for public-sector producers to undertake the supply of these goods and services.' Comment.
4 Would you agree that the existence of public-sector producers can be justified only on the grounds that more resources are thereby utilized than would be otherwise?
5 Discuss the main problems in the private-enterprise system that public enterprise is designed to solve, and outline alternative solutions to these problems.

6 What are the main differences between the way in which resources are allocated in private and public-enterprise systems?

7 'The price mechanism operates so as to allocate resources in accordance with society's needs.' Discuss.

8 What economic arguments may be advanced for and against nationalization? How would you apply these arguments to banking?

9 Evaluate, with reference to particular products, the arguments for and against the setting by public-sector producers of prices that are insufficient to cover the costs of production.

10 Why have so many countries embarked on a programme of privatization in recent years? Do you see any dangers in such programmes?

## Objective Test Questions: Set No. 3

For answers see page 274.

1 Which of the following conditions must be fulfilled if a producer is to increase his profits by means of a policy of price discrimination?

1 There should be no leakage between the two markets.
2 The two markets must have similar elasticities of demand.
3 The costs of supplying the two markets must be identical.

A 1, 2 and 3
B 1 and 2 only
C 1 only
D 3 only

2 If a firm maintained its price but reduced its costs in order to earn higher profits this would be an example of

A price discrimination
B cost differentials
C price-minus costing
D economies of scale

3 Question 3 is based on Figure 1 in which AC and MC denote the average and marginal cost of labour and MRP denotes marginal revenue productivity. Which of the following statements is/are true?

1 The equilibrium wage rate is $OW_1$
2 The amount of labour employed is $OQ_1$
3 The supply of labour is perfectly elastic

A 1 and 2 only
B 2 and 3 only
C 1 only
D 3 only

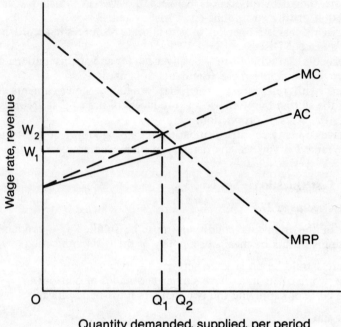

Fig. 1

4 Which of the following might result from the introduction of a minimum wage for young workers at a level above the wage currently paid to these workers?

1 The total income of all young people of working age falls
2 Firms substitute older for younger workers
3 Firms substitute capital for young workers.

A 1, 2 and 3
B 1 and 2 only
C 2 and 3 only
D 1 and 3 only

5 Which of the following applies/apply to an open market?

1 Price leadership usually exists
2 Price is determined by the interaction of aggregate demand and supply
3 Individual suppliers cannot control the price

A 1 and 2 only
B 2 and 3 only
C 1 only
D 3 only

6 In order to stabilize producers' income, buffer stocks should be used to make demand elasticity

A higher
B lower
C closer to unity
D zero

7 Which of the following is true of the profit maximizing firm in both monopoly and perfect competition?

A Price equals marginal revenue
B Equilibrium output is at minimum average cost
C Equilibrium output is where marginal cost equals marginal revenue
D Equilibrium output is where average cost equals average revenue

Questions 8 to 10 are based on Figure 2. At which of the four levels of output, A, B, C, D,

8 are profits maximized?

9 are profits zero?

10 is revenue maximized?

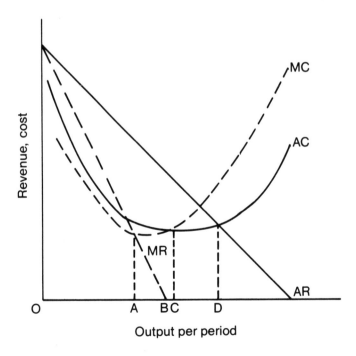

Fig. 2

Questions 11 and 12 are based on Figure 3. At which price A, B, C, D, are profits

11  maximized?

12  zero?

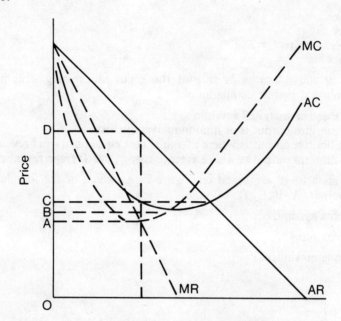

Fig. 3

13  If average variable cost is constant, as output increases

    1  average variable cost equals marginal cost
    2  average total cost is constant
    3  average fixed cost is constant

    A  1 and 2 only
    B  2 and 3 only
    C  1 only
    D  3 only

14 Where AC denotes average cost, MC marginal cost, AR average revenue, and MR marginal revenue, the long-run profit maximizing position in monopolistic competition is where

A  MC = AC = MR = AR
B  MC = MR; AC = AR
C  MC = MR; AR > AC
D  MR > MC; AR = AC

15 Where AC denotes average cost, MC marginal cost, AR average revenue and MR marginal revenue, the profit maximizing position in monopoly is where

A  MC = MR; AC = AR
B  MR > MC; AR > AC
C  MC = MR; AR > AC
D  MC = AC; MR = AR

16 The parties to a collective restrictive agreement can attempt to justify the agreement on any of the following grounds *except* that

A  the agreement is in the national interest
B  the removal of the restriction would be likely to cause a substantial reduction in export earnings
C  the restriction is necessary to enable fair terms to be negotiated with a large supplier or purchaser
D  the restriction is necessary to protect the public against injury

17 A manufacturer can attempt to justify resale price maintenance on all of the following grounds *except* that in the absence of r.p.m.

A  the quality or variety of goods available for sale would be substantially reduced
B  the number of retail establishments in which the goods were sold would be substantially reduced
C  the rate of innovation would decline
D  the retail prices of the goods would increase

Questions 18 and 19 relate to Figure 4 in which D indicates the demand for, and S the supply of, a factor of production.

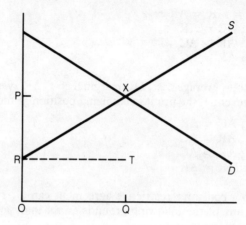

Fig. 4

18 The economic rent obtained by the factor is:

A  ORTQ
B  OPXQ
C  RPXT
D  RPX

19 The transfer earnings of the factor are:

A  ORTQ
B  RPX
C  RPXT
D  ORXQ

20 An increase in the demand for one factor of production could arise following:

1 an increase in the productivity of that factor
2 an increase in the price of the products made by that factor
3 an increase in the price of other factors

A  1, 2 and 3
B  1 and 2 only
C  2 and 3 only
D  1 and 3 only

# 12. *The Measurement of Economic Activity*

## 12.1 Introduction

In Chapter 1 we presented a highly simplified model of a national economy. This model showed that the owners of resources supply inputs to producers in return for rewards (income) of various kinds, and that these resources are transformed into a flow of output (goods and services) which are supplied to consumers in exchange for payment. In many countries, including the U.K., economic statisticians measure three of these four flows; the level of economic activity is expressed in terms of the value of incomes, output and expenditure.

We examine the U.K. national accounts below. But first we demonstrate the principles underlying the construction of these accounts.

## 12.2 Value Added

### 12.21 *Output*

In converting inputs to outputs, producers add value to the goods and services that they supply. Value added is defined as sales receipts (the value of sales) minus the cost of bought-in materials. As a simple example the value added during the production and sale of canned tomatoes is shown in Table 12.1.

In order to simplify the analysis it is assumed that at the beginning of the period the growers have already acquired the tomato plants, fertilizer etc. that they need, so that they do not need to buy any materials during this period. They grow tomatoes which they sell to the manufacturers (canners) for £700,000. Since we have assumed that the cost of bought-in materials is zero, all of this £700,000 constitutes value added.

*Table 12.1 Value Added in Production (£)*

|  | Cost of bought-in materials | Sales receipts | Value added |
|---|---|---|---|
| Farming | – | 700,000 | 700,000 |
| Manufacturing | 700,000 | 1,500,000 | 800,000 |
| Retailing | 1,500,000 | 2,000,000 | 500,000 |
|  |  |  | 2,000,000 |

The canners process the tomatoes and sell them to retailers for £1,500,000. The value added at the manufacturing stage is therefore £800,000 (£1,500,000 minus £700,000). The retailers store and display the tomatoes which they sell to consumers for £2,000,000. The value added by retailers is therefore £500,000 (£2 million minus £1,500,000). Note that the value of the final sales, £2 million, equals the sum of the value added at the various stages of the process of production and distribution.

This example ignores many of the inputs required to produce and sell canned tomatoes, such as the cost of the greenhouses in which the tomatoes are grown, the cost of the empty cans purchased by the manufacturers and the shelves on which the cans are displayed in the shops. Nevertheless, although highly simplified, the example does illustrate the principle that underlies the output approach to the measurement of economic activity.

### 12.22 *Income*

The value added at each stage of production and distribution is available as payment to the factors of production used at the stage. Continuing to simplify, we assume that only two factors are required: labour, which receives wages; and capital, which receives profit. The distribution of value added between wages and profit is shown in Table 12.2

*Table 12.2 The Distribution of Value Added (£)*

|  | Value added | Wages | Profit |
|---|---|---|---|
| Farming | 700,000 | 400,000 | 300,000 |
| Manufacturing | 800,000 | 600,000 | 200,000 |
| Retailing | 500,000 | 300,000 | 200,000 |
|  | 2,000,000 | 1,300,000 | 700,000 |

### 12.23 *Expenditure*

Expenditure is the third approach to the measurement of economic activity noted in the introduction. In fact, in this example all final expenditure is undertaken by a single group, consumers. (It will be remembered that we have ignored investment spending e.g. the purchase of greenhouses.)

### 12.3 The United Kingdom National Accounts: Expenditure

We have discussed the principles used in the construction of a country's national accounts. We now examine the national accounts of the United Kingdom, beginning with the measurement of expenditure. The various expenditure flows are shown in Figure 12.1, and the magnitude of the flows in 1988 is shown in Table 12.3. (The letters attached to the various flows in the diagram correspond to those in the table.)

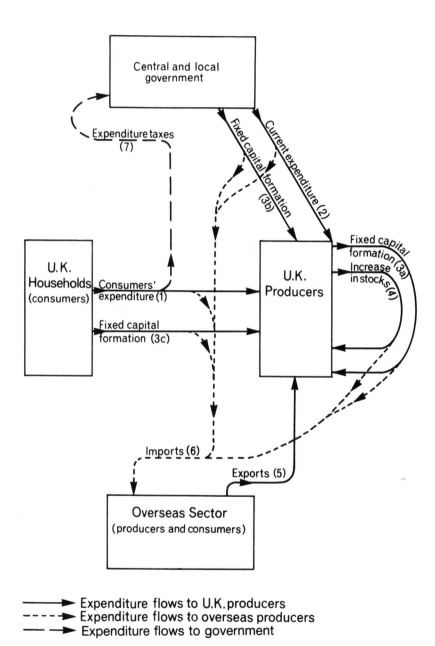

Fig. 12.1 The pattern of expenditure

*Table 12.3 National Product by Category of Expenditure (£000 million)*

| | |
|---|---|
| (1) Consumers' expenditure | 293.6 |
| (2) General government final consumption | 91.8 |
| (3) Gross domestic fixed capital formation | 88.8 |
| (4) Value of physical increase in stocks and work in progress | 4.4 |
| (5) Exports of goods and services | 108.5 |
| (6) *less* Imports of goods and services | − 125.2 |
| Statistical discrepancy (expenditure adjustment) | 2.1 |
| Gross Domestic Product at Market Prices | 463.9 |
| (7) *less* Taxes on expenditure (net of subsidies) | − 69.1 |
| Gross Domestic Product at Factor Cost | 394.8 |
| Net property income from abroad | 5.6 |
| Gross National Product at Factor Cost | 400.4 |

*Source: United Kingdon National Accounts*

## 12.31 *Consumers' Expenditure*

Table 12.3 shows that consumers' expenditure (designated 1) is by far the largest expenditure flow, accounting for almost two-thirds of gross domestic product (G.D.P.) at market prices. Consumers' expenditure includes virtually all the items that one would expect: food, clothing, washing machines, leisure activities etc. The one exception is expenditure on new housing which is included in investment expenditure. Note that the expenditure of £293 billion did not lead to an equivalent value of resources being employed by U.K. producers, for there are two 'leakages'. The first is imports (6), discussed below. The second leakage comprises various types of taxes on expenditure (7). An allowance has to be made for these two leakages before we can identify the value of resources employed by U.K. producers in satisfying the demands of U.K. consumers.

## 12.32 *General Government Final Consumption*

General (i.e. central and local) government final consumption (2) is current expenditure on goods and services which in 1988 amounted to £92 billion. About 60 per cent was spent by the central government and almost 40 per cent by local authorities. Most of these goods and services are *not* provided at prices that reflect their cost of production, and indeed many are provided free. Consequently it is conventional to value them in the national income accounts in terms not of their prices but of their 'cost of production'.

## 12.33 *Investment*

The third expenditure flow that gives rise to the utilization of resources is investment expenditure. This comprises two elements – gross domestic fixed capital formation (3) and the physical increase in stocks (4). As can be seen from Table 12.3, the former is by far the more important of these two elements.

The bulk of investment expenditure takes the form of payments by one producer to another, indicated by the loops (3a) and (4) in Figure 12.1. About a quarter of fixed capital formation is undertaken by the government (3b). Finally, investment is also undertaken by 'households', indicated by the flow (3c). This partly comprises expenditure on the purchase of new houses by private individuals, and partly capital expenditure by unincorporated businesses. The treatment of these two flows as investment by households is a convention adopted in the construction of the U.K. national income accounts.

### 12.34 *Foreign Trade*

We noted above that some spending by consumers is devoted to imported goods and services. These imports represent a leakage of expenditure from the U.K. Similar, though smaller, leakages also occur in the form of imports arising from the current spending by the government and from investment spending.

Table 12.3 shows that our total imports of goods and services in 1988 amounted to £125 billion. On the other hand, we exported goods and services to the value of £108.5 billion. This expenditure by overseas consumers and producers, designated (5), represents an injection into the U.K.'s economic system.

When we add together the three expenditure flows – consumers' expenditure (1), government consumption (2), and investment expenditure (3 and 4), and when we make an allowance for exports (5) and imports (6), and also for errors in measurement (statistical discrepancy) we arrive at the value for *gross domestic product at market prices*. After making a further allowance for expenditure taxes and subsidies (7), we arrive at the value of *gross domestic product at factor cost*. As the term implies, this is a measure of the value of domestic resources utilized during the period in question.

In order to obtain the value of the *gross national product at factor cost* we make a final allowance for property income paid to, and received from, overseas countries. Table 12.3 indicates that the U.K. had a positive net balance on this item of £5.6 billion in 1988.

We shall examine the determinants of each of these expenditure flows in subsequent chapters. But first we discuss briefly the other approaches to the measurement of economic activity, namely payments to resources or factors of production, and the flow of output.

## 12.4 Payments to Factors of Production: National Income

The monetary flows discussed in the previous section represent payments for goods and services. A second important set of monetary flows constitutes payments to the factors of production utilized in the production of these goods and services. To have included these flows in Figure 12.1 would have made it too complicated, but an indication of their magnitude is given in Table 12.4.

The total for gross national product, £400.4 billion, corresponds to that given in the bottom line in Table 12.3. But we have also included in Table 12.4 a figure for capital consumption, and thus obtained the value of the *national income*. Capital consumption, or depreciation, denotes that during the year the nation's capital assets suffered a loss in value as they were utilized in the

*Table 12.4 National Income (£000 million)*

| | |
|---|---:|
| Income from employment | 249.8 |
| Income from self-employment | 42.6 |
| Gross trading profits of companies | 70.2 |
| Gross trading profits of public corporations* | 7.2 |
| Rent | 27.5 |
| Imputed charge for consumption of non-trading capital | 3.4 |
| *less* Stock appreciation | − 6.1 |
| Statistical discrepancy (income adjustment) | 0.2 |
| Gross Domestic Product at Factor Cost | 394.8 |
| Net property income from abroad | 5.6 |
| Gross National Product at Factor Cost | 400.4 |
| *less* Capital consumption | − 54.8 |
| National Income | 345.6 |

\* Including trading surplus of general government enterprises

*Source: United Kingdom National Accounts*

production of goods and services. National income can, therefore, be seen as a measure of the value of production, an allowance having been made for capital 'used up'.

By far the most important form of income is income from employment, accounting for about 72 per cent of national income. Company profits accounted for about 20 per cent, but this figure is reduced when allowance is made for the replacement of the assets used up in production.

## 12.5 The Flow of Output

The final approach to the measurement of economic activity is via the flow of output. The value of output produced by the various industries or sectors of the economy is shown in Table 12.5.

Table 12.5 shows clearly that the U.K. can no longer be seen as predominantly a manufacturing nation. Manufacturing now accounts for less

*Table 12.5 Gross Domestic Product by Industry (£000 million)*

| | |
|---|---:|
| Agriculture, forestry and fishing | 5.6 |
| Energy and water supply | 21.8 |
| Manufacturing | 93.4 |
| Construction | 25.7 |
| Distribution, hotels and catering; repairs | 55.1 |
| Transport and communication | 28.7 |
| Banking, finance, insurance, business services and leasing | 76.9 |
| Ownership of dwellings | 21.4 |
| Public administration, national defence and compulsory social security | 27.0 |
| Education and health services | 35.2 |
| Other services | 25.8 |
| Statistical discrepancy | 0.2 |
| Gross Domestic Product at Factor Cost | 394.8 |

than a quarter of total output, being far outweighed in value by the service sector.

## 12.6 Changes in Living Standards

In the previous sections we have examined various measures of the level of economic activity. Changes in the level of economic activity are an indicator of changes in living standards. However, they are by no means a perfect indicator, for various reasons.

### 12.61 *Monetary and Real Changes*

The data in Tables 12.3 to 12.5 are at current prices, i.e. they denote the actual values of the transactions recorded for that year. For many purposes it is essential to have information in this form. However when we wish to measure economic activity in real, or volume, terms, we need to make our measurements in constant prices.

Let us assume that a manufacturer of chocolates makes in a given year 1 million boxes of chocolates which he sells at £2 a box, giving a total turnover of £2 million. In the following year he raises his price by 10 per cent to £2·20. He again sells a million boxes (which might well happen if incomes rose by 10 per cent). His turnover rises to £2·2 million, but this is, of course, entirely due to the higher price. His volume of sales, his real level of activity, is unchanged. To show this we need to deflate the sales figure by a price index. The initial price is given the value 100. Since price has risen by 10 per cent we have

$$\frac{£2,200,000}{110} = £2,000,000$$

It is interesting to note that when the first edition of this book was written it showed national income for 1974 as £75 billion. A comparison with Table 12.4 reveals that in current prices national income is now more than four times as large as in 1974. But most of this represents higher prices. In real terms the increase is only about 18 per cent.

### 12.611 *Price Indices*

Of the several price indices which are published regularly, the best known is the Retail Price Index (R.P.I.). In constructing the R.P.I. the Central Statistical Office obtains each month the prices of about 600 goods and services. These goods and services are given weights according to their share in the expenditure of an 'average' household.

The R.P.I. is not necessarily the best available cost of living index, since it does not take account of changes in direct taxes or national insurance contributions. Both price and tax changes are covered by the Tax and Price Index. Nevertheless, the R.P.I. continues to be used in the calculation of index-linked pensions and is the index most often quoted in wage negotiations.

The C.S.O. also publishes a price index for the goods bought by an average pensioner household. This information is available to the government when it decides the rates of retirement pensions.

### 12.62 *The Provision of Products without Payment*

Some goods (a term which here includes services) are provided without payment and so do not enter into the national accounts. Examples include the services provided by housewives to their families, food grown in householders' gardens for own consumption, and many charitable activities.

### 12.63 *Economic Bads*

Economic activity gives rise to both economic goods and economic 'bads', such as pollution of various kinds, traffic congestion and the destruction of recreational areas. If an increase in the output of goods is accompanied by an increase in the output of bads then any measure which takes the former into account but ignores the latter will overstate the increase, or improvement, in the standard of living. Conversely, if in a given period there is a reduction in the output of bads, as happened when smokeless zones were introduced, the improvement in living standards will be greater than indicated by the change in the consumption of goods.

### 12.64 *The Distribution of Income*

National income is, of course, an aggregate measure, an indicator of overall living standards. In all economies one finds a wide range of incomes. A rise in national income might be accompanied by a widening of income differentials; indeed the poor could become poorer in both relative and absolute terms.

### 12.7 International Differences in Living Standards

An additional difficulty arises in trying to compare living standards between countries. Since the national income of the various countries is expressed in different currencies – sterling, dollars, marks, yen, etc. – it is necessary to find a common denominator. The official exchange rate may seem to be the obvious candidate, and in fact it is frequently used. However it is an imperfect tool, as can be seen from the following example.

*Table 12.6 International Living Standards*

|  | National income per head | | |
|  | Country A | Country B | Country B |
| Exchange rate | $ | £ | $ |
| --- | --- | --- | --- |
| £1 = $2 | 10,000 | 6,000 | 12,000 |
| £1 = $1·50 | 10,000 | 6,000 | 9,000 |

National income per head is $10,000 in country A and £6,000 in country B. With an exchange rate of £1 = $2 B's national income per head would be $12,000, higher than that of A. With an exchange rate of £1 = $1·50 B's national income per head would be $9,000, less than that of A. In recent years changes of this magnitude in the exchange rate have been known to occur within a period of a few months. But it would be absurd to imagine that within such a short period a corresponding change would occur in relative living standards, as would be suggested by Table 12.6.

Moreover even in periods when exchange rates are stable, they may be an imperfect guide to the relative values of currencies and hence to comparative living standards.

We noted above that within a given country the distribution of income may change over time. At any given time substantial differences in income distribution exist between countries, and these reduce the value of comparisons made in terms of average income.

Another factor referred to above – the provision of products without payment – can also affect international comparisons. In less developed countries a large proportion of the population is engaged in subsistence agriculture, and estimates of the value of their output are likely to be highly inaccurate.

There are several other factors which reduce the value of national income as an indicator of relative living standards. For example differences in taste mean that Americans eat large quantities of expensive meat, whereas Indians eat cheap rice and East Africans eat cheap maize. Spending on heating homes in cold countries or on air conditioning in hot countries is included in national income, whereas it would be better seen as being required to overcome the disadvantages of living in these countries.

It is clear, then, that great care must be taken in interpreting statistics relating to international living standards. The World Bank has estimated that the official figure of India's national income should be raised by a factor of three in order to compare it with that of the U.S.A., and other observers have suggested even higher adjustment figures.


## 12.8 Summary and Conclusions

In this chapter we defined value added and showed how the value added approach is used in estimating the flows which are contained in the national accounts: the flow of expenditure, of income and of output. The accounts are constructed so that these three flows should in principle have the same value.

We showed how estimates of these flows are used in the construction of various measures of economic activity: gross domestic product, gross national product and national income. The relationships between these measures were also explained.

The connection between national income and living standards was discussed, and the difficulties of comparing living standards, over time and between countries, were explored.

## Further Reading

Artis, M. J., Ed. *The U.K. Economy* (London: Weidenfeld and Nicolson 11th Edn, 1986), Ch. 1.

Begg, D., Fischer, S. and Dornbusch, R., *Economics* (London: McGraw-Hill, 2nd Edn, 1987), Ch. 19.

Hardwick, P., Khan, B. and Langmead, J., *An Introduction to Modern Economics* (London: Longman, 2nd Edn, 1986), Ch. 17.

Lipsey, R. G. and Harbury, C., *First Principles of Economics* (London: Weidenfeld and Nicolson 1988), Ch. 26.

Livesey, F., *A Textbook of Economics* (London: Longman, 3rd Edn, 1989), Ch. 13.

Maunder, P., Myers, D., Wall, N. and Miller, R. L., *Explaining Economics* (London: Collins, 1987), Ch. 13.

## Revision Exercises

1 Outline the three approaches to the measurement of the national income and explain how they relate to each other.

2 Using Table 12.3 as a guide, draw a diagram showing expenditure flows between the following sectors: U.K. households, U.K. producers, the government sector, the overseas sector. Show how an increase in the level of government consumption would be likely to affect each of the following: consumers' expenditure, exports, imports, gross domestic fixed capital formation.

3 Applying the procedures adopted in the U.K. national accounts to the hypothetical data in Table 12.7, calculate (a) gross domestic product at market prices, (b) gross domestic product at factor cost, (c) gross national product at factor cost, (d) national income.

*Table 12.7 National Income Accounts of Suburbia (£000 million)*

| | |
|---|---|
| Consumers' expenditure | 50 |
| Public authorities' current expenditure on goods and services | 6 |
| Gross fixed capital formation | 5 |
| Value of the physical increase in stocks | 1 |
| Exports of goods and services | 6 |
| Imports of goods and services | 4 |
| Expenditure taxes | 3 |
| Subsidies | 1 |
| Property income received from abroad (net) | 2 |
| Capital consumption | 9 |

4 'If company profits were halved, workers would be about 10 per cent better off.' Discuss.

5 To what extent are changes in gross national product a reasonable indicator of changes in living standards?

6 'Any increase in national income, whatever its origin, represents an increase in consumers' welfare.' Discuss.

7 Explain why it is difficult to make an accurate comparison of living standards in two countries.

8 Do you think that the output of economic bads is likely to increase or decrease in the U.K. over the next ten years? Explain your answer.

9 Explain why estimates of economic activity should take account of (a) expenditure taxes, (b) property income from abroad, (c) capital consumption.

10 Discuss the proposition that exports from the U.K. are of benefit only to overseas consumers, while imports are of benefit only to UK consumers.

# 13. *Consumption*

## 13.1 Introduction: the Determinants of Consumption

We saw in Chapter 12 that consumption, i.e. consumers' expenditure on goods and services, is the single most important component of total expenditure, accounting for almost two-thirds of the gross national product at market prices. In this chapter we explore the main determinants of consumers' expenditure. We are concerned here with total, or aggregate, consumption, not with its pattern. This means that we take as given the various factors which influence expenditure on particular goods and services. These factors have, of course, been discussed at length in earlier chapters.

## 13.2 The Level of National Income

The most important determinant of the volume of consumption is undoubtedly the level of national income; the higher the level of national income the greater the volume of consumption. Using symbols we can express this relation as:

$$C = f(Y)$$

where C represents consumption,
  Y represents national income,
   f indicates that consumption depends upon (is a function of) national income.

The results of statistical analysis suggest that the relation takes the form: $C = a + bY$; a, a constant, is positive, denoting that consumption would be positive even if consumers currently received no income. Such consumption would be financed out of savings accumulated in past years.

The extent to which consumption changes as income changes is denoted by b. More precisely, $b = dC/dY$, where C represents consumption, Y represents national income, and d denotes a (small) change in these variables. So if a 10 per cent change in income was accompanied by a 7 per cent change in consumption, the value of b would be 0·7. The economic term for this relationship is the *marginal propensity to consume*.

The *average propensity to consume* is defined as total consumption divided by total national income (C/Y). In Table 13.1 we show, for a range of incomes, the values of total consumption, average propensity to consume and marginal propensity to consume, which are obtained from the following consumption function:

$$C = £1,000 \text{ million} + 0·7Y$$

The data in Table 13.1 are plotted in Figure 13.1. CC is a straight line because the value of b (the marginal propensity to consume) does not change. The fall in the average propensity to consume (C/Y), which occurs as income rises, can easily be derived from the diagram by considering the situation at two different income levels. For example, NM/OM is clearly greater than RS/OS.

*Table 13.1 A Hypothetical Schedule of Income and Consumption*

| National income (£000 million) | Consumption (£000 million) | Average propensity to consume | Marginal propensity to consume |
|---|---|---|---|
| 0 | 1·0 | – | – |
| 1 | 1·7 | 1·70 | 0·7 |
| 2 | 2·4 | 1·20 | 0·7 |
| 3 | 3·1 | 1·03 | 0·7 |
| 4 | 3·8 | 0·95 | 0·7 |
| 5 | 4·5 | 0·90 | 0·7 |
| 6 | 5·2 | 0·87 | 0·7 |
| 7 | 5·9 | 0·84 | 0·7 |
| 8 | 6·6 | 0·83 | 0·7 |
| 9 | 7·3 | 0·81 | 0·7 |
| 10 | 8·0 | 0·80 | 0·7 |

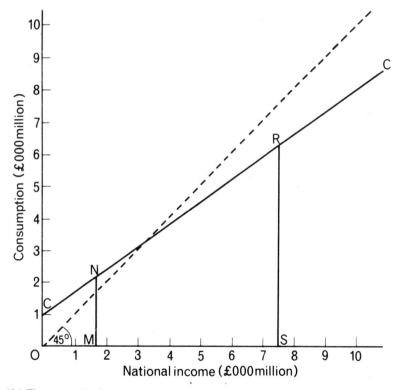

Fig. 13.1 The consumption function

The dotted line in Figure 13.1 is drawn at 45° to the axes, and indicates what consumption would be if national income were always spent entirely on consumption (if saving were always zero). In fact, as can be seen from Table 13.1, when income is £3,000 million or less, consumption is greater than income (dis-saving occurs). Conversely, when income is £4,000 million or above, consumption is less than income (saving occurs).

### 13.21 *Post-Keynesian Theories of Consumption*

The above analysis was first developed by J. M. Keynes many years ago. There is considerable evidence of a stable relationship between income and consumption, i.e. that MPC is constant, when a long period is considered. However, the relationship is by no means so stable when shorter periods are considered. The short-run response to a change in income is not usually as great as the long-run response, i.e. MPC has a lower value in the short run.

This is illustrated in Figure 13.2 where $C_S$ and $C_L$ represent the short- and long-run consumption functions. When income increases from $Y_1$ to $Y_2$ consumption first increases from $C_1$ to $C_2$ in accordance with the short-run consumption function. Subsequently, if the higher level of income persists, consumption increases further to $C_3$. Similarly if income were to fall, the decline in consumption would be greater in the long than the short run.

Three alternative explanations of the situation illustrated in Figure 13.2 have been suggested.

### 13.211 *The Permanent Income Hypothesis*

This theory was developed by Milton Friedman, who argued that consumption depends upon average long-run ('permanent') income. Consumption will not respond fully to a change in income, e.g. from $C_1$ to $C_3$ in Figure 13.2, unless people believe that the change in income will be maintained. If they believe the change to be only temporary, the response will be less, e.g. consumption will increase from $C_1$ to $C_2$ in Figure 13.2, and consumers will save a higher proportion of the additional income.

### 13.212 *The Life-cycle Hypothesis*

Developed by Modigliani and Ando, this resembles the permanant income hypothesis. It assumes that people estimate their lifetime income and formulate lifetime consumption plans in the light of the estimates. According to this hypothesis a change in current income will affect current consumption only if it causes the household to modify its estimate of lifetime income. This theory recognizes that expenditure may vary at different stages of the household's life

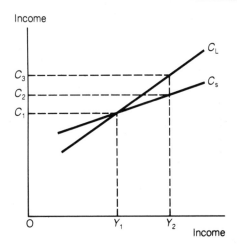

Fig. 13.2 Short and long-run consumption factors

cycle, and that for part of the time expenditure may exceed income, the excess being met by borrowing or out of savings. Consequently this theory draws attention to a range of factors not so far considered, including the availability of credit and rates of interest. These factors are discussed further below.

Both of these theories could explain data that cannot be explained by the Keynesian theory, and they might therefore be considered to have improved upon that theory. However, it would be extremely difficult to subject either the permanent income or the life-cycle hypothesis to a rigorous test since they both incorporate individuals' expectations for a long period ahead. To understand the difficulties involved in such a test, try to estimate your own lifetime earnings. Even if you are currently in employment or if you know the salary or wage at which you are likely to start work, you will not find it an easy task.

### 13.213 *The Relative Income Hypothesis*

This theory assumes that current consumption is determined by the individual's income relative to his or her previous peak income and to other people's consumption.

The peak income becomes important when income falls. In Figure 13.3 $C_L$ is the long-run consumption function and $C_S$ is a short-run function (of which there might be several). If income falls from $Y_1$ to $Y_2$ consumption falls from $C_1$ to $C_2$ in accordance with the short-run function $C_S$. If income subsequently returns to $Y_1$ consumption returns to $C_1$. Any further increase in income leads to an expansion of consumption in line with the long-run function $C_L$.

### 13.3 Taxation and Government Expenditure

Taxation leaves less money in consumers' pockets, thus reducing consumption. On the other hand, certain types of government expenditure, known as transfer

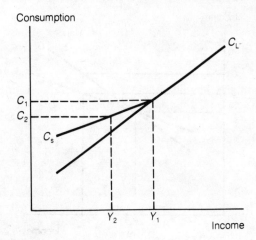

Fig. 13.3 Consumption influenced by relative income

payments, put money into consumers' pockets and so lead to an increase in consumption.

## 13.4 The Distribution of Income

Different members of the community may have different propensities to consume, owing to a number of factors – age, size of family, etc. It would seem that an increase in the community's propensity to consume would be likely to follow from a redistribution of income (and wealth) from the richer members to the poorer, since there is some evidence that the latter's propensity to consume is above average.

## 13.5 Price Changes

If consumers expected prices to continue to rise, they might increase their spending (MPC would rise), in order to 'beat' future increases. On the other hand, if the price increases created uncertainty in the minds of consumers about future economic conditions, they might react by reducing their consumption in order to put something aside 'for a rainy day' (see also the following section.)

## 13.6 The Real Wealth Effect

Consumption may be affected by the level of consumers' wealth. Inflation results in a fall in the real value of existing wealth. If consumers attempt to restore the value of their wealth, this will lead to an increase in the marginal propensity to save (MPS). Since MPC + MPS = 1, this implies a fall in the propensity to consume. In the U.K. rapid inflation in the 1970s was accompanied by a rise in the propensity to save and a fall in the propensity to consume.

## 13.7 The Rate of Interest

The rate of interest is the price, or cost, of borrowed money. In practice different rates of interest will apply to different forms of borrowing. The rate of interest may affect consumption in two ways. First, it may influence consumers' willingness to borrow money in order to finance consumption. Second, it may influence the decisions of other consumers on how they divide their income between consumption and saving.

## 13.8 The Availability of Credit

In some circumstances consumers may not be able to borrow as much money as they would like in order to finance consumption. The supply of credit may be restricted either by the policies of individual suppliers – banks, hire-purchase companies, etc. – or because of government regulations and control. A change in these policies, which are discussed in greater detail in Chapter 17, will influence consumption, especially of consumer durables, whose purchase is often credit-financed. A factor contributing to the higher propensity to consume in the 1980s, noted above, was the spread of new credit mechanisms e.g. credit cards.

## 13.9 Summary and Conclusions

We have examined in this chapter the various factors that influence the level of consumption. The level of income was identified as the most important of these factors. It appears that over much of the postwar period consumers spent a given proportion of any increase in income that was considered to be permanent – the long-run marginal propensity to consume was constant. This meant that as income increased, the average propensity to consume tended to decline.

Consumption (and therefore saving) is also affected by other factors, whose influence is especially strong over short periods. These factors include price changes, the rate of interest and the availability of credit. On the other hand the effect of a change in income is usually less over a shorter than over a longer period.

### Further Reading

Artis, M. J., Ed., *The U.K. Economy* (London: Weidenfeld and Nicolson, 11th Edn, 1986), Ch. 1.
Begg, D., Fischer, S. and Dornbusch, R., *Economics* (London: McGraw-Hill, 2nd Edn, 1987), Ch. 20.
Griffiths, A. and Wall, S., *Applied Economics* (London: Longman, 1986), Ch. 11.
Hardwick, P., Khan, B. and Langmead, J., *An Introduction to Modern Economics* (London: Longman, 2nd Edn, 1986), Ch. 19.
Lipsey, R. G. and Harbury, C., *First Principles of Economics* (London: Weidenfeld and Nicolson, 1988), Ch. 21.
Livesey, F., *A Textbook of Economics* (London: Longman, 3rd Edn, 1989), Ch. 14.

Maunder, P., Myers, D., Wall, N. and Miller, R. L., *Economics Explained* (London: Collins, 1987), Ch. 15.

## Revision Exercises

1 Discuss the main determinants of consumption.
2 If consumption equals £10 million + 0·5Y, where Y is the level of national income (in £ million), calculate consumption when national income is

   (a) £20 million;   (b) £10 million;   (c) zero.

3 Given a consumption function of the form C = a + bY, define (a) the average propensity to consume; (b) the marginal propensity to consume.

*Table 13.2*

| National income (£000 million) | Consumption (£000 million) |
|---|---|
| 0 | 2 |
| 1 | 2·6 |
| 2 | 3·2 |
| 3 | 3·8 |
| 4 | 4·4 |
| 5 | 5·0 |
| 6 | 5·6 |

4 On the basis of the consumption schedule presented in Table 13.2,

   (a) calculate the average propensity to consume at each level of national income;
   (b) calculate the marginal propensity to consume at each level of national income;
   (c) plot the consumption function on a diagram;
   (d) express the consumption function as a numerical formula.

5 Why is the value of the short-run consumption function likely to differ from its long-run value?
6 Define and discuss the permanent income, life cycle and relative income hypotheses.
7 How would a redistribution of income from richer to poorer members of the community be likely to affect the level of consumption?
8 If the marginal propensity to consume is constant, explain how the average propensity to consume is likely to change as income changes.
9 If the marginal propensity to save is constant, explain how the average propensity to save is likely to change as income changes.
10 'If MPC + MPS ≡ 1·0, consumption can never exceed income.' Discuss.

# 14. *Investment*

## 14.1 Introduction

When the man in the street uses the term investment, he usually means the purchase of financial securities, e.g. shares. But in the national accounts investment refers to physical productive assets. Most investment comprises fixed capital formation e.g. plant, machinery, vehicles, buildings. (We noted in Chapter 12 that consumers' expenditure on housing is also treated as investment, not consumption.) A small part comprises additions to stocks of raw materials, components etc. About two-thirds of fixed capital formation is accounted for by businesses or producers (including public corporations but not the government), and in this chapter we are mainly concerned with the factors affecting business investment.

## 14.2 Replacement Investment

Productive assets, such as machines and buildings, gradually wear out through use and the passage of time, a process known as depreciation or capital consumption. If a country's economic capacity is to be maintained, new assets must be purchased to replace those that wear out.

## 14.3 Net Investment

Net investment is that investment which results in an expansion of capacity. Gross investment equals net plus replacement investment. So if, for example, gross or total investment were £20 billion and capital consumption (and hence replacement investment) were £14 billion, net investment would be £6 billion. In the rest of this chapter 'investment' refers to gross investment, except where another meaning is specified.

## 14.4 Investment and Profitability

In general terms we can say that investment will be undertaken if additional profits will thereby be generated. More precisely, investment will be undertaken if the rate of return from that investment exceeds its cost. (An alternative motive for investment would be to increase sales or market share.)

Figure 14.1 indicates the volume of investment that would be expected to yield given rates of return. The most profitable projects available, represented by the volume of investment $Q_1$, are expected to yield a rate of return $R_1$. Other projects are expected to yield lower returns – those which are represented by the volume of investment $Q_1Q_2$ would yield rates of return between $R_1$ and $R_2$. Finally, at $Q_3$, no investment opportunities with positive rates of return remain.

The term *marginal efficiency of capital* is sometimes used to denote the rate of return from a given volume of investment.

The amount of investment undertaken in a given period will depend upon not only the prospective rate of return, or yield on investment, but also the availability and cost of investment funds. The interaction of these two factors is considered below, but first we examine each factor separately, beginning with the determinants of the rate of return.

## 14.5 Factors Influencing the Rate of Return on Investment

### 14.51 *Changes in the Level of the National Income*

In order to show the effect of a change in national income let us imagine first that the investment demand curve schedule shown in Figure 14.1 refers to a given year, t, and was constructed on the assumption that the national income in that year would be the same as in the previous year, t − 1.

If national income is not expected to change, there will be no need to increase total capacity. Some individual producers may increase their capacity, in order

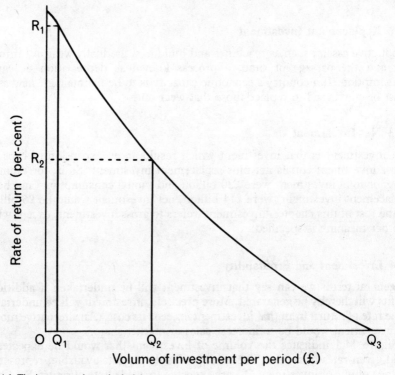

Fig. 14.1 The investment demand schedule

to supply new products, for example; but their additional capacity will be balanced by a reduction in capacity (disinvestment) by firms whose products will be replaced in consumers' budgets by the new products. Consequently only replacement investment will be undertaken.

It may seem strange to think of replacement investment as having a return. In fact rate of return is to be interpreted here as the loss of profitability that would have occurred had this investment not taken place.

If national income is expected to increase in the following year, t + 1, additional investment opportunities will be created. More precisely, the volume of investment expected to yield any given rate of return will increase. The investment demand schedule will therefore shift to the right, from $I_t$ to $I_{t+1}$, as indicated in Figure 14.2. That figure also indicates that in year t + 2 national income is expected to be less than in year t + 1, causing the investment demand schedule to shift to the left.

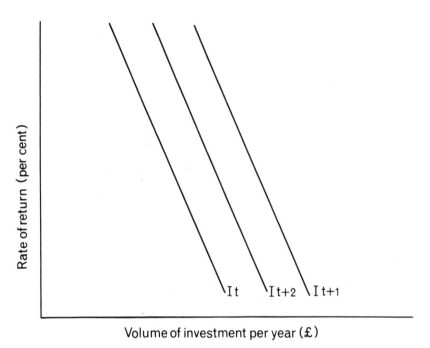

Fig. 14.2 Changes in the investment demand schedule

### 14.511 *The Accelerator*

The change in national income could take the form of a change in any of its elements; as an example let us consider a change in the most important element, consumers' expenditure. The effect of this change on investment can be illustrated by reference to one particular product, say potato crisps.

Let us assume that, during a period in which national income is stable, the annual sales of crisps are £1 million, and that to produce this output ten machines, each costing £1 million, are required (i.e. the capital-output ratio is 10:1.) The useful life of each machine is ten years, and one machine is replaced each year, so that replacement investment is £1 million a year.

Subsequently, as national income increases by 10 per cent, the annual demand for crisps (at present prices) rises to £11 million. If producers wish to satisfy this demand, they will require eleven machines. In this year, therefore, investment demand will be £2 million, £1 million being required for replacement purposes and £1 million for net investment. Note that this doubling of investment demand was the result of an increase of only 10 per cent in national income and consumers' expenditure. (Investment that occurs in response to a change in income is known as *induced investment*.)

This relationship between a change in national income and a change in investment expenditure is known as the accelerator principle. Expressed formally,

$$dI = a(dY)$$

where I is investment,
    Y is national income,
    d indicates a (small) change in these variables,
    a is the accelerator (capital-output) ratio.

Putting into the equation the figures used in the above example we have

$$dI = a(dY)$$

$$100 \text{ per cent} = 10 \ (10 \text{ per cent})$$

As noted above, we have assumed here that producers wish to expand their capacity in order to meet the higher demand. They might not do so if they thought that the increase was only temporary. We have also assumed that no spare production capacity existed. If there had been spare capacity, producers might simply have utilized this in order to produce the additional output required. Finally we have assumed that the producers of crisps were able to obtain the additional machines i.e. that capacity was available in the engineering industry. All these conditions have to be met if the accelerator is to work freely. (If they are not met, the operation of the accelerator is dampened.)

To look further ahead, if in the following year the demand for crisps remains at the new level of £11 million, investment demand will fall back to £1 million of replacement investment. There is no need for further net investment, since producers now have sufficient capacity to meet the higher demand.

This analysis suggests that, even though the relationship between consumers' and investment expenditure may not be as direct as assumed in our hypothetical example – even though the operation of the accelerator may be dampened – nevertheless investment expenditure is likely to be more volatile than consumers' expenditure. Empirical evidence does in fact confirm the existence of a relationship of the kind shown in Figure 14.3.

### 14.512 *An Inventory Accelerator*

We have concentrated so far on changes in fixed-capital formation. A second

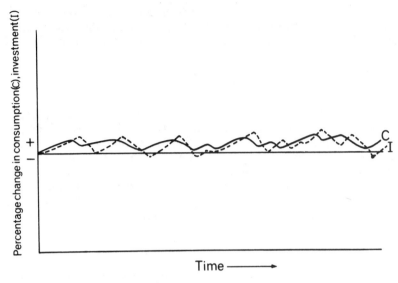

Fig. 14.3 Fluctuations in consumption and investment

element of investment is expenditure on stocks of components and materials, i.e. inventory. Firms often try to maintain a given ratio of inventory to output, in the same way as they have a desired ratio of fixed capital to output. Consequently changes in output are likely to lead to fluctuations in expenditure not only on fixed capital but also on inventory. We can, in fact, think of the inventory accelerator as a mechanism similar in character to the fixed-capital accelerator. Indeed it is sometimes useful, as a matter of convenience, to speak about 'the accelerator', this being understood to encompass the two individual accelerators.

However, caution should be exercised in the interpretation of statistics on inventories. In the national accounts inventory includes stocks of finished goods: Finished goods are, of course, usually produced by manufacturers, and stocked by distributors, in anticipation of demand. If demand turns out to be less than expected, suppliers will be left with more finished goods (and probably more materials) than they expected. In some instances, therefore, an increase in stocks may be unplanned, reflecting an unfavourable rather than a favourable change in demand.

### 14.52 *A Change in the Relative Cost and the Availability of Inputs*

If a change occurs in the cost of capital assets relative to the cost of other inputs, profit maximization requires that the mix of inputs be changed. This in turn implies that the rate of investment should change. For example, if in real terms labour became more expensive, one would expect more capital and less labour to be employed. A more extreme instance of substitution among factors is where one factor becomes extremely scarce: a scarcity of highly skilled craftsmen, for example, will encourage the introduction of machines to take their place. In all these instances the change in investment opportunities that occurs could be represented by means of an outward shift in the investment-demand schedule, similar to that shown in Figure 14.2.

## 14.6 Sources of Finance

A broad distinction can be made between internal sources of finance, generated by the current trading activities of the firm, and external sources, or 'new' money. *Internal* sources comprise depreciation provisions, retained profits and funds released by sales of, and reductions in, assets. Although identified separately in company accounts, all these sources represent money the firm could distribute to shareholders but retains within the business. To some extent the sources of *external* finance that are available to a business depend upon its legal form. We examine the most important of these forms in turn.

### 14.61 *Unincorporated Businesses: Sole Traders and Partnerships*

It has been estimated that there are around $1\frac{1}{4}$ million unincorporated businesses in the U.K., making this by far the most important form numerically. However, they are almost all very small, and together account for only about one-tenth of the capital expenditure undertaken by private-sector businesses.

Finance for one-man businesses (sole traders), which are particularly common in distribution, farming and the building trades, is largely short-term in nature, comprising bank loans, trade credit, hire-purchase credit, etc. Longer-term credit may sometimes be obtained by means of a mortgage on land or buildings. Permanent capital is restricted to the savings of the owner and the profits retained in the business.

Sources of finance for partnerships, which are very common in the professions – law, medicine etc. – are similar to those for the one-man business. But a partnership usually has more permanent capital, since it can have up to twenty partners. (For accountants and solicitors this figure may be exceeded.)

### 14.62 *Joint-stock Companies*

About 750,000 companies are registered in the U.K. They are of two types: private limited companies, which are the most important numerically, and public limited companies (often abbreviated to plc or PLC and not to be confused with public corporations), which are more important in terms of aggregate size. All the sources of finance available to unincorporated businesses are also available to joint-stock companies. In addition, joint-stock companies are able to raise permanent capital in return for the issue of shares.

There are two main types of share – preference shares and ordinary shares. Preference shares usually attract a fixed rate of dividend, and holders are paid in full before ordinary shareholders receive anything. Preference shareholders are, however, paid after holders of debentures (long-term loans) and usually receive a slightly higher payment in compensation. Ordinary shares generally do not carry a fixed rate of dividend, and receive a share of profits only after all other claims have been met. Consequently ordinary shares can represent a risky form of investment. On the other hand, ordinary shareholders tend to receive the greatest rewards when business is flourishing and profits are high.

Only a public company can make a public offer of shares. Moreover, unlike those of the private company, the securities issued by public companies can be freely traded. This applies to equity (permanent capital) and debentures (long-term loans), and is an important incentive to investors.

### 14.63 *The Stock Exchange*

Most trading in the securities of public companies takes place on the Stock Exchange. (In the U.K. the main International Stock Exchange is located in London, and there are smaller Exchanges in a number of other cities.) The U.K. Stock Exchange also provides a market for U.K. government (gilt-edged) securities, for other public sector securities and for securities issued by a number of foreign companies and governments.

Stock Exchange member firms, whether broker-dealers or market-makers, are able to act in a dual capacity. They can deal direct with investors, buying and selling securities from their own book, or they can act as agent on behalf of a client. (Many member firms are part of financial services conglomerates, a number of which include a U.K. or foreign bank.)

### 14.64 *The New Issue Market*

Transactions on the Stock Exchange do not in themselves affect the resources, or the capital employed, of the companies whose securities are traded, for the Stock Exchange is not itself a source of new money. Nevertheless, as we said above, the ability of investors to trade freely encourages them to subscribe new money when additional securities are issued by companies. These new issues can take several forms.

### 14.641 *Public Issue by Prospectus*

Here the company itself offers, directly to the public, a fixed number of shares (or debentures) at a stated price. A prospectus must be published, setting out the nature of the company's business, and giving details of its past turnover, profits, etc.

### 14.642 *Offer for Sale*

This is very similar to the public issue, but here the company sells the shares to an issuing house (usually a merchant bank), which in turn offers them to the general public.

### 14.643 *Placing*

The shares are again acquired by an issuing house, but instead of being offered to the general public, they are 'placed' with clients of the issuing house and with market makers. The shares are subsequently traded on the Stock Exchange, the general public then being able to buy.

### 14.644 *Offer for Sale by Tender*

This method tends to be used when investors' attitudes are very volatile, making it difficult to judge which price would be likely to equate demand with supply. The stated price is the minimum at which a tender will be accepted. If investors believe that the shares are worth more than this minimum, they will put in higher bids in order to try to ensure an allocation of shares.

### 14.645 *Rights Issue*

Rights issues are confined to existing shareholders, who are offered additional shares in proportion to their holdings in the company concerned. Since these shares are offered at a price below the price of existing shares, a rights issue can be seen as a reward to shareholders. However, the company also benefits, since administrative costs are usually lower than for other types of issue.

Rights issues should not be confused with bonus or scrip issues, which do *not* raise new money. In these instances the new shares are issued free to existing shareholders, but after the issue the market price is adjusted downwards to take into account the greater number of shares in issue. (The main benefit of a rights issue is that it improves the marketability of shares by increasing the number issued.)

### 14.65 *The Unlisted Securities Market*

In 1981 the Stock Exchange established the Unlisted Securities Market. This was partly an attempt to form a regulated market for stocks that were traded outside the official Stock Exchange list, and partly a response to the dearth of new quoted companies. Companies can seek a quotation on the U.S.M. with a record of profits for only three years, as compared with five for fully listed stocks. Moreover they need sell a minimum of 10 per cent of the equity, as compared with 25 per cent on the full market.

There are 300–400 companies quoted on the U.S.M. The actual figure varies as new companies enter the market and others leave. (Some leavers graduate to a listing on the main market, others are absorbed by mergers or acquisitions and a few fail.)

The costs of U.S.M. entry depend upon a number of factors, including the method of entry (e.g. offer for sale, placing) and the amount raised. On average companies pay about 2.5 per cent of their market capitalization in flotation expenses, which is about a quarter to a third less than the costs that firms of comparable size might incur in joining the main market.

### 14.66 *The Third Market*

Firms that are too small or speculative to enter the U.S.M. may apply to have their shares traded on the Third Market, established in 1987. In order to enter the Third Market a company must produce accredited accounts for at least one year (or as a 'greenfields' company prove that it requires capital to finance a viable project), be incorporated in the U.K. with at least three directors, and be sponsored by a Stock Exchange member firm.

## 14.7 The Relative Importance of the Various Sources of Finance

Internally generated funds (undistributed income) account for around two thirds of companies' capital requirements. In most years bank borrowing is the major external source of funds. The importance of this source has increased as banks have introduced a wider range of vehicles for lending, including term lending for periods of up to twenty years. Capital issues – debentures and shares – are a relatively minor source of finance. However their importance tends to increase in periods when higher company profits make new issues more attractive to investors.

Debentures are a relatively safe form of investment, since they yield a fixed rate of interest. Moreover should the company go bankrupt, debenture holders have a prior claim, ahead of shareholders, on the proceeds of the sale of the company's assets.

From the company's point of view the debenture is useful in enabling it to tap the funds of those investors for whom security is of prime importance. Moreover the interest payments on debentures (as on other loans) can be offset against tax, thus reducing the company's tax liability and, therefore, the real cost of this form of finance.

However, there are dangers in being 'highly geared', i.e. having a high proportion of funds subscribed by way of fixed interest capital. If profits fluctuate substantially, it may be impossible in a bad year to meet the interest payments on loans, and this may lead to the company going bankrupt.

As noted above, ordinary shares represent the most risky form of investment, both because there is no guarantee that dividends will be paid, and because ordinary shareholders have the last call on the assets of the company in cases of bankruptcy. To compensate for these disadvantages, shareholders can normally expect to obtain a higher return in the long run than debenture holders, always provided, of course, that they choose their companies wisely!

## 14.8 The Shareholders

Until comparatively recently the importance of individual, private shareholders had shown a consistent, long-term decline. Between 1963 and 1981 private investors' shares of total holdings of ordinary shares fell from 54 to 28 per cent. One of the main reasons for this decline was the enormous growth of indirect saving, especially contributions to pension funds and insurance companies.

But this decline has now been reversed. The proportion of the adult population owning shares is estimated to have risen from·7 per cent in 1979 to over 20 per cent today. A number of factors contributed to this rise. Probably most important was the government's privatization programme, discussed in Chapter 11. In 1989 13 per cent of all adults held shares in privatized companies (including 5 per cent whose only shareholding was in such companies).

A second factor was the granting of favourable tax treatment for employee share schemes; in 1989 3 per cent of the adult population held shares in the company for which they worked (about one in ten employees in the corporate sector).

Finally, since 1987 shareholding has been encouraged by tax concessions on holdings in personal equity plans (PEPs).

A further boost to shareholding has occurred as building societies have taken advantage of recent legislation to convert themselves into companies. Shareholders in the societies have been offered shares in the newly-formed companies on favourable terms.

### 14.81 *Investment Trusts*

Investment trusts are companies that obtain money by the issue of shares and debentures. This money is used, however, not in the purchase of plant, equipment, materials, etc., but in the purchase of securities, especially ordinary shares, in other companies. The advantage of the investment trust for the investor is that it enables him to spread his risks.

### 14.82 *Unit Trusts*

This spreading of the investor's risk has been one of the main reasons for the growth of unit trusts. They do not issue share capital and are not limited companies, but they issue units giving the owners the right to participate in the ownership of the trusts' assets. The investor's risk is minimized, not only because the trust's funds are invested in a wide range of companies but also because the units are highly marketable. Buying and selling prices for the units are quoted daily by the trust managers.

### 14.83 *Life Assurance and Pension Funds*

Despite the recent increase in the number of shareholders, individuals have continued to channel most of their savings into life assurance and pension funds (LAPFs). Much of this money is used to purchase shares, and the holdings of the LAPFs now exceed those of private shareholders.

### 14.84 *Merchant Banks*

Merchant banks are less important as suppliers of finance than the institutions considered above. Nevertheless the wide range of financial services they provide gives them a very important role in the British, and indeed the international, financial system.

These services include advising companies about the best means of financing particular projects, and bringing these companies into contact with institutions that are able to provide the necessary finance. Sometimes merchant banks may themselves provide capital, but this is normally on a small scale. It is essentially 'nursery' finance, provided until such time as the company can generate sufficient finance from other sources, perhaps from retained earnings or by making a public issue of shares.

A number of merchant banks provide short-term finance by accepting bills of exchange or commercial bills. The banks who specialize in this activity are known as accepting houses. Other functions undertaken by merchant banks include advising on mergers and take-overs, managing investments on behalf of clients, dealing in foreign exchange, gold and silver bullion markets, and acting as trustees.

### 14.85 *The Divorce between Ownership and Control*

The fact that institutions are far more important than private individuals as shareholders is an important aspect of the 'divorce between ownership and control'. An associated aspect is the relatively small number of shares held by the directors of many companies.

Institutional investors have been criticised because they tend to take a passive attitude towards the running of companies in which they have an important stake. In fact they are more prepared to exercise their power publicly than they were in the past. For example the pension funds forced Habitat to explain the rationale of the merger with Mothercare; they persuaded Burton to drop a controversial beneficial property deal for its top executives; they, together with other institutions, instituted litigation in an effort to block a golden handshake of £560,000 to a former managing director of Associated Communications Corporation. Moreover pressure is undoubtedly exerted behind the scenes on many companies.

It still remains true, however, that institutions often express their dissatisfaction with the performance or prospects of a company by selling their shares. Given the size of their holdings, this can lead to substantial fluctuations in share prices.

## 14.9 The Availability and Cost of Finance

### 14.91 *Retained Earnings*

Given the importance of internally generated funds, it is not surprising that econometric studies have found that changes in the level of retained earnings are often followed by changes in investment. In fact we should expect to find a link, not only because retained earnings are a source of funds for investment but also because rising profits usually indicate more favourable economic conditions, causing the investment-demand schedule to shift to the right.

If investment is entirely financed from retained earnings, it might appear that the cost of finance is zero. But this would be an invalid conclusion. By spending money on capital assets firms are foregoing other opportunities, such as putting money on deposit at the bank, buying shares in other companies, distributing bigger dividends to shareholders, and so forth. The return that could have been earned from the most profitable of these alternatives, i.e. the *opportunity cost*, is the true cost of using retained earnings to finance investment.

### 14.92 *External Finance*

Where insufficient internal funds are available, outside funds must be used, and the cost of capital will depend upon the nature of these funds. For example, if money is borrowed from a bank, the cost is the rate of interest charged by the bank (adjusted to take account of the fact that interest payments reduce the company's tax liability). If money is raised by the issue of shares, the cost is the return shareholders would expect to get in future years.

### 14.10 The Volume of Investment

As we noted above, the volume of investment undertaken in a given period depends upon both the demand for investment funds, which reflects the expected return from investment projects, and the supply of such funds. The interaction of these two sets of forces is illustrated in Figure 14.4.

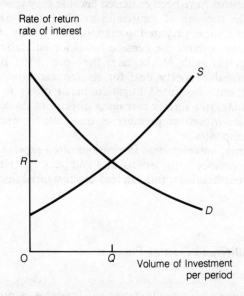

Fig. 14.4 Equilibrium rate of interest and volume of investment

The investment demand schedule, D, indicates the demand for investment funds. The supply of funds, S, is positively related to the rate of interest or, more generally, the cost of finance. At the equilibrium point the return, R, from the last unit of investment undertaken equals the cost of the funds required for that investment. The total amount of investment undertaken is Q. The yield from any further investment would be less than the cost of the funds required for that investment.

The demand and supply schedules in Figure 14.4, which may apply only for a single period, incorporate the many factors discussed in this chapter. We can draw together the various points discussed by considering the effect of a change in these factors. We do this with reference to Figure 14.5 in which the initial demand and supply curves are $D_1$ and $S_1$. The value of investment is $Q_1$ and the rate of interest is $R_1$. This figure shows an increase in demand and supply; in practice, of course, both demand and supply may either increase or decrease from one period to another.

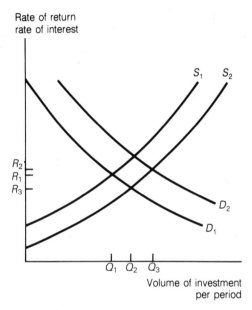

Fig. 14.5 Changes in the rate of interest and volume of investment

### 14.101 *An Increase in Demand*

An increase in demand, represented by a shift of the demand curve from $D_1$ to $D_2$, occurs because of an increase in the prospective returns or yields of investment projects. This could be due to: an increase in national income and hence in demand; the impact of technological change in the form of new products or processes; an increase in the cost of other inputs, and especially labour, for which capital is substituted; an improvement in business confidence – this might relate to some of the other factors, but it is identified separately to emphasize the fact that the demand curve reflects *prospective* yields, and also because it is known that in practice the level of business confidence affects investment decisions. Finally, we should note that if the capital stock increases over time, this will eventually lead to an increase in the level of replacement investment (assuming a constant rate of depreciation per unit of capital stock). The result of the shift in the investment demand schedule would be an increase in investment to $Q_2$, and a rise in the rate of interest to $R_2$.

## 14.102 *An Increase in Supply*

An increase in the supply of investment funds, represented by a shift of the supply curve from $S_1$ to $S_2$, may occur because of an increase in the total money supply within the economy. (The factors affecting the money supply are discussed in Chapter 18.) A higher level of national income is also likely to mean an increase in the level of savings and hence in the supply of funds for investment (as well as an increase in demand, as noted above).

We showed in Chapter 13 that changes can occur in the propensity to save and to consume. It follows that in principle the level of saving could increase even if national income did not change. This would increase the supply of investment funds. But it would also be likely to cause a fall in the demand for these funds because of the fall in consumption.

We saw earlier that the saving of companies, i.e. undistributed income, forms a major source of funds for investment. It follows that increased company profitability in one period may lead to an increased supply of investment funds in a subsequent period. (An increase in profits in one period may also lead to an increase in business confidence and hence to a higher demand for investment funds.)

With the demand schedule $D_1$, the shift of the supply schedule from $S_1$ to $S_2$ would lead to a fall in the rise of interest to from $R_1$ to $R_3$ and an increase in investment from $Q_1$ to $Q_3$.

## 14.11 Consumers' Investment: Expenditure on Housing

Consumers' spending on new houses is treated as investment in the national accounts. The justification for this is that there is an analogy between houses and the buildings and machines bought by firms, in that they all give rise to a flow of services or benefits over a long period of time. But note that, on the same grounds, consumers' expenditure on cars and other durable goods might also be classed as investment, although it is in fact treated as consumption.

When we consider the factors that influence spending on new houses, we must make a distinction between the long and the short run. In the long run the prime determinants of the demand for housing are the size of the population and the national income. In the short run the prime determinant is the availability of finance, in particular the volume of funds supplied by the building societies and banks.

## 14.12 External Benefits and Costs

The activities of producers, including investment, may give rise to 'external benefits' for other members of the community. The primary purpose of a dam included in a hydro-electric scheme may be to increase the supply of electricity and hence the revenue of the producer. But people may also benefit if the dam adds to the recreational facilities of the area – more interesting walks, opportunities for bird watching, etc. Conversely, investment may give rise to 'external costs'. The building of a dam might equally well reduce an area's recreational facilities, force people to move their homes, reduce the availability of farming land, and so forth.

The return to the community from investment may not equal the sum of the returns to the individual firms making that investment, a factor that explains the increasing importance of social cost-benefit analysis.

### 14.13 Summary and Conclusions

In general investment is undertaken if the expected benefits exceed the expected costs. In the private sector the excess of benefits over costs is measured in terms of additional profits. In parts of the public sector investment yields external benefits.

The rate of return on investment is influenced by changes in the relative cost and availability of inputs. The cost of the funds to finance investment depends upon the source of those funds.

### Further Reading

Artis, M. J., Ed. *The U.K. Economy* (London: Weidenfeld and Nicolson, 11th Edn, 1986), Ch. 1.

Begg, D., Fischer, S. and Dornbusch, R., *Economics* (London: McGraw-Hill, 2nd Edn, 1987), Ch. 20.

Griffiths, A. and Walls, S., *Applied Economics* (London: Longman, 2nd Edn, 1986), Ch. 12.

Lipsey, R. G. and Harbury, C., *First Principles of Economics* (London: Weidenfeld and Nicolson, 1988), Ch. 27.

Livesey, F., *A Textbook of Economics* (London: Longman, 3rd Edn, 1989), Ch. 16.

Maunder, P., Myers, D., Wall, N. and Miller, R. L., *Economics Explained* (London: Collins, 1987), Ch. 15.

### Revision Exercises

1 Explain what is shown by an investment demand curve, and indicate what factors might cause the curve to shift upwards and to the right.
2 How are changes in the level of national income likely to influence the rate of return on investment?
3 Define the accelerator principle and indicate how the operation of the principle may influence the pattern of investment expenditure.
4 In what circumstances will the operation of the accelerator be dampened?
5 Explain the statement that the amount of investment undertaken in any period depends upon the prospective rate of return and also on the availability and cost of investment funds.
6 'If a firm is able to finance investment internally, its cost of capital is zero.' Discuss.
7 Explain how a change in the cost of capital is likely to affect the volume of investment undertaken.
8 The Victoria Line extension to the London underground system was built

despite the knowledge that the additional revenue would not cover the cost of constructing and operating the line. Does this mean that the total costs outweighed the total benefits of the line?

9 Examine the possible effect of a fall in consumption on (a) net investment and (b) replacement investment.

10 'While an increase in saving makes an increase in investment more possible, it also makes it less likely.' Discuss.

# 15. *The Determination of National Income*

## 15.1 Introduction

In the previous two chapters we have examined the various factors that influence consumption and investment. We now show how these two variables, together with overseas transactions and government expenditure, interact so as to determine national income.

## 15.2 Expenditure, Output and Income

We saw in Chapter 12 that the level of economic activity can be measured in terms of expenditure on goods and services, the income received by the owners of resources utilized in the production of goods and services, or the value of the output of goods and services. The relationship between these alternative measures is shown in Figure 15.1. This figure assumes that a change in income is accompanied by an equal change in output. As shown later, this relationship will not hold when part of the change in expenditure and income represents a change in prices (see Figure 15.10).

Total expenditure is measured on the vertical axis. For each level of expenditure there is a corresponding level of output and income. For example, expenditure $E_1$ corresponds to output and income $Q_1$. Note that, since the line E is drawn at 45° to the two axes, any two corresponding points will be exactly equal numerically. If $E_1$ represents expenditure of £3 million, $Q_1$ will also represent £3 million. This simply reflects the fact that we are measuring, for a given time period, different aspects of a circular flow.

Figure 15.1 is therefore simply a record of what transpired, a summary of transactions, during a past period. It tells us nothing about the future behaviour of the system, whether income is likely to remain at $Q_1$ (whether $Q_1$ is the equilibrium level of income), or whether it will rise above or fall below $Q_1$.

## 15.3 The Equilibrium Level of National Income

In order to determine what is the equilibrium level of income we need to examine the relationship between the income received in one period of time (t) and the expenditure *planned* in the following period (t + 1). The condition for equilibrium is that planned expenditure in period t + 1 should equal income in period t. When this condition is met, the circular flow continues at a constant rate from one period to the next. This is shown in Figure 15.2, where income is

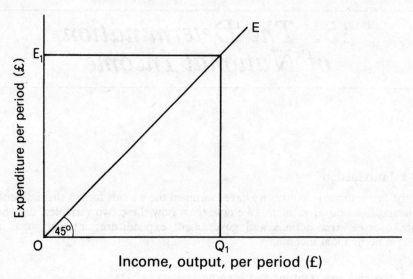

Fig. 15.1 Expenditure related to income and output

denoted by Y and expenditure by E.

If planned expenditure is less than the previous period's income, then income will gradually decline. For example, Figure 15.3 shows the situation where planned expenditure is always 80 per cent of income in the previous period. Conversely, if planned expenditure is greater than income, income gradually rises. The expenditure which cannot be met from the current income, must be financed out of past savings.

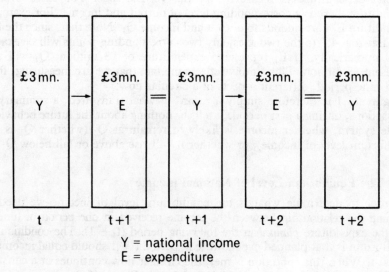

Y = national income
E = expenditure

Fig. 15.2 Constant equilibrium level of national income

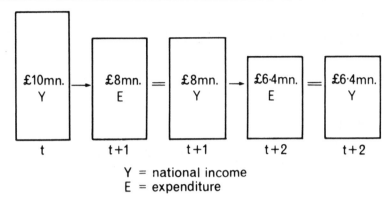

Y = national income
E = expenditure

Fig. 15.3 Falling level of national income

Returning to the 45° diagram, we have drawn, in Figure 15.4, a total *planned* expenditure function. (The shape of this function will be explained below.) We can see that only at income $Y_E$ are income and planned expenditure equal. If income is above $Y_E$, planned expenditure is less than income, and therefore the level of income will decline. Conversely, if income is below $Y_E$, planned expenditure is greater than income, and the level of income will rise.

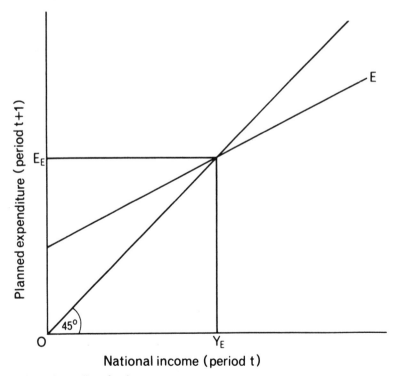

Fig. 15.4 Planned expenditure function

## 15.4 The Expenditure Function

### 15.41 *Consumption*

We showed in Chapter 13 that the relation between income and consumption most commonly takes the form

$$C = a + bY$$

This relation is presented in diagrammatic form in Figure 15.5. As before, a indicates the level of consumption at zero income, and b (which is the marginal propensity to consume) determines the slope of the consumption line. With the consumption line $C_1$ (to ignore for the moment all other forms of expenditure), the equilibrium national income is $Y_1$. If the marginal propensity to consume were greater, e.g. if the consumption line were $C_2$, the equilibrium level of income would be greater, at $Y_2$.

### 15.42 *Investment*

We showed in Chapter 14 that investment is likely to rise as the level of national income rises. For the moment we assume that the level of investment is *constant* at all levels of income. Our total expenditure function now takes the form shown in Figure 15.6. Investment is represented by the horizontal line I. When investment is added to the consumption line C, we obtain the total expenditure

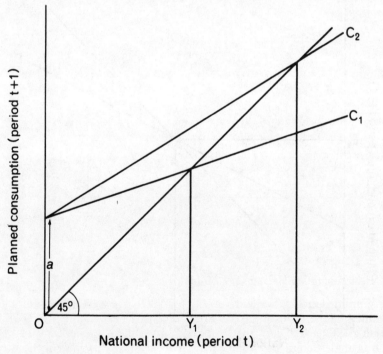

Fig. 15.5 Planned consumption function

line E. (Another way of looking at this is that investment represents the vertical distance between lines C and E.) As before, the equilibrium level of income ($Y_E$) is that at which planned expenditure in period t + 1 equals income in period t.

### 15.43 *The Multiplier*

Looking again at Figure 15.6, we see that had there been no investment expenditure, the equilibrium income would have been $Y_1$ rather than $Y_E$. The additional expenditure resulting from the investment is $E_1E_E$, or RT. But notice that this increase in expenditure is greater than the amount of investment, ST. The remainder of the additional expenditure, RS, consists of an increase in consumption resulting from the increase in income. This magnification of the initial increase in (investment) expenditure is known as the multiplier effect.

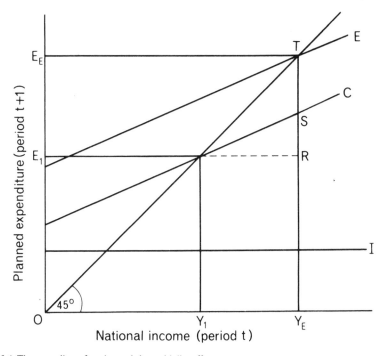

Fig. 15.6 The expenditure function and the multiplier effect

### 15.44 *Determining the Value of the Multiplier*

In the simplified model that we have adopted so far, the value of the multiplier is determined by the value of the marginal propensity to consume. Let us assume first that MPC is 0.2, and that additional investment expenditure of £1,000 million is undertaken, beginning in period t. (Since this investment is *not* a response to a change in income it is known as autonomous investment.)

Expenditure and therefore income having increased by £1,000 million in period t, consumers spend an additional £200 million in period t + 1. Since investment continues at £1,000 million, total expenditure in period t + 1 is £1,200 million, £200 million more than in period t (Figure 15.7). This additional income generates a further increase in consumption of £40 million (£200 million × 0.2) in period t + 2, total expenditure being £1,240 million. In period t + 3, expenditure and income is £1,248 million. It can be seen that the rate of increase in income declines over time, and that eventually income would cease to grow.

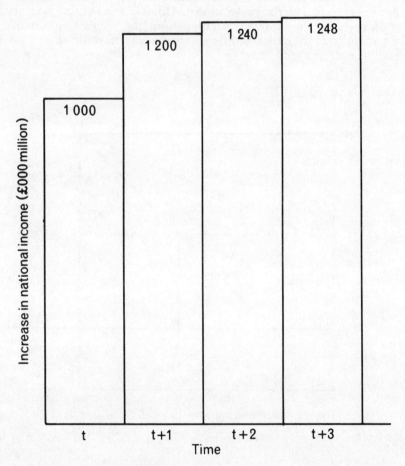

Fig. 15.7 Determining the value of the multiplier

We can calculate the eventual limit to income from the multiplier formula, which is

$$K = \frac{1}{1 - MPC}$$

In this instance, with MPC = 0·2, the multiplier, K, is

$$\frac{1}{1 - 0·2} = \frac{1}{0·8} = 1·25$$

Applying the multiplier to the initial increase in investment expenditure of £1,000 million, we deduce that the eventual increase in income would be £1,250 million, of which £1,000 million would constitute investment and £250 million consumption expenditure.

With a higher MPC, more of each addition to income would be spent; it would re-enter the circular flow, and so the eventual increase in income would be greater. For example, if MPC = 0·75, the value of the multiplier would be

$$K = \frac{1}{1 - 0·75} = \frac{1}{0·25} = 4$$

Investment expenditure of £1,000 million would now give rise to an eventual increase in income of £4,000 million.

We showed in Chapter 13 that the marginal propensity to consume plus the marginal propensity to save equals unity, or 1 − MPC = MPS. We can therefore construct an alternative formulation of the multiplier, using the same figures as above, as follows:

$$K = \frac{1}{MPS} = \frac{1}{0·25} = 4$$

This £4,000 million would comprise £3,000 million of consumption expenditure and £1,000 million of investment expenditure. Another way of expressing this situation is to say that, of an additional income of £4,000 million, consumers plan to spend £3,000 million and to save £1,000 million. The additional saving equals the additional investment. Hence we have an alternative definition of the equilibrium level of income, namely that level at which *planned saving and planned investment are equal*.

### 15.45 *An Extension of the Model*

This model can be used to show the effect on income of changes in other forms of expenditure. In the previous example we could substitute government expenditure or exports for investment. Given MPC = 0·75, an increase in government expenditure (or exports) of £1,000 million would give rise to an eventual increase in income of £4,000 million.

### 15.46 *Injections and Withdrawals*

It will be useful now to summarize the argument to date in terms of our 45° diagram. In Figure 15.8, if consumption were the only form of expenditure, the equilibrium income would be $Y_1$. The effect of the three *injections* – investment (I), government expenditure (G) and exports (X) – is to increase the equilibrium income from $Y_1$ to $Y_E$. As we said earlier, we can define equilibrium income as that level at which *planned expenditure in one period equals income in the previous period*.

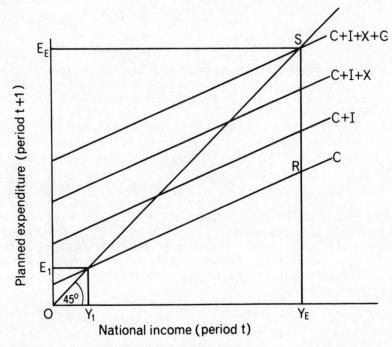

Fig. 15.8 The equilibrium level of income and the effect of injections

We previously noted an alternative definition of equilibrium income as that level at which planned saving equals planned investment. In terms of our expanded model the equilibrium income is that level at which *planned withdrawals equal planned injections*. In addition to saving, the other withdrawals from the circular flow of income are taxation and imports. We can therefore deduce that in Figure 15.8, with equilibrium income $Y_E$, planned withdrawals must equal RS, since this is the total planned injections.

Incidentally, a more developed formulation of the multiplier takes into account all three forms of withdrawal. Where the marginal propensity to withdraw is the sum of the marginal propensities to save, to taxation and to import

$$\text{i.e. MPW} = \text{MPS} + \text{MPT} + \text{MPM, then K} = \frac{1}{\text{MPW}}.$$

## 15.5 Further Consideration of the Expenditure Function

In the previous sections we made the simplifying assumption that each injection into the circular flow of income was constant at all levels of income. In practice it is likely that the level of each injection will rise as income rises. This is illustrated in Figure 15.9.

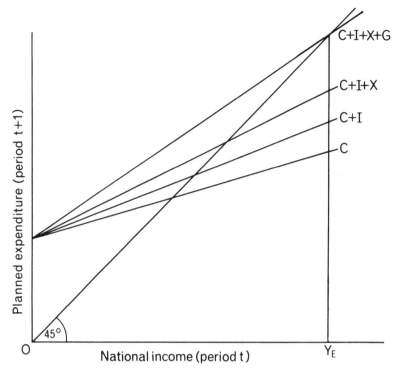

Fig. 15.9 An extension of the multiplier model

The fact that each form of expenditure is positively related to income implies that an increase in any one form will cause all the other forms of expenditure to increase.

## 15.6 Real versus Money Income

We have assumed so far in this chapter that a change in expenditure is matched by an equivalent change in the *volume* of output, and therefore in *real* income. This is a reasonable assumption in very depressed economic conditions, when many resources are lying idle. In much of the postwar period, however, increases in expenditure between one period and another have reflected partly an increase in the volume, and partly a rise in the price of this output. Another way of putting this is to say that the rise in money income is greater than the rise in real income, the difference being accounted for by the rise in prices.

This situation can be demonstrated by combining the usual 45° diagram with a diagram showing the behaviour of prices. In the lower part of Figure 15.10 the aggregate supply curve for all commodities (S) indicates the price at which various quantities of output would be supplied. Producers would be willing to supply up to $Q_1$ at price $P_1$. In order to bring forth a higher supply a higher

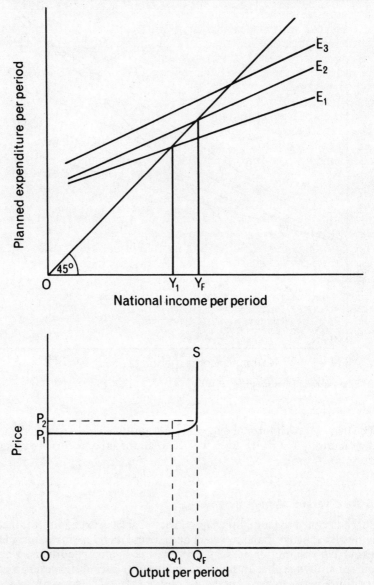

Fig. 15.10 Real income related to money income

price would be required, for several reasons. First, at higher rates of output less efficient resources, both material and human, would be brought into use. Second, the greater the demand for resources, the more likely it is that the price of these resources, especially labour, will rise. Finally it is also possible that suppliers will take advantage of the demand conditions to increase their profit margins.

We suggested earlier that the most likely response when demand for one firm's products increases is that price will remain stable. But the prices of resources are much less likely to rise in that situation than when many firms are seeking to employ more resources, as here.

An increase in price means that any increase in money income beyond $Y_1$ (which corresponds to output $Q_1$) will not be fully matched by the increase in real income. For example, following a rise in expenditure from $E_1$ to $E_2$, money income rises by 20 per cent ($Y_1$ to $Y_F$). But prices rise by 10 per cent (from $P_1$ to $P_2$) between the corresponding output levels $Q_1$ and $Q_F$. Consequently real income rises by only 10 per cent.

Indeed there will come a point where no further increase in real income is possible because no additional output can be produced, whatever the level of demand. It is conventional to designate this point the *full employment level of income*. This is shown as income $Y_F$ in Figure 15.10, with $Q_F$ as the corresponding level of output. If expenditure were to rise from $E_2$ to $E_3$, this would entirely represent an increase in prices.

Of course this limit to output, and to real income, will change over time. As the productive capacity of the economy increases, the capacity limit is shifted to the right, so that the effect on prices of a given increase in expenditure will depend upon the period of time over which that increase takes place. The longer the period is (i.e. the slower the rate of increase in expenditure), the greater is the possibility of expanding productive capacity.

## 15.7 Potential and Actual National Income

We must stress that the term 'equilibrium' as applied to national income (and indeed to any economic variable) indicates stability, an absence of any tendency to change. There is no implication that the equilibrium level of national income is the 'right' level or the highest level that could be attained. Indeed Keynes demonstrated very clearly that national income could reach an equilibrium at a point at which substantial resources, especially labour, remained unemployed. To put it another way, the actual national income could be less than the potential national income.

## Further Reading

Artis, M. J., *The U.K. Economy* (London: Weidenfeld and Nicolson, 11th Edn, 1986), Ch. 1.

Begg, D., Fischer, S. and Dornbusch, R., *Economics* (London: McGraw-Hill, 1987), Ch. 20.

Hardwick, P., Khan, B. and Langmead, J., *An Introduction to Modern Economics* (London: Longman, 2nd Edn, 1986), Ch. 18.

Lipsey, R. G. and Harbury C., *First Principles of Economics* (London: Weidenfeld and Nicolson, 1988), Chs 28 and 29.

Livesey, F., *A Textbook of Economics* (London: Longman, 3rd Edn, 1989), Ch. 18.

Maunder, P., Myers, D., Wall, N. and Miller, R. L., *Explaining Economics* (London: Collins, 1987), Chs 14 and 16.

**Revision Exercises**

1 Under what conditions will national income attain an equilibrium level?
2 Explain why income will decline when planned expenditure in any period is less than income in the previous period.
3 Outline the injections into and withdrawals from the circular flow of income and discuss their effects.
4 Explain the likely impact on the level of national income of an increase in the average propensity to consume.
5 Define the multiplier and show how a fall in its numerical value will affect the level of income.
6 'The national income will be in equilibrium when savings equal investment.' Discuss.
7 Explain why the level of injections may vary as the level of income varies, and outline the implications of this fact for the theory of income determination.
8 Show how a reduction in the cost of capital is likely to affect the level of national income.
9 'The effect on the level of national income of an increase in government expenditure will depend upon the form of that expenditure.' Discuss.
10 In a given period money expenditure increased by 10 per cent while output increased by only 5 per cent. Using diagrams, explain the implications of these changes.

# 16. *Demand Management*

## 16.1 Introduction

We have shown that Keynesian analysis suggests that the level of total expenditure or aggregate demand is an important influence on the level of output and employment. For much of the post-war period government policy followed the prescriptions of Keynesian analysis. When unemployment showed a tendency to rise, governments stimulated aggregate demand. Conversely, when unemployment was deemed to be too low, leading to rapidly rising prices, governments took steps to reduce, or at least moderate the rise in, aggregate demand. (The policy measures used to influence demand are discussed in the following chapters.) By 'managing' aggregate demand the government attempted to keep inflation and unemployment at a target level.

## 16.2 A Trade-off between Inflation and Unemployment

The idea that there is a trade-off between inflation and unemployment received support from the results of research into the behaviour of the U.K. economy over the period 1862 to 1958 undertaken by Professor A. W. Phillips. When Phillips plotted the rate of change of wages (a strong influence on the rate of change of prices) against the level of unemployment he found the relationship illustrated in Figure 16.1.

It appeared that the government could choose to have a very low rate of wage (and price) increase, $W_L$, if it was prepared to tolerate heavy unemployment, $U_H$. Alternatively it could reduce unemployment to a low level, $U_L$, if it was prepared to accept a higher rate of inflation, $W_H$.

## 16.3 Improving the Terms of Trade-off

In order to try to improve the terms of trade-off between inflation and unemployment, governments might adopt two sets of policies.

### 16.31 *Prices and Incomes Policies*

Prices and incomes policies have been used to try to prevent prices (including the price of labour) from rising at too rapid a rate when aggregate demand was high. Unfortunately, as shown in Chapter 9, these policies have frequently failed to achieve their objective.

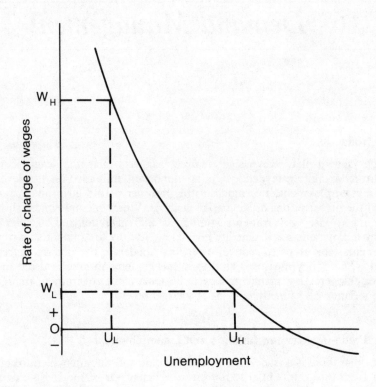

Fig. 16.1 The Phillips curve

### 16.32 *Policies to Increase Productive Capacity*

The reason for attempting to increase productive capacity is as follows. Prices begin to rise rapidly when the point is approached at which capacity would need to be fully utilized in order to meet demand. Consequently the greater the capacity, the greater demand (and therefore output and employment) can be without prices rising at an unacceptable rate.

An increase in productive capacity can be achieved in two ways. First, the efficiency or quality of the existing volume of resources can be increased. This may involve an increase in educational and training programmes (see Chapter 9), policies designed to increase the degree of competition in order to facilitate the expansion of more efficient firms (Chapter 10), and intervention in firms' decisions on location (Chapter 21).

An increase in capacity can also be achieved by increasing the volume of resources available. As far as labour is concerned, although the size of the total population is not very responsive to government policies (except over a very long period), the size of the working population may be responsive to policies concerning taxation, education and training, etc. In general, however, governments have less influence on the total volume of the labour input than they have on the capital input. They are able to influence the rate of investment in buildings, machines, etc., by means of a wide range of policies (see Chapters 17, 18 and 21).

## 16.4 A Sound Balance of Payments

If prices rise more quickly than those of our competitors, we may fail to achieve another aim of government policy – a sound balance of payments. The balance of payments comprises the value, during a given period, of transactions with overseas countries causing monetary flows into or out of the U.K. If the sum of cash outflows exceeds the sum of cash inflows, an adverse (negative) balance results. If cash inflows exceed outflows, a favourable (positive) balance results.

In many instances an objective of a sound balance of payments implies that the balance should be positive. However, it is important to recognize that a positive balance for the U.K. necessarily implies a negative balance for another country (or countries). Moreover, large balances, whether negative or positive, may have undesirable consequences for the international system of trade and payments. Consequently, a sound balance of payments should usually be interpreted to mean a *modest* surplus, or simply the avoidance of a deficit.

We have already noted that a rate of price increase greater than that of our international competitors is likely to result in a balance of payments deficit. Looking at the other side of the coin, a potential balance of payments deficit may prevent governments from adopting policies designed to increase the level of expenditure.

Again, the balance of payments position may inhibit policies designed to expand the level of capacity. This may seem strange, in view of the fact that additional capacity would enable a greater volume of exports to be produced. Problems may arise, however, because the increase in the volume of imports, which often occurs as a result of economic growth, normally precedes the increase in exports. This puts a strain on the balance of payments, and although this strain may only be temporary, i.e. exports may eventually catch up with imports, we may not be able to take the risk inherent in this policy, unless our reserves of gold and foreign currencies are very strong.

## 16.5 The Challenge to the Keynesian Analysis

In the late 1970s and the 1980s, the onset of 'stagflation' and 'slumpflation' severely dented confidence in the ability of governments to influence inflation and unemployment. Moreover the theory underpinning government policy was challenged by the emergence of alternative theories. Especially important was the development of the natural rate of unemployment hypothesis.

Milton Friedman and other economists have argued that the long term level of employment, and hence the long term or natural level of unemployment, is determined by the *real* wage rate. It is likely that an increase in aggregate expenditure will cause all prices, including the price of labour, to rise to the same extent. Consequently real wages, and therefore employment, will be unchanged. The only long-term effect of the increase in expenditure will be higher prices.

This is illustrated in Figure 16.2. With aggregate demand $D_1$, $Q_1$ goods and services are produced at an average price level $P_1$. Keynesian analysis suggests that if there is spare capacity, including unemployed workers, output would increase following an increase in aggregate demand. With an upward sloping aggregate supply curve $S_1$, output would increase to $Q_2$ and average price to $P_2$. (This process was illustrated in the Chapter 15 – see the increase from $Q_1$ to $Q_F$ in Figure 15.10.)

The upward sloping supply curve indicates, of course, that higher prices have been offered to attract the additional resources, including labour, required to produce the extra output. Additional workers accept jobs in response to the offer of higher wages. However, this response occurs only in the short term. As time goes on, firms increase the prices of goods and services to cover their increased costs. Workers then realize that real wages have not changed, i.e. they have fallen back to their original level. Consequently the number of workers willing to work will also be unchanged, i.e. it will return to its original level. This is indicated by the vertical supply curve $S_2$. This also means, of course, that output returns to $Q_1$. However, this output is now sold at a higher average price $P_3$.

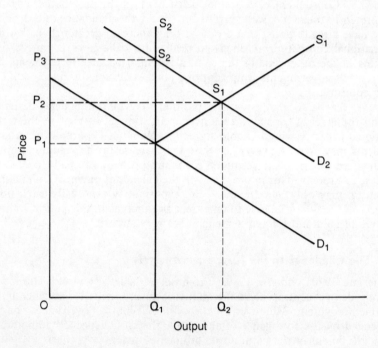

Fig. 16.2 The impact of an increase in aggregate demand

We have met a vertical supply curve before (Figure 15.10). But there the supply curve became vertical at the full employment level of output. The analysis presented in this section suggests that the supply curve may become vertical even when resources, including labour, remain unemployed.

### 16.51 *The Policy Implications*

Many economists do not believe that this analysis could be applied to the U.K. economy in recent years. They point out that some workers would be prepared to accept jobs at the existing real wage, if such jobs became available. However, all economists agree that this alternative view of the economy, this challenge to the Keynesian analysis, has had one benefit. It has led to greater attention being paid to measures that affect the supply side of the economy. The aim of these measures is to enable more goods and services to be produced at any given price level. This would be shown by a shift of the supply curve – whether vertical or upward sloping – to the right.

## 16.6 Supply-side Measures

Several sets of measures can be considered under this heading. These measures are discussed in different chapters and it will therefore be helpful to summarize them here.

### 16.61 *Measures to Increase the Efficiency of the Labour Market*

We showed in Chapter 9 that governments have sought to increase efficiency by encouraging more training of labour and by trying to ensure that training is directed towards the acquisition of skills for which demand seems likely to exceed supply. We also briefly examined industrial relations legislation designed to reduce the number of strikes and to weaken the monopoly power of the trades unions. Finally, we saw that government Jobcentres put people seeking work in touch with employers seeking workers.

### 16.62 *Measures to Increase the Efficiency of Industry*

The presumption underlying competition policy, discussed in Chapter 10, is that an increase in competition usually leads to an increase in efficiency. This belief is also one of the factors which led to the privatization programme outlined in Chapter 11.

### 16.63 *Measures to Increase Incentives*

Most of the measures designed to increase incentives come under the heading of fiscal policy which is discussed in Chapter 17. Since 1979 the basic rate of income tax has been reduced from 33 to 25 per cent, while nine higher rates of income tax running up to 83 per cent have been replaced by a single higher rate of 40 per cent. The aim of these tax reductions was to create a greater incentive for individuals to work hard, to exercise their initiative and to take the risks that are often involved in establishing and running a company.

In the same period the main rate of corporation tax has been cut from 52 to 35 per cent, one of the lowest in the world, while for small companies the rate has been reduced from 42 to 25 per cent.

Several measures have been taken to increase the incentive to save, and in particular the incentive to invest savings. Changes to the capital gains tax have reduced the burden of the tax, and lower rates of inheritance tax have made it easier to pass family businesses on to the next generation. As pointed out in Chapter 14, wider share ownership has been encouraged by favourable tax treatment of personal equity plans and employee share schemes, and by the privatization programmes. Wider share ownership helps to improve the efficiency of capital markets. The efficiency of capital markets has also been enhanced by the various measures to aid the financing of small firms, discussed in Chapter 10.

## 16.7 Summary and Conclusions

Keynesian analysis suggests that by increasing aggregate demand, unemployment can be reduced, but that this will be accompanied by an increase in the rate of inflation. The terms of the trade-off between inflation and unemployment can be improved by supply-side policies, intended to increase productive capacity. Other economists have challenged this analysis, suggesting that an increase in aggregate demand will cause prices to rise but will eventually leave unemployment unchanged. These economists would put more emphasis on supply-side policies than would Keynesians.

## Further Reading

Begg, D., Fischer, S. and Dornbusch, R., *Economics* (London: McGraw-Hill, 2nd Edn, 1987), Chs 21, 25 and 30.

Hardwick, P., Khan, B. and Langmead, J., *An Introduction to Modern Economics* (London: Longman, 2nd Edn, 1986), Chs 25 and 27.

Livesey, F., *A Textbook of Economics* (London: Longman, 3rd Edn, 1989), Ch. 19.

Maunder, P., Myers, D., Wall, N. and Miller, R. L., *Explaining Economics* (London: Collins, 1987), Ch. 18.

## Revision Exercises

1 Explain what you understand by the term demand management.
2 Why was it believed that there was a trade-off between inflation and unemployment?
3 How might governments seek to improve the trade-off between inflation and unemployment?
4 Analyse the impact on the inflation rate of policies designed to increase productive capacity.
5 Analyse the impact on the balance of payments of policies designed to increase productive capacity.
6 Why may a substantial balance of payments surplus be undesirable?

7 Why might a potential balance of payments deficit prevent governments from adopting policies designed to increase the level of expenditure?

8 Explain what is likely to happen to employment if all prices, including the price of labour, rise to the same extent.

9 Explain why less reliance is now placed on economic policies based on Keynesian analysis.

10 What is the likely effect on unemployment of greater flexibility in the labour market?

**Objective Test Questions: Set No. 4**

For answers see p. 274.

1 Which of the following statements is true?

A  The average propensity to consume cannot exceed one
B  The average propensity to consume always equals the marginal propensity to consume
C  The average propensity to consume plus the average propensity to save always exceeds one
D  The marginal propensity to consume plus the marginal propensity to save always equals one.

2 The formula $K = \dfrac{\Delta Y}{\Delta J}$ gives the value of the multiplier K. Where $\Delta Y$ represents a change in income $\Delta J$ represents a change in

A  the volume of savings
B  government expenditure
C  consumption expenditure
D  injections into the circular flow of income.

3 Given a marginal propensity to save of 0·2, a marginal propensity to import of 0·15 and a marginal propensity to taxation of 0·05, the value of the multiplier would be

A  0·2
B  0·4
C  2·5
D  5·0

4 Which of the following is most likely to lead to a fall in the value of the multiplier?

A  More even distribution of income
B  More even distribution of wealth
C  Lowering of tariff barriers in the country
D  Reduction in interest rates

5 Question 5 is based on Figure 1; from the diagram we can conclude that

   A the average propensity to consume is constant
   B the marginal propensity to consume falls as income increases
   C the marginal and average propensities to consume are equal when
      income is A
   D dis-saving occurs when income is less than A.

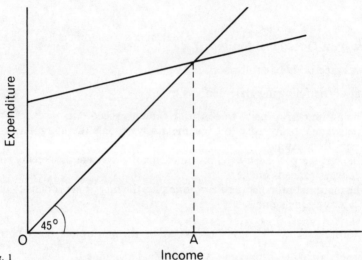

Fig. 1

6 Which of the following statements is true? The marginal propensity to consume

   A can never exceed unity
   B may exceed unity when dis-saving occurs
   C can never exceed the average propensity to consume
   D is the reciprocal of the marginal propensity to save

7 Of the following, the best definition of the accelerator hypothesis is that the change in investment is a function of the

   A rate of interest
   B rate of interest and the marginal efficiency of capital
   C level of national income or output
   D rate of change of national income or output

8 *Period*      *National Income*

     1            150
     2            200
     3            250

If the value of the accelerator is 2, new investment in period 3 will be

A   50
B   100
C   150
D   200

9 In which of the following situations, other things remaining equal, is a rise in national income most likely to occur?

A An increase in the multiplier and a fall in the accelerator
B A fall in the multiplier and an increase in the accelerator
C A fall in both the multiplier and the accelerator
D An increase in both the multiplier and the accelerator.

10 When national income is at an equilibrium level, this implies that
A actual expenditure in a given period equals planned expenditure in the previous period
B planned expenditure in a given period equals actual income in the previous period
C actual income in a given period equals planned income in the previous period
D actual income in a given period equals planned income in that period.

11 Given the potential gross national product, real gross national product at any given time will be determined mainly by the level of

A consumption
B investment
C aggregate demand
D prices

12 Which of the following is/are likely to cause a change in the volume of planned savings?

1 An increase in the rate of interest
2 An increase in the national income
3 A change to a more even distribution of income

A 1, 2 and 3
B 1 and 2 only
C 1 and 3 only
D 2 and 3 only.

13 Which of the following is/are included in investment expenditure?

  1 The purchase of a machine by a company
  2 The purchase of a new house by an individual consumer
  3 The purchase of a new car by an individual consumer

  A 1, 2 and 3
  B 1 and 2 only
  C 1 and 3 only
  D 2 and 3 only

14 Substantial fluctuations in the profits of a company are most likely to result in fluctuations in the payments received by the holders of

  A ordinary shares
  B preference shares
  C cumulative preference shares
  D debentures

15 A company may raise additional capital by means of a

  1 bonus issue
  2 scrip issue
  3 rights issue

  A 1 and 2 only
  B 2 and 3 only
  C 1 only
  D 3 only

16 Which of the following may raise money by the issue of shares to the general public?

  A Co-operative society
  B Partnership
  C Private company
  D Public limited company

17 To derive net domestic product from gross domestic product it is necessary to subtract

  A imports
  B indirect taxes
  C subsidies
  D depreciation

18 In order to convert gross domestic product at factor cost into gross national product at factor cost it is necessary to make an allowance for

1 net property income from abroad
2 taxes on expenditure and subsidies
3 depreciation

A 1 and 2 only
B 2 and 3 only
C 1 only
D 3 only

19 The major source of funds for companies' capital requirements is

A bank loans
B issues of shares
C issues of debentures
D undistributed income

20 The Phillips Curve purported to explain the relationship between

A the rate of change of prices and the rate of change of wages
B the rate of change of wages and unemployment
C the level of aggregate demand and employment
D the level of investment and the change in national income.

# 17. *Fiscal Policy*

## 17.1 Introduction

In the previous chapter we explained why governments may try to influence aggregate demand, the level of total expenditure. In this and the following chapter we discuss the various policies that they might adopt. We begin with fiscal policy which encompasses measures relating to taxation and government expenditure.

## 17.2 Fiscal Policy and Total Expenditure

In Figure 17.1 $E_F$ is the level of total expenditure required in order to bring national income to the full employment level, $Y_F$. If, when the Chancellor of the Exchequer came to prepare his annual budget, it appeared that, given

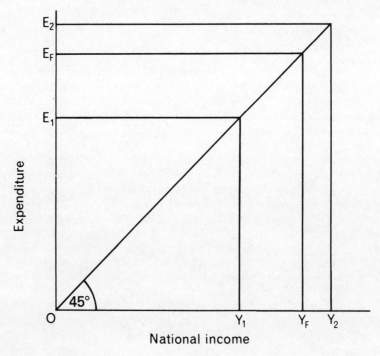

Fig. 17.1 Fiscal policy and total expenditure

existing government policies, total expenditure was likely to be $E_1$, he would be faced with the prospect of substantial unemployment. When expenditure is less than required to yield the full employment level of income, we say that a deflationary gap exists. In Figure 17.1, $E_1E_F$ represents the deflationary gap.

Faced with the prospect of unemployment, the Chancellor might adopt a policy designed to bring total expenditure nearer to $E_F$ in order to absorb unemployed resources. This increase in total expenditure might be achieved in one of two ways. First, the government could contribute to an increase in total expenditure by increasing its own expenditure. In addition this would, via the multiplier and accelerator mechanisms, lead to an increase in consumption and investment. Alternatively the government could reduce taxation. A reduction in company taxation usually encourages investment and subsequently, via the multiplier, consumption. A reduction in personal taxation usually stimulates consumption and, via the accelerator, investment.

If it appeared that, under existing policies, total expenditure would probably be $E_2$, the government would almost certainly wish to change these policies so as to reduce total expenditure. When expenditure is higher than necessary for full employment, an inflationary gap is said to exist. In Figure 17.1 $E_FE_2$ represents the inflationary gap. The required reduction in expenditure might be achieved either by a reduction in government expenditure or by an increase in taxation, or both.

## 17.21 *The Balance between Government Expenditure and Taxation*

Major changes in fiscal policy are normally announced in the budget statement made by the Chancellor in the Spring (March or April). This statement sets out the government's objectives for the coming year and indicates how it intends to achieve those objectives. In recent years the Chancellor has often had to resort to a mini-budget later in the year. This is, perhaps, an indication that governments are finding the control of the economy an increasingly difficult problem.

If the Chancellor intends that government expenditure should exceed revenue from taxation, he is said to plan for a *budget deficit*. This is most likely to happen when the government wishes to stimulate the economy, i.e. to increase total expenditure (but see section 17.6). A *budget surplus* occurs when revenue from taxation exceeds government expenditure. This normally indicates a desire by the government to dampen the rate of economic activity – to moderate the rise in total expenditure or even to cause it to fall.

If the Chancellor intends that government expenditure should exactly equal revenue from taxation, he is said to plan for a *balanced budget*. If the marginal propensity to consume of those people whose incomes are increased as a result of government expenditure equals the marginal propensity to consume of those people whose incomes are reduced by taxation, then a balanced budget will have. a neutral effect, leaving total expenditure unchanged.

In fact, this condition (of equal MPCs) is most unlikely to be met. Fiscal policy *usually* has a redistributive effect, transferring income from higher to lower income groups. Since the MPC of the latter group is likely to be above average (and that of the former group below average), the redistribution of income is likely to cause total expenditure to rise. This tendency will be strengthened if people meet their higher tax liability by reducing saving rather than consumption, as may well happen, at least in the short run. Consequently, in the short run a balanced budget is likely to lead to a (modest) increase in total expenditure.

Having analysed the likely overall impact of changes in fiscal policy, we now examine the composition of government receipts (of which the most important is taxation) on the one hand, and expenditure on the other.

## 17.3 Government Receipts and Expenditure

The relationship between general (central and local) government receipts and expenditure is shown in Table 17.1. It can be seen that there was a substantial budget surplus, receipts exceeding expenditure by almost £4 billion.

*Table 17.1 General Government Receipts and Expenditure 1988 (£ million)*

| Receipts | | Expenditure | |
|---|---|---|---|
| Taxes on income | 61,143 | Final consumption | 91,547 |
| Taxes on expenditure[1] | 75,131 | Fixed capital formation[2] | 5,491 |
| Taxes on capital | 4,818 | Subsidies | 5,862 |
| Social security contributions | 31,551 | Grants and transfers | 61,192 |
| Gross trading surplus, rent and royalties | 3,979 | Debt interest | 18,149 |
| Interest, dividends and miscellaneous | 6,690 | | |
| Imputed charge for consumption of capital | 2,452 | | |
| Total | 186,192 | | 182,241 |
| Surplus | 3,951 | | |

[1] Includes local authority rates
[2] Includes change in book value of stocks and work in progress
*Source*: Financial Statistics

As indicated above, a budget surplus often implies a desire by the government to dampen the rate of economic activity. However, the surpluses achieved in the late 1980s had a somewhat different origin.

### 17.31 *Public Sector Borrowing Requirement and Debt Repayment*

The public sector borrowing requirement is related to, but is not precisely the same as, the budget deficit. It is the net difference between the expenditure and income of the public sector as a whole. In the 1970s the budget was invariably in deficit, and these deficits were associated with a series of public sector borrowing requirements, as shown in Figure 17.2. The long-term aim of the Conservative government elected in 1979, was to have a balanced budget. But in the shorter term a series of budget surpluses, such as that shown in Table 17.1, enabled the repayment of money borrowed previously, and hence a reduction of the national debt. The swing from public sector borrowing requirement to public sector debt repayment is shown in Figure 17.2.

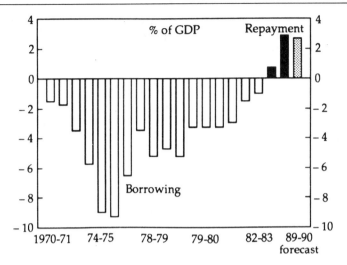

Fig. 17.2 Public sector borrowing requirement and debt repayment
*Source*: The Treasury, *The Budget in Brief*, 14 March 1989

## 17.4 Government Expenditure

Table 17.1 identifies five major forms of expenditure: consumption, capital formation, subsidies, grants and other transfers, and debt interest.

### 17.41 *Final Consumption*

Half of total expenditure was accounted for by final consumption, i.e. current expenditure on goods and services. This expenditure enters directly into the circular flow of income and so contributes directly to the national income. Government final consumption, together with government spending on capital formation, is designated as G in the 45° diagrams Figures 15.8 and 15.9.

While it is difficult to effect significant short-term changes in the pattern of current expenditure, more substantial shifts can occur over longer periods of time. Since the early 1960s the share of current expenditure going to military defence has fallen substantially, largely due to the reduction in the U.K.'s overseas military commitments. During the same period eduction's share has risen, partly because of an increase in the number of people in the relevant age group and partly because of a belief that a well-educated workforce is more efficient and productive. In the 1990s education's share will probably fall again as the number of young people declines.

### 17.42 *Fixed Capital Formation*

Fixed capital formation is the major element of investment spending. The most important areas of spending are housing, roads and public lighting, education, health and environmental services.

Capital expenditure is often concerned with projects that take several years to complete, so that it is especially difficult to effect substantial short-term changes in its volume or pattern. But as with consumption spending, more substantial changes can occur over longer periods. Since the mid 1970s capital spending has fallen from 12 to less than 4 per cent of total government expenditure. This was due partly to lower spending on the building of houses and schools, and partly to increased spending on the remaining categories, considered below.

### 17.43 *Subsidies, Grants and Other Transfers*

Subsidies and grants now account for over one third of total government expenditure. Since these payments are not made in return for a productive activity, but merely transfer income from some individuals (via the payment of taxes, etc.) to other individuals, they are known as transfer payments. (Some writers prefer not to classify subsidies as transfer payments, but confine the term to grants.)

Transfer payments do not directly enter into the circular flow of income and are not included within government expenditure (G) in 45° diagrams. They do, however, indirectly contribute to national income in that the spending power of the recipients – individuals or companies – is increased. This increased spending power enters the circular flow in the form of increased consumption (C) or investment (I). (There is, of course, a corresponding withdrawal from the circular flow in the form of taxation (T)).

Social security benefits – retirement pensions, unemployment benefits, supplementary benefits, etc. – account for over two-thirds of total grants, suggesting that this category of expenditure is an important means of redistributing income. Income may also be redistributed via subsidies. However these are much smaller in total than grants. Moreover, producers receive a much higher proportion of expenditure on subsidies than on grants, suggesting that an increase in economic efficiency may be a relatively more important objective of subsidies than of grants.

### 17.44 *Debt Interest*

Debt interest, also a transfer payment, accounted for 10 per cent of government expenditure. Increased government borrowing in the 1970s and early 1980s, together with higher rates of interest, resulted in an increase in the proportion of expenditure accounted for by interest payments and this led to concern about the 'growing burden of the national debt'.

In fact the ratio of the national debt to national income is not high by historical standards. Moreover, although interest payments do in one sense represent a burden, they simply cause a redistribution of income within the community if the debt is held by members of the community. On the other hand insofar as part of the debt is in the hands of foreign holders, interest payments constitute an outflow on the balance of payments account (see Chapter 19).

## 17.5 Government Receipts

Three-quarters of total receipts comprised revenue from taxes of various forms. A further 17 per cent comprised social security contributions, sometimes treated as a form of taxation.

### 17.51 *The Objectives of Taxation*

### 17.511 *To raise revenue*

Almost one third of total revenue from taxation comes from income tax, and there is no doubt that this tax will continue to be a major source of government revenue. However, it has been suggested that high rates of income tax may lead to a fall in tax revenue. The most notable proponent of this view is Arthur Laffer, an American economist. Laffer has argued that the higher the proportion of income that is paid in tax, the less effort will be put into income-generation activities, causing total tax revenue to fall (Figure 17.3).

The disincentive effect of high tax rates has several aspects. The most obvious is that where individuals have discretion in the length of their working week, they may choose to work shorter hours e.g. by refusing to work overtime. People on piece work, whose earnings depend on the amount produced, may work less hard.

Fig. 17.3 A Laffer curve

Much of the effort of senior managers is devoted to activities designed to increase employment in their companies. If the managers work less hard because of high tax rates this may result in a fall in income, not only of these managers but also of those people whose employment opportunities are reduced. This argument was one of the justifications advanced for the reductions in the highest rates of tax made in the U.K. in the 1980s. (A similar argument could be applied to any tax on the earnings of companies, such as corporation tax.)

A study by Professor Lindsey showed that in the U.S.A. tax cuts as a whole had led to a fall in tax revenue. However, a cut in the top rate of tax from 70 to 50 per cent in 1982 had led to a substantial increase in revenue from the top tax brackets. In 1984 high-income earners paid $42 billion, whereas it is estimated that under the higher rates about $34 billion would have been paid. About one-third of the increase was estimated to have resulted from additional work, the so-called supply-side response, the rest from reduced tax avoidance.

In the U.K. the percentage of tax revenue contributed by the top 1 per cent of taxpayers increased slightly from 11 per cent in 1978/79 to 12 per cent in 1985/86 despite a cut in the maximum tax rate from 83 to 60 per cent. The top rate has since been reduced to 40 per cent and it will be interesting to see what impact this will have on revenue.

At the other end of the income tax scale it has been argued that levying tax on low income earners may dissuade them from seeking employment. This is especially likely to happen when an increase in income from employment means that the worker loses his or her eligibility to benefits such as free school meals, rent rebates, etc. It can be shown that in some instances entering employment would actually leave a person or family worse off financially, an extreme example of the operation of the *poverty trap*.

In order to reduce the disincentive effect of taxation on employment and effort, three steps have been taken. First, the standard rate of tax has been reduced to 25 per cent. Second, the income at which tax becomes payable has been raised, at least in line with inflation. Third, income tax is now levied on unemployment benefit, provided, of course, that the recipient's total income is above the minimum threshold level.

It is clear, then, that taxing income from employment could operate to reduce effort. It is also clear that the net effect of higher rates of tax could be to reduce total tax revenue, partly because of a fall in the incomes on which tax is levied, and partly because people spend less and therefore pay less to the government in the form of expenditure taxes. Tax revenue could also fall because of increased tax evasion. These disincentive effects of direct taxation have influenced government policy, especially in recent years. However, although there is agreement about how these effects *could* operate, there is no agreement about how important they have been in practice.

In the 1980s the rates of corporation tax were reduced, as also were various allowances against tax. As the economy expanded and company profitability increased, the yield of corporation tax increased, and it currently accounts for around a tenth of total tax revenue.

To maximize revenue from indirect (expenditure) taxes, the highest tax rates should be imposed on products whose price elasticity of demand is low (although other considerations may militate against this policy as shown below).

This explains the high rates of duty on hydrocarbon oils (including petrol), tobacco and alcoholic drinks, which together yield around 10 per cent of total revenue. The major revenue earner within this category is, however, value added tax, accounting for 14 per cent of the total.

### 17.512 *To Influence the Level of Expenditure*

As pointed out above, the level of expenditure is influenced by the balance between taxation and expenditure. Since it is often difficult to alter expenditure in the short-run, the burden of adjustment often falls on taxation. It is especially useful for the government if it can utilize mechanisms that automatically increase taxation as national income increases. One such *automatic stabilizer* is a progressive system of personal taxation – a system under which the *proportion* of income paid in tax increases as income increases. (A regressive system is one under which the proportion of income paid in tax falls as income increases.)

### 17.513 *To Influence the Pattern of Expenditure*

Expenditure taxes have frequently been used as a means of influencing the pattern of consumption. A common form of discrimination is the imposition of higher tax rates on luxury products than on necessities, a policy that has been justified as being 'fair' or 'equitable'. Other justifications for higher rates of tax on particular products have included saving foreign exchange by discouraging the consumption of imports, encouraging economy in use (e.g. higher tax on oil to encourage energy saving), and discouraging the consumption of products thought to have adverse effects either on consumers (e.g. tobacco), or on other members of the community (e.g. pollution caused by vehicles.) These aims are reflected in the fact that foodstuffs and other basic necessities do not attract VAT (technically, they are zero-rated), and in the high taxes and excise duties levied on vehicles, petrol, tobacco and alcoholic drinks. (In the 1989 Budget the tax on unleaded petrol was reduced as an anti-pollution measure.)

### 17.514 *To Redistribute Income*

The acceptance of the view that fiscal policy should have a role in redistributing income by taking it from the richer and giving it to the poorer members of the community has two major implications for taxation policy. First, direct (and especially income) taxes will constitute an important part of the general system of taxation, since it is easy to ensure that they are progressive in nature.

Second, the structure of indirect taxation will be such that heavier taxes are imposed on products of the greatest *relative* importance in the budget of richer people, and lighter or zero taxes, or even negative taxes (subsidies), will be imposed on products that are of greatest relative importance in the budget of poorer people.

The capital gains tax, levied on profits made from the buying and selling of securities and other assets, could in principle be seen as a device for redistributing income. But the relatively low tax rates and the exemptions allowed reduce the yield to a very low level.

The main objective of inheritance tax is to redistribute wealth and income by taxing money left by people when they die and gifts made up to seven years before death. (The term 'inheritance tax' is somewhat misleading since it suggests that the tax is levied on the amount inherited by one person, whereas in fact it is levied on the total amount given by the donor.) Although the tax is levied at 40 per cent, it is paid only above an (indexable) threshold, and it is unlikely that the tax will have a marked effect on the distribution of wealth.

## 17.6 The Expenditure and Financing of Local Authorities

The expenditure and financing of local authorities has been a constant source of friction between these authorities and central government. Friction often occurs because the spending plans of the local authorities conflict with the central government's overall plans. For example, the government may believe that the economy is in danger of overheating and that a reduction in expenditure is required, while local authorities, wishing to meet the needs of their local communities, would prefer to increase their spending. The friction is made worse by the fact that central government has provided the bulk of the local authorities' income (see below).

Despite differing forms of control imposed by different governments, local authority expenditure increased at a much faster rate than the economy as a whole for much of the post-war period. Although this no doubt enabled improvements to be made in some of the services provided by the local authorities, the increased expenditure has also been seen by some observers as a sign of falling efficiency.

### 17.61 *The Financing of Local Authorities*

Between 1963 and 1986 rates revenue doubled in real terms. But expenditure rose even more, and the local authorities became increasingly reliant on central government finance. By 1980 central government grants accounted for around two-thirds of the local authorities' current expenditure. During the 1980s, with a change of government, this proportion fell to under a half, but government grants remained the major source of income, well ahead of rates.

### 17.62 *The Pattern of Local Authority Spending*

Almost three-quarters of expenditure comprises spending on goods and services, by far the most important heading being education, followed by public order and safety, and housing and community amenity. Although some discretion is exercised at the local level, the broad parameters of spending are established centrally. For example, the basic structure of the education service is determined by the Department of Education and Science, and the system for administering law and order by the Home Office.

The heavy involvement of central government, both in the provision of finance and in influencing the pattern of expenditure, has led to the suggestion that it should take full responsibility for some of the services currently provided by local authorities, e.g. education. Such a change would also make it easier for central government to control spending on those services and therefore public spending as a whole. However, an alternative view has also been expressed, namely that a strong system of local government is essential for democracy and that ways should be found of increasing the proportion of expenditure financed locally.

### 17.63 *Alternative Forms of Finance*

The system of rates in force in the 1980s had several deficiencies. The amount paid by a household did not reflect its use of local services. It was regressive, i.e. in general people on low incomes paid a higher proportion of their income in rates than higher-income earners. Finally, it failed the test of democratic accountability. Rates were paid by householders, not by all voters. Moreover, half of the rates income came from industry, which had no voting rights.

### 17.64 *The Community Charge*

Various alternative systems were discussed, e.g. a local income tax, a sales tax, but eventually the government introduced, with effect from 1990 in most of England and Wales (1989 in Scotland), the Community Charge (commonly known as the poll tax). It was estimated that the tax would be paid by 33 million people in England and Wales, of whom 20 to 25 per cent would obtain a full or partial rebate, mainly on the ground of low income. (This is intended to moderate the regressive effect of a flat-rate tax.)

The Community Charge is expected to account for about one-fifth of a local authority's income. Most of the remainder would be provided centrally, partly as a central government grant and partly as a business rate collected nationally and redistributed in accordance with each authority's population.

## 17.7 The Public Sector Borrowing Requirement

In section 17.21 we showed that according to the Keynesian analysis a budget deficit would lead to an increase in aggregate expenditure. However, critics of this analysis have argued that a budget deficit can lead to other changes which cancel out the expansionary effects. The argument usually refers to the public sector borrowing requirement rather than the budget deficit, but in fact there is a close connection between the two.

### 17.71 *The Financing of the Public Sector Borrowing Requirement*

There are three major sources of financing the P.S.B.R.: the non-bank private sector (companies and households), the monetary sector (banks) and the overseas sector. Finance is provided in exchange for the issue of a variety of securities, including gilts, local authority bonds, Treasury bills and National Saving Certificates.

### 17.72 *The Impact of Public Sector Borrowing*

Supply-demand analysis tells us that an increase in the supply of securities causes a fall in their price. Putting the matter the other way round, an increase in the demand for money causes its price, i.e. the rate of interest, to rise. This rise in interest rates makes borrowing by industrial and commercial companies more expensive and causes them to reduce their investment expenditure. Also, perhaps less importantly, there may be a reduction in consumption.

This process, whereby higher government spending leads to a reduction in other forms of spending is known as 'crowding out'. In the extreme case, where the net effect is to leave aggregate expenditure unchanged, crowding out is said to be complete or absolute.

### 17.73 *The Public Sector Borrowing Requirement and the Money Supply*

If the P.S.B.R. is financed, entirely or partly, by the banking sector, this will cause an increase in the money supply. As we show in the next chapter, an increase in the money supply is likely to lead to an increase in prices. It was for this reason that in the 1980s the government took steps to reduce the size of the P.S.B.R. Indeed by the end of the decade, revenue exceeded government expenditure, giving rise to a negative P.S.B.R. (public sector debt repayment).

### 17.8 Fiscal Policy and Unemployment

As noted at the beginning of the chapter, Keynesian analysis suggests that by stimulating aggregate demand fiscal policy can reduce unemployment. However, as pointed out above, if crowding out occurs, aggregate demand and hence unemployment may remain unchanged. Moreover, as we showed in Chapter 16, some economists claim that even if aggregate demand does increase, leading to an increase in employment, this will be followed by an increase in prices which will cause employment to fall (and unemployment to rise) to its previous level.

Although this alternative view is not held by all economists, there is general agreement that unemployment is less responsive to changes in fiscal policy than once appeared to be the case. Consequently it seems unlikely that future governments will rely as heavily on fiscal policy as a means of reducing unemployment as some governments have in the past.

### 17.9 Summary and Conclusions

Keynesian analysis suggests that the balance between government expenditure and revenue from taxation influences aggregate demand. As well as paying careful attention to this balance, governments use fiscal policy to achieve a range of other objectives. These objectives were discussed with reference to the pattern of both expenditure and taxation.

Critics of the Keynesian analysis have argued that a budget deficit, and hence a positive public sector borrowing requirement, can affect both the level of interest rates and the money supply. The impact of changes in the money supply are discussed in the following chapter.

**Further Reading**

Artis, M. J. Ed., *The U.K. Economy* (London: Weidenfeld and Nicolson, 11th Edn, 1986), Ch. 2.
Begg, D., Fischer, S. and Dornbusch, R., *Economics* (London: McGraw-Hill, 2nd Edn, 1987), Chs 21 and 24.
Lipsey, R. G. and Harbury, C., *First Principles of Economics* (London: Weidenfeld and Nicolson, 1988), Ch. 31.
Livesey, F., *A Textbook of Economics* (London: Longman, 3rd Edn, 1989), Ch. 20.
Maunder, P., Myers, D., Wall, N. and Miller, R. L. *Economics Explained* (London: Collins, 1987), Ch. 32.

**Revision Exercises**

1 What do you understand by the term 'deflationary gap'? Outline the possible implications of a deflationary gap for government economic policy.
2 Can fiscal policy solve the unemployment problem?
3 In what circumstances is the government most likely to plan for a budget deficit?
4 Compare and contrast the likely impact of different forms of government expenditure.
5 What factors may affect the pattern of government expenditure?
6 Discuss the effect of transfer payments on the circular flow of income.
7 Discuss the relative advantages and disadvantages of direct and indirect taxation.
8 What are the major objectives of taxation? In what ways might these objectives conflict with other objectives of government policy?
9 Explain what you understand by the term crowding out and explain its significance.
10 Why is so much attention given to the size of the public sector borrowing requirement?

# 18. *Monetary Policy*

## 18.1 Introduction

Monetary policy encompasses any measure designed to affect the level of economic activity by influencing the supply or the cost of money. Much of this chapter is devoted to a discussion of the factors influencing the demand for, and supply of, money. But as a preliminary to this discussion we must define what we mean by money.

## 18.2 Money: A Simple Definition

Anything can be classified as money which (a) is generally acceptable in exchange for goods or in settlement of debts, and (b) acts as a store of value. History reveals many examples of commodities once accepted as money but subsequently discarded – shells in primitive societies, 'old' marks in Germany in the 1920s, cigarettes in Germany after 1945, etc. Conversely, we have seen in recent years the emergence of new forms of money, both at the domestic and the international level. Consequently, although our definition may be timeless, its applicability will change over time. (In the U.K. at the present time several 'monetary and liquidity aggregates' can be identified, as shown in Figure 18.1.)

## 18.3 The Demand For Money

Following Keynes, we can specify three motives for liquidity preference, i.e. three reasons why individuals or firms may wish to hold money rather than use it to acquire assets such as shares, debentures, goods, property, etc., which would yield a positive return. These reasons are the transactions, precautionary and speculative (or asset) motives.

| | |
|---|---|
| MO: | Narrow money. Notes and coin in circulation plus bankers' balances at the Bank of England. |
| nibMl: | Notes and coin plus residents' sterling non-interest bearing sight deposits. |
| M2: | Notes and coin plus residents' sterling retail deposits with banks and building societies. |
| M4: | Notes and coin plus residents' sterling deposits with banks and building societies. |
| M4c: | Like M4 but also includes foreign currency deposits. |

*Source: Economic Progress Report*, August 1989
Fig. 18.1 The main monetary aggregates

### 18.31 *The Transactions Demand*

Consider an individual who receives a salary of, say, £800 per month, and who knows that during that month he is likely to make regular payments, e.g. for food, of £400, and irregular payments, e.g. clothes, car tax, gas bill, etc., of a further £400. He will probably keep the whole of the £800 as money, perhaps initially by depositing his salary cheque in his current bank account and drawing out a few pounds.

A second example of the transactions demand is when a firm keeps some of the money received from the sale of goods or services in order to make future payments for wages, raw materials, rates, etc. The total value of transactions undertaken by all individuals and firms will vary in accordance with the national level of output and income, and we can in fact identify national income as the main determinant of the transactions demand.

Two other determinants can be identified. The first is the nature of any penalty resulting from a failure to meet one's financial obligations. A failure to pay the labour force at the end of the week is likely to lead to an immediate cessation of work, whereas it may be possible to delay the payment of a bill for materials for several weeks. Second, the transactions demand is likely to be influenced by the efficiency of the financial system. Especially important is the extent to which opportunities are available for individuals and, probably more importantly, firms to lend money for very short periods of time. The greater these opportunities, the lower the transactions demand is likely to be.

### 18.32 *The Precautionary Demand*

The precautionary demand arises because future financial obligations cannot always be foreseen with a high degree of certainty. The distinction between precautionary and transactions demands can be illustrated by a very simple example. A family setting off for a day's car ride would take a given amount of money, in the form of cash or cheques, to pay for meals and petrol (transactions demand). They would also, if they were sensible, take an additional amount to cover the possibility of a breakdown or accident requiring expenditure on repairs, train fares, etc. (precautionary demand). The availability of short-term lending opportunities might have a relatively greater influence on the precautionary than the transactions demand. Otherwise the influencing factors are very similar.

### 18.33 *The Speculative or Asset Demand*

Keynes suggested that each wealth-holder would have a view about what the price of bonds (and hence the rate of interest) would be in the future. If he felt that bonds would fall in price (the rate of interest would rise), he would sell bonds, i.e. his speculative demand for money would increase. Conversely, if he felt that bond prices were likely to rise, he would buy bonds, i.e. his speculative demand for money would fall.

It is more usual today to use the term asset demand to describe the third motive for holding money. Government stock (bonds) and money are not the only forms of wealth. Wealth may also be held in the form of debentures and shares issued by companies, property, etc. These different forms of assets offer different forms of return – interest, dividends, capital gains etc. However, as before, the choice is between holding one or more assets which yield a positive return, and holding money which does not (the asset demand).

Since the rates of interest on all loans – government stock, debentures etc. – tend to move together, Keynes's analysis can be extended to these other forms of loan. It cannot, however, be extended so easily to other assets which yield different forms of return, e.g. the yields on shares and debentures sometimes move in opposite directions.

A further limitation of Keynes's analysis arises from the assumption that holdings of money yield no return. This assumption has become increasingly dubious in the light of recent changes in the financial system, e.g. the introduction by banks of interest-bearing current accounts.

Finally, the links between the major international financial institutions are much closer today than they were in Keynes's day. These institutions are now able to quickly switch funds from one country to another. So, for example, when deciding whether to buy U.K. government stock, investors will take into account the returns on the stock issued by the governments of the U.S.A., Germany, Japan etc., together with the yield on other assets, such as shares, issued in all these other countries.

### 18.34 *The Combined Demand for Money*

In Figure 18.2 the demand for money (measured along the horizontal axis) is related to the rate of interest (measured along the vertical axis), for a given level of national income. Curve L represents the combined demand for money, which can be seen to be higher as the rate of interest drops (i.e. the higher the current price of bonds). D represents the transactions and precautionary demands, which we have suggested are only slightly interest-elastic. The horizontal distance between the lines D and L represents the speculative or asset demand, which is far more responsive to current rates of interest.

The equilibrium rate of interest is that at which the demand for and supply of money are equal. If we assume that the supply is S, then the equilibrium rate will be R. If, for example, the transactions or precautionary demand fell, owing perhaps to an increase in the opportunities for short-term lending, curve D, and therefore curve L, would shift to the left, and the equilibrium rate would fall.

Figure 18.2 takes the level of national income as given. If national income increases, the demand for money will increase, and L will shift to the right, causing an increase in the rate of interest. Conversely, a fall in national income will cause L to shift to the left.

### 18.4 The Supply of Money

Figure 18.3 demonstrates that, with a given demand for money (L), the rate of

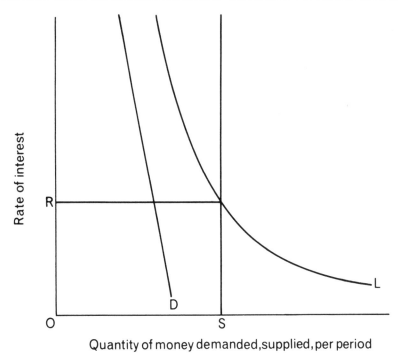

Fig. 18.2 Demand for, and supply of, money

interest ($R_1$ and $R_2$) changes as the money supply ($S_1$ and $S_2$) changes. We now discuss the factors that influence the supply or stock of money. We pay particular attention to the British economy, but we begin with a more general discussion of the role of banking systems.

## 18.5 The Role of Banking Systems

A short historical account of the origins of banking systems provides a useful insight into their current role. The initial role of banks (which were often goldsmiths) was to safeguard coin and other valuables deposited by their customers, a role for which they charged a fee. When these deposits were made, the bank issued a receipt, promising to repay the deposit upon demand. In time these receipts began to be accepted in the settlement of debts, circulating and functioning as money.

### 18.51 *The Creation of Credit*

Up to this point one form of money (bank notes) had simply been substituted for a less convenient form (coin and other valuables). The total stock of money had not changed. However, the next stage brought about a radical change in the banks' role, whereby their activities resulted in an increase in the stock of

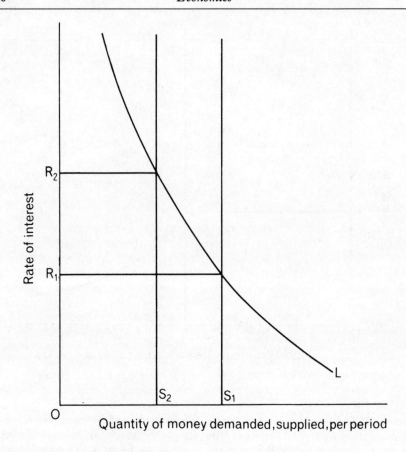

Fig. 18.3 Supply of money and rate of interest

money. The more enterprising banks realized that in any given period only a proportion of the notes they had issued were presented for repayment, and that they could therefore issue a greater volume of notes than was covered by the coin deposited in their vaults. In this way the banks actually created credit.

If experience suggested that a cash:assets ratio of less than 1:1 was required, then the bank would be able to make loans, i.e. to create credit. For example, a 1:10 cash:assets ratio would enable credit to be created up to nine times the initial level of deposits, as shown in Table 18.1.

This table indicates that the notes issued by the bank when making loans are subsequently deposited with the bank. This will usually happen after the notes have changed hands in the settlement of debts. When this process has been completed, at the end of Stage 2, the liabilities of the bank comprise the £1,000 liable to be paid to the initial depositors and £9,000 liable to be paid to the depositors of the additional notes subsequently issued.

*Table 18.1 Credit Creation in a Single bank-System*

| Liabilities (£) | | Assets (£) | | Cash/assets ratio |
|---|---|---|---|---|
| | | *Stage 1* | | |
| Initial deposits | 1,000 | Coin | 1,000 | 100 per cent |
| | | *Stage 2* | | |
| Initial deposits | 1,000 | Coin | 1,000 | 10 per cent |
| Created deposits | 9,000 | Loans | 9,000 | |
| | 10,000 | | 10,000 | |

### 18.511 *Multi-Bank systems*

In a multi-bank system, when one bank creates credit by making loans (by issuing 'notes'), a higher proportion of these notes is likely to be presented for repayment. Let us imagine, for the sake of simplicity, that our system comprises two banks, A and B, and that A makes loans of nine times its initial deposits, as did the single bank in our previous example. As before, the loans made by the bank will be used for repaying debts. Some of these transactions will be between people who bank at A. In this respect the situation will remain as in the previous situation, since the people who accept the notes will, if they wish to deposit them, do so with bank A. However, other transactions will lead to the transfer of notes to customers of bank B, who may present the notes at bank A, to be exchanged for coin. Alternatively they may deposit their notes with B, which will then present them to A, to be exchanged for coin. Whichever happens, the demand for coin from A will be much greater than under the single-bank system.

Consequently, in a multi-bank system, if only one bank creates credit, it will have to keep a higher cash ratio, i.e. it can create less credit than in the single-bank system. But in practice we would expect all the banks in the system to create credit, and in these circumstances the degree of credit creation will be virtually (but not entirely) the same as in the single-bank system.

This is illustrated in Table 18.2. At the first stage each bank receives deposits of coin to the value of £500. Subsequently, working to a 10 per cent cash:assets ratio, each bank makes loans to the value of £4,500. Let us assume that in each case half the loans are used to settle debts with depositors at the other bank – customers of bank A receive notes to the value of £2,250 issued by bank B, while customers of bank B receive notes to the value of £2,250 issued by bank A. In a modern banking system these 'notes' will in fact largely comprise cheques, and people receiving cheques deposit them in their own bank accounts. Consequently, we reach a situation where bank A and bank B each hold notes, to the value of £2,250, issued by the other bank. These notes will simply be exchanged on a one-for-one basis, and neither bank has to dip into its precious reserves of coin. When this process is completed, the situation will be that at stage 2. The exchange or clearing of cheques is the function of the modern 'clearing-house'.

Of course, there is a possibility that things may not work out as smoothly as this. If bank A's customers have a higher level of indebtedness to customers of bank B than vice versa, B will end up with more notes issued by A than the

*Table 18.2 Credit Creation in a Multi-bank System*

| | Bank A | | | | Bank B | | | |
|---|---|---|---|---|---|---|---|---|
| Liabilities (£) | | Assets (£) | | Liabilities (£) | | Assets (£) | | Cash/assets ratio |
| | | | *Stage 1* | | | | | |
| Initial deposits | 500 | Coin | 500 | Initial deposits | 500 | Coin | 500 | 100 per cent |
| | | | *Stage 2* | | | | | |
| Initial deposits | 500 | Coin | 500 | Initial deposits | 500 | Coin | 500 | 10 per cent |
| Created deposits | 4,500 | Loans | 4,500 | Created deposits | 4,500 | Loans | 4,500 | |
| | 5,000 | | 5,000 | | 5,000 | | 5,000 | |

reverse. When the banks have exchanged what notes they can, B will present the surplus to A to be exchanged for coin. This possibility of imbalance in any one period will cause the banks to maintain a slightly higher cash ratio than would be maintained in a single-bank system.

### 18.6 The British Banking System

#### 18.61 *The Assets of the Banking Sector*

Table 18.3 gives a breakdown of the sterling assets of the U.K. offices of those banks which report monthly, i.e. banks with a balance sheet of £100 million or more, or eligible liabilities of £10 million or more. These include the large London clearing banks, National Westminster, Barclays, Midland, Lloyds.

*Table 18.3 The Sterling Assets of Banks in the U.K., March 1989*

| | £ million | per cent |
|---|---|---|
| Notes and coin | 2,782 | 0·6 |
| Special and cash ratio deposits with Bank of England | 1,124 | 0·3 |
| Other balances with Bank of England | 284 | 0·1 |
| Market loans | 118,416 | 26·6 |
| (of which, loans to discount houses) | (10,370) | (2·3) |
| Bills | 9,824 | 2·2 |
| Advances | 264,835 | 59·5 |
| Investments | 20,431 | 4·6 |
| Miscellaneous assets | 27,396 | 6·2 |
| Total | 445,092 | 100 |

*Source*: Financial Statistics

The assets structure represents a compromise between conflicting objectives, since liquidity and profitability are normally inversely related. The best example of this principle is the cash (notes and coin) which is held by the banks. If the banks are to retain public confidence, it is essential that they should be able to meet demands for cash immediately (their liquidity should be adequate). However, the cash held for this purpose does not, of course, make a direct contribution to the banks' profits. A similar point applies to the 'other' balances held at the Bank of England, which are used mainly for settling inter-bank indebtedness. Since these settlements are made daily, following the clearing of cheques, each bank must always maintain a positive balance at the Bank of England. Again, these highly liquid assets do not yield any return.

The banks know from experience what proportion of their deposits it is prudent to cover by cash. If the banks feel that their holdings of cash are in danger of falling below this level, they will supplement these holdings by realizing some of their other highly liquid assets. The first line of defence is provided by the money the banks have lent 'at call' (part of the 'market loans' item). This money is lent to various financial institutions, the most important of which are the discount houses.

At the other extreme are those assets that are illiquid but more profitable. 'Advances' account for almost 60 per cent of total sterling assets. Advances are of two main types – loans and overdrafts. With a loan, the customer's account is credited with the amount of the loan. Interest is, of course, charged on the full amount of the loan. With an overdraft, the bank allows the customer to overdraw or to go into debt, on this current account, up to a pre-determined limit. Interest is charged only on the amount overdrawn.

The rate of interest on advances is fixed in relation to the bank's *base rate*. The margin charged above base rate varies according to the nature and status of the customer, but is usually between 1 and 5 per cent. Although the margin over base rate is fixed for the life of the loan, the bank is free to change the base rate. Such changes are usually, but not always, accompanied by a change in the rate of interest paid by the bank on deposit accounts.

## 18.7 The Objectives of Monetary Policy

When we consider monetary policy in detail we will see that it may influence the *pattern* of economic activity, e.g. by making it easier to borrow money for particular purposes. However the main objective is to influence the *level* of economic activity.

If the government wishes to stimulate economic activity it will make it easier to obtain money (especially by borrowing) and reduce its cost. Conversely in order to restrict economic activity, or to reduce its rate of growth, the government will make it more difficult to obtain money, and increase its cost.

### 18.71 *The Quantity Theory of Money*

The quantity theory, as originally formulated by Irving Fisher, was

$$M.V = P.T$$

where M = the quantity of money
V = the velocity of circulation of money
P = the price level
T = the volume of transactions

The classical view was that V was fixed. Consequently a change in M was reflected in a change in P or T. Since T was also assumed to be fixed in the short run, there was a direct relationship between the quantity of money (M) and the price level (P).

Modern 'quantity theorists', such as Milton Friedman, do not believe that velocity is rigid and unchanging. However they do regard it as being relatively stable in the longer term. Moreover although they accept that the volume of transactions may change, they point out that it is extremely difficult to increase the volume of transactions when there is little excess or spare capacity in the economy. Consequently they argue that if the money supply increases faster than the rate at which productivity is increasing in the economy, the result will inevitably be an increase in the price level. Indeed it is claimed that any increase in output and employment that may initially occur following an increase in the money supply will subsequently be reversed, and that the only permanent effect will be higher prices.

The implication of this analysis is that the government's best hope of increasing the level of employment lies in supply side policies. The role of monetary policy is to ensure that the money supply and aggregate expenditure do not grow at a rate that causes prices to rise. This objective can be illustrated by reference to Figure 18.3. The government can attempt to restrict the growth of aggregate expenditure in two ways.

First, it can cause the money supply to fall from $S_1$ to $S_2$. In terms of our earlier analysis (see Table 18.2) the government would restrict the volume of loans that the banks could make on the basis of a given volume of initial assets. With a given demand for money, L, its price (the rate of interest) would rise from $R_1$ to $R_2$.

Alternatively (or additionally) the government could cause the interest rate to rise from $R_1$ to $R_2$. At this higher price less money would be demanded, and this in turn would cause the money supply to fall from $S_1$ to $S_2$. In Table 18.2 the higher rate of interest would cause a fall in the demand for loans and hence in the amount of created deposits.

In some instances the government may seek to advance on both fronts, i.e. to simultaneously influence both the money supply and the rate of interest.

Having explained the fundamentals of monetary policy we now examine various measures in greater detail. We continue to assume that policy is restrictive; in some periods, e.g. when there is heavy unemployment, it may be expansionary, the government's aim being a faster rate of growth in the money supply and a fall in interest rates.

## 18.8 Monetary Policy and the Money Supply

Governments, together with the Bank of England, have attempted to control the money supply in various ways.

### 18.81 *Direct Controls*

On occasion the Bank of England has put limits on the volume of bank lending.

The disadvantages of direct controls is that they inhibit competition and lead to disintermediation.

### 18.82 *Regulations Relating to Balance Sheet Ratios*

Regulations have been introduced requiring the banks to maintain a given ratio of specified assets, e.g. balances at the Bank of England, to total assets or deposits. (These regulations have sometimes been bolstered by the use of Special Deposits.) In principle the existence of these regulations enables the authorities to curb lending. By engaging in open-market operations (selling securities to the public, who pay by drawing on their bank deposits) they can reduce the bank's liquid assets, (e.g. their balances at the Bank of England). In order to restore the liquidity ratio to the specified level, the banks have to engineer a multiple contraction of deposits. (This is the converse of the process of credit creation described above.)

### 18.83 *Measures to Limit the Growth of Deposits*

The supplementary special deposits scheme or 'corset' penalized any bank whose deposits grew at a faster rate than the target specified by the authorities.

### 18.84 *Measures to Influence Interest Rates*

All financial markets are interlinked. Consequently the authorities have sought to influence interest rates in general by controlling key rates such as Bank Rate in the past and, more recently, Minimum Lending Rate. The use of MLR is currently suspended. However a similar mechanism now operates, as described in the following section.

### 18.85 *The Current Situation*

The authorities influence the money supply and the rate of interest mainly via the operation of the money market. The money market comprises the institutions that deal in short term securities and loans – discount houses, money brokers, gilt-edged dealers and banks. Since August 1981, in order to ensure the efficient operation of the market, all eligible banks have been required to maintain an average of 6 per cent (and never less than 4 per cent) of eligible liabilities as secured money with the discount houses and/or secured call money with money brokers and gilt-edged dealers. Moreover all banks with eligible liabilities of £10 million or more are required to hold at least ½ per cent of eligible liabilities as non-operational, non-interest bearing deposits with the Bank of England (cash ratio deposits, Table 18.3). In addition Special Deposits can be called for when deemed appropriate by the authorities.

As noted above, the authorities can in principle make use of such required balance-sheet ratios to limit bank lending, and hence the money supply. In practice, however, they have operated mainly to influence interest rates, and in particular the rate on very short term (up to 7 days) money. If the money supply is rising faster than desired, the Bank of England raises the rate of interest at which it is willing to supply money – either by buying bills or by very short-term lending – to the discount houses. This change affects other short-term, and eventually long-term, interest rates. The higher interest rates are intended to dampen the demand for money and hence lead to a reduction in the rate of growth of the money supply.

The operation of the system is illustrated in Figure 18.4. The rate of interest is that at which the Bank of England discounts eligible bills (bills accepted by any of more than 100 banks deemed eligible by the Bank). In period 1 the Bank buys bills at prices equivalent to rates of interest between $R_1$ and $R_2$. In period 2 the Bank decides that higher interest rates would be appropriate, in order to dampen spending and/or counteract a fall in the sterling exchange rate. Consequently it reduces its demand for bills at those prices, causes prices to fall and interest rates to rise to within the band $R_3$ to $R_4$. Alternatively if the Bank provides funds by direct lending, it raises its lending rate.

## 18.9 An Assessment of Monetary Policy

Much greater emphasis was given to monetary policy in the 1980s than in the preceding decades, and this provided an opportunity to assess the effectiveness of the policy.

There is no doubt that the 1980s saw a reversal of the undesirable economic trends that marked the 1970s. By comparison with the previous decade, the 1980s saw improvements in the rate of growth of output, productivity, the rate of inflation and the balance of payments. Only in terms of unemployment did the situation worsen. Overall, therefore, economic performance improved markedly in the 1980s.

However, one cannot say that this was entirely, or even mainly, due to monetary policy, since the economy was also affected by other factors, including changes in the prices of imported raw materials and foodstuffs, the development of North Sea oil, and the introduction of measures designed to increase aggregate supply, described in earlier chapters.

Moreover, towards the end of the 1980s, as consumption rose rapidly, the rate of inflation increased and substantial balance of payments deficits occurred. Advocates of monetary policy claim that this was due not to any inherent defect in monetary policy, but to the fact that the policy was administered badly; had a tougher policy been enforced, e.g. if higher interest rates had been introduced, the economy would not have got out of control. However, other commentators feel that monetary policy, and especially such a heavy reliance on changes in interest rates, was in itself inadequate. They suggest that other measures to control demand, e.g. limitations on bank lending, higher tax rates, should have been introduced.

## 18.10 Summary and Conclusions

Money may be demanded for various reasons. Modern banking systems are able to meet this demand by creating credit. Changes in the demand for, or the supply of, money, affect the rate of interest. Monetary policy attempts to influence aggregate expenditure via changes in interest rates and/or the supply of money. Government policy, together with the banks' desire for liquidity and profitability, influence the structure of the banks' assets.

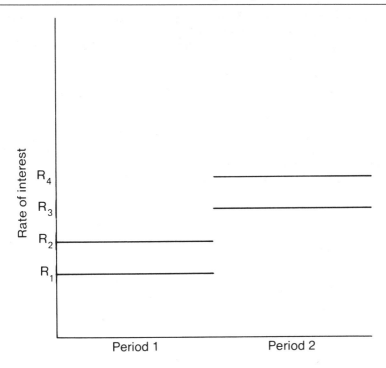

Fig. 18.4 Changes in money market interest rates

## Further Reading

Artis, M. J., Ed., *The U.K. Economy* (London: Weidenfeld and Nicolson, 11th Edn, 1986), Ch. 2.

Begg, D., Fischer, S. and Dornbusch, R., *Economics* (McGraw-Hill, 2nd Edn, 1987), Chs 22–4.

Hardwick, P., Khan, B. and Langmead, J., *An Introduction to Modern Economics* (London: Longman, 2nd Edn, 1986), Chs 20–2.

Lipsey, R. G. and Harbury, C., *First Principles of Economics* (London: Weidenfeld and Nicolson, 1988), Chs 15 and 16.

Livesey, F., *A Textbook of Economics* (London: Longman, 3rd Edn, 1989), Ch. 21.

Maunder, P., Myers, D., Wall, N. and Miller, R. L., *Economics Explained* (London: Collins, 1987), Ch. 31.

## Revision Exercises

1 Discuss the major determinants of the demand for money.
2 'All changes in national income involve changes in both real and monetary variables.' Discuss.
3 Examine the effect on the rate of interest of a fall in national income.

4 How can banks create credit? Show how the limits to credit creation may differ between a single- and a multi-bank system.

5 Examine the effects on the level of national income of changes in the money supply.

6 Discuss the factors that influence the structure of bank assets and show how these factors are reflected in the structure of the assets of the U.K. banking system.

7 Explain why the authorities may wish to control the money supply.

8 By what means may the authorities attempt to control the money supply?

9 Explain the statement that the assets structure of the banks represents a compromise among conflicting objectives.

10 What factors should a government take into account when deciding whether to use fiscal or monetary policy in order to increase the level of economic activity?

## Objective Test Questions: Set No. 5

For answers see p. 274.

1 The government's budget is said to be balanced when

A national income is in equilibrium
B national income equals national expenditure
C government expenditure equals government revenue from taxation
D government expenditure equals government revenue from taxation plus borrowing.

2 Which of the following is/are direct taxes

1 Value Added Tax
2 Excise duty
3 Personal (income) tax

A 1 and 2 only
B 2 and 3 only
C 1 only
D 3 only

Questions 3 to 7 each comprise two statements. Answer

A if both statements are true
B if the first statement is true and the second statement is false
C if the first statement is false and the second statement is true
D if both statements are false

3 Both corporation tax and personal (income) tax are direct taxes.
Both corporation tax and personal (income) tax are levied directly on individuals.

4 An increase in either direct or indirect taxation is likely to lead to a reduction in the pressure on resources.
An increase in either direct or indirect taxation is equally likely to cause prices to rise.

5 A doubling of the rate of indirect taxation on a product for which demand is elastic must, other things remaining equal, cause the total yield from the tax to fall.

An increase in the price of a product for which demand is elastic will cause the quantity demanded to fall.

6 There will be no tendency for national income to change as a result of equal changes in tax revenues and government expenditure.

The short-run effect of equal changes in tax revenues and government expenditure is that total withdrawals and total injections change by equal amounts.

7 Equality of aggregate demand and aggregate supply requires that the government's budget should be balanced.

A balanced budget implies that government expenditure equals government revenue from taxation.

8 All the following will give rise to a transactions demand for money *except* the intention by

A investors to buy bonds when their price falls
B firms to pay wages
C firms to buy raw materials
D households to buy food

9 The demand for money is influenced by the

1 level of income
2 rate of interest
3 opportunity cost of holding money

A 1, 2 and 3
B 1 and 2 only
C 1 and 3 only
D 2 and 3 only

10 A banking system comprises five banks, each of which maintains a minimum cash ratio of 10 per cent. If each of the banks received additional cash deposits of £100, the system could create further deposits up to a maximum of

A £5,000
B £4,500
C £1,000
D £500

11 The minimum bank lending rate is the minimum rate of interest charged when money is lent by the

A commercial banks to members of the general public
B Bank of England to the discount houses
C commercial banks to the discount houses
D Bank of England to members of the general public

12 Question 12 is based on Figure 1, in which E represents total expenditure. If F represents the full employment level of national income, the deflationary gap is

A GF
B YZ
C XZ
D XY

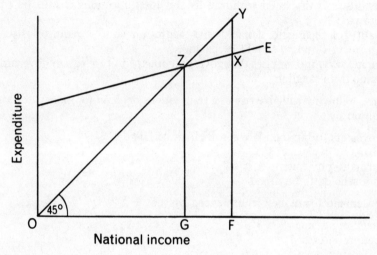

Fig. 1

13 Question 13 is based on Figure 2, in which C represents consumption expenditure and J total injections. Given that OM is the full employment level of national income, an increase in injections from $J_1$ to $J_2$ would lead to an increase in

1 output
2 employment
3 prices

A 1, 2 and 3
B 1 and 2 only
C 2 and 3 only
D 1 and 3

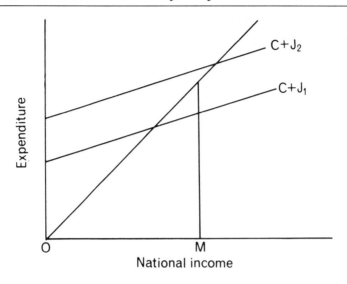

Fig. 2

14 A level of expenditure in excess of that required to keep factors of production fully occupied indicates the existence of

A dis-saving by consumers
B a budget surplus
C an inflationary gap
D a tendency for national income to fall

15 Which of the following, if increased, would be likely to reduce an inflationary gap?

1 Consumption
2 Exports
3 Direct taxation

A 1 and 2 only
B 2 and 3 only
C 1 only
D 3 only

16 An increase in the gross domestic product would result from an increase in

1 imports
2 net property income from abroad
3 exports

A 1 and 2 only
B 2 and 3 only
C 1 only
D 3 only

17 Transfer payments include all the following except

A unemployment benefit
B sickness benefit
C social security contributions
D retirement pensions

18 Which of the following constitutes a leakage from the circular flow of incomes?

A Imports
B Transfer payments
C Subsidies to business
D Interest paid on bank deposits

19 Which of the following forms of government spending contribute(s) directly to the national income?

1 Transfer payments
2 Final consumption
3 Gross capital formation

A 1 and 2 only
B 2 and 3 only
C 1 only
D 3 only

20 Question 20 is based on the table below:

| Year | Index of GNP (current prices) | Price Index |
|------|-------------------------------|-------------|
| 1 | 100 | 100 |
| 2 | 105 | 105 |
| 3 | 110 | 106 |
| 4 | 120 | 118 |

Which of the following statements is/are correct?

1 Real GNP was higher in year 4 than year 1
2 The increase in real GNP was bigger in year 4 than in year 3
3 Real GNP increased in years 2, 3 and 4

A 1 and 2 only
B 2 and 3 only
C 1 only
D 3 only

# 19. *International Trade*

## 19.1 Introduction

This chapter falls into two major parts. In the first we examine the determinants of international trade, using a very simple hypothetical model. This model explores the conditions under which trade will take place between two countries each of which can produce only two products. In the second part we examine the trading pattern of the United Kingdom. While drawing upon the analysis presented in the first part, we introduce additional considerations that are important in the current international economic system. Finally, in a brief concluding section, we discuss government policy in relation to the balance of payments.

## 19.2 The Determinants of International Trade

### 19.21 *Uneven Distribution of Resources*

As we noted in Chapter 1, human and material resources are distributed unevenly around the world. This means that the real cost of producing goods and services varies from country to country. In order to understand why these cost differences may result in international specialization and trade, consider the three situations presented in Table 19.1 for countries X and Y.

*Table 19.1 Alternative Production Possibilities*

|   | Country X | Country Y |
|---|---|---|
| A | 100 fish, or | 60 fish, or |
|   | 10 rabbits | 12 rabbits |
| B | 120 fish, or | 60 fish, or |
|   | 24 rabbits | 20 rabbits |
| C | 100 fish, or | 50 fish, or |
|   | 20 rabbits | 10 rabbits |

This table shows the outputs that could be produced, in each of the two countries, by a given quantity of labour in a given period of time. In situation A country X is more efficient (i.e. its real costs are lower) than country Y in catching fish, while Y is more efficient than X in hunting rabbits. In such a situation, where each country has an *absolute advantage* in the production of one product, the gains from specialization and trade are obvious. If X specialized in fishing and Y in hunting the total output would be 100 fish and 12 rabbits, whereas if the inhabitants of each country divided their time equally between fishing and hunting, total output would be only 80 (50 + 30) fish and 11 (5 + 6) rabbits.

### 19.22 *The Principle of Comparative Advantage*

Situation B is less straightforward. Country X has an absolute advantage in both fishing and hunting, but it has a *comparative advantage* in fishing (120/24 > 60/20), while Y has a comparative advantage in hunting (20/60 > 24/120). By this we mean that X's relative efficiency is greater in fishing. It is easy to show that total output can be increased if countries specialize in the product in which they have a comparative advantage. If each country allocates half its resources to fishing and half to hunting, total output will be 90 (60 + 30) fish and 22 (12 + 10) rabbits. If, on the other hand, X allocates eleven-twelfths of its resources to fishing and one-twelfth to hunting, while Y specializes completely in hunting, total output will be higher, as shown in Table 19.2.

*Table 19.2 Output with and without specialization*

|  | Fish | Rabbits |
|---|---|---|
| Without specialization: |  |  |
| X | 60 | 12 |
| Y | 30 | 10 |
| Total | 90 | 22 |
| With specialization: |  |  |
| X | 110 | 2 |
| Y | – | 20 |
| Total | 110 | 22 |

Finally, in situation C country X has an absolute advantage in the production of both fish and rabbits, but has no comparative advantage in either product. (The opportunity cost ratios are identical in the two countries.) In these circumstances no advantage would be gained from specialization and trade.

Since international trade brings financial transactions into play, we now recast our data in monetary terms. From now on we shall confine our attention to situation B in which X can produce 120 fish or 24 rabbits, and Y 60 fish or 20 rabbits. If the costs of the resources used are reflected in the prices of goods produced, then in country X rabbits will be five times as expensive as fish. If X's currency is 'singles' (s), the prices could be, for example, one fish = 1s, one rabbit = 5s. Similarly in Y, rabbits would be three times as expensive as fish. If Y's currency is 'doubles' (d), the prices might be one fish = 1d, one rabbit = 3d.

For every rabbit that X catches it has to forgo 5 fish. Consequently, it will specialize in fishing, provided that it can sell 5 fish at a price that will enable it to buy more than 1 rabbit. Similarly for every 3 fish that Y catches it has to forgo 1 rabbit. Consequently, it will concentrate on hunting, provided that it can sell a rabbit at a price that will enable it to buy more than 3 fish. In the light of these requirements, let us consider the situations presented in Table 19.3.

*Table 19.3 International Specialization and Trade*

| | X | | Y | |
|---|---|---|---|---|
| | Fish | Rabbits | Fish | Rabbits |
| Domestic prices | 1s | 5s | 1d | 3d |
| Import prices when: | | | | |
| 1s = 0·5d | 2·00s | 6s | 0·5d | 2·5d |
| 1s = 0·8d | 1·25s | 3·75s | 0·8d | 4d |
| 1s = 1·5d | 0·67s | 2s | 1·5d | 7·5d |

Line 1 of this table shows, for reference purposes, the domestic prices, i.e. the prices that would rule in each country in the absence of trade. The remaining figures relate to the price of imports at three different exchange rates. If the exchange rate were 1s = 0·5d, X would be able to export both fish and rabbits, since the price in Y of both would be cheaper than when produced by Y. Conversely, with a rate of 1s = 1·5d, Y would be able to export both fish and rabbits, since the price in X of both would be cheaper than when produced by X. In neither of these situations would trade continue, since one country could not earn the foreign currency with which to pay for its imports from the other country. (But see also Section 19.224.)

The only exchange rate of the three at which international trade would occur is when 1s = 0.8d. At this rate X would export fish to Y, which would in turn export rabbits to X. We can see, then, that the pattern of international trade is influenced by domestic costs and prices, and also by the exchange rate, which can be seen as the price of one currency in terms of another.

### 19.223 Transport Costs

In the above example we made no reference to transport costs. In practice international trade in any product will occur only so long as transport costs do not outweigh the price differential. For example, we saw that with 1s = 0.8d country X would sell fish in Y at a price of 0.8d per unit. However, if it cost 0.2d per unit to transport fish, exporters from X would no longer be able to sell at a price below that charged by domestic producers.

In practice transport costs differ from one product to another, tending to be highest (in relation to the price of the product) for products with a low price–volume ratio. Consequently they inhibit trade in some products (e.g. bricks, cement) far more than in others (e.g. watches, jewellery).

### 19.224 Multilateral Trade

The above example related to a situation of bilateral trade, i.e. trade between two countries. In practice trade is multilateral. For example, the U.K. sells whisky to the U.S.A. and uses the proceeds to buy machinery from Germany, oranges from Israel etc. This means that a country need be less concerned about the balance of its trade with any one other country than under bilateral trade.

Moreover, the wider the basis for trade, the greater is likely to be the scope for the application of the principle of comparative advantage, and thus for an increase in total economic welfare.

## 19.3 The Equilibrium Rate of Exchange

The equilibrium rate of exchange is that at which, given the relative costs of the countries concerned, each country's balance of payments is in equilibrium. The components of a country's balance of payments are examined below, but, in terms of our simple model, a balance of payments equilibrium implies that the value of the goods imported by a country equals the value of the goods exported by that country.

It is clear that an exchange rate of 1s = 0·5d is not an equilibrium rate. Indeed it would represent a situation of fundamental disequilibrium, Y's prices being far too high. Neither is 1s = 1·5d an equilibrium rate, since X's prices are now too high. How can an exchange rate in disequilibrium be corrected? Several alternative adjustment mechanisms can be identified.

### 19.31 *A Change in Relative Prices*

If Y's currency was overvalued in relation to that of X, Y's prices would tend to fall *relative to those of X*. The flow of money into X, following from its trade surplus, would tend to lead to an increase in the level of economic activity, and hence to higher costs and prices. Conversely, the outflow of money from Y would tend to lead to a contraction of economic activity, and to lower costs and prices. Assuming that the changes in costs affected all products to the same extent, there would eventually come a point at which X could still export fish to Y, but at which Y could export rabbits to X.

This can be seen as a natural process of adjustment, the system being brought into equilibrium by the free play of market forces. But if the government is dissatisfied with the speed of adjustment it may take additional measures. It may, for example, increase income tax in order to reduce expenditure, including expenditure on imports.

### 19.32 *Barriers to Trade*

Governments may also intervene more directly, by erecting barriers to international trade. These barriers are mainly designed to limit imports, and thus to improve the balance of trade. An improvement in the balance of trade is likely in turn to lead to a higher exchange rate.

### 19.321 *Tariffs*

A tariff is a tax on imports. Making imports more expensive tends to reduce the quantity demanded (especially when home-produced substitutes are available). In this respect a tariff has similar consequences to a rise in the costs and prices of foreign producers, although now the additional revenue accrues to the government of the importing country.

A government may apply a uniform tariff on all imported goods, but more commonly tariffs are used selectively, to discourage the import of particular types of commodity. For example the U.K., an important manufacturing nation with relatively few natural resources, has normally levied higher tariffs on manufactured goods than on raw materials and foodstuffs. Indeed these latter types of commodity were usually admitted duty-free until the U.K. entered the European Economic Community.

Often tariffs are applied even more selectively, e.g. certain types of manufactured goods attract a higher tariff than others. This usually happens for one of two reasons. First, if a long-established industry suffers such severe competiton from overseas producers that bankruptcies and unemployment seem likely, a tariff may be imposed in order to protect the domestic producers. Second, if a country is trying to set up an industry that has been long-established in other countries, it may apply a tariff in order to protect the 'infant industry'. When the infant industry has grown to maturity, and its producers have become as efficient as overseas competitors, the tariff is (or may be) removed.

### 19.322 *Quotas*

Quotas are imposed on specific categories of product, and determine how much (by volume or value) of a product may be imported in a given period – say a year. The quota may apply to the total imports of the products concerned, or it may apply only to imports from certain countries whose products are particularly cheap. The quota is, of course, a method of protecting domestic producers by reserving part of the total market for them. Domestic producers are also likely to gain an indirect benefit in that a restriction of supply tends to lead to higher prices.

### 19.323 *Other Barriers*

Several rounds of negotiations under the auspices of GATT (see Chapter 20) have led to reductions in tariffs and quotas. On the other hand some countries have attempted to restrict imports by other means. These include the imposition of technical requirements or specifications which are met more easily by domestic than overseas suppliers, and giving preference to domestic suppliers in government contracts.

Barriers to trade may be imposed even if the trade balance is satisfactory and the exchange rate does not need supporting. For example, it is argued that Japan has erected many non-tariff barriers in order to protect domestic producers despite the fact that the yen has been strong. The erection of barriers in such circumstances is, of course, a highly unpopular policy, and invites retaliation from other countries.

### 19.324 *Voluntary Export Restraints*

A voluntary export restraint (VER) is an arrangement between two parties (governments or industries) whereby one 'voluntarily' agrees to restrict the volume of its exports to the other country. Quotas are difficult to sustain under GATT rules, and the spread of VERs can be seen as an attempt to evade these rules.

### 19.325 *The Costs of Protection*

We have drawn attention to the benefits of import barriers. But protection also gives rise to costs. If the barriers imposed by country A against imports from country B, are matched by barriers imposed by B, neither country benefits. Indeed both countries are worse off because of (a) the cost of administering the protection, (b) interference with the operation of the principle of comparative advantage.

If protection by one country does not give rise to retaliation, it might be thought that that country would benefit. But protection also gives rise to costs which in principle might outweigh the benefits.

One of the major costs is the higher prices paid by consumers. This applies not only to imported goods but also to the prices of domestic goods which are protected from foreign competition. These higher prices reduce consumers' real income and cause a fall in the volume of consumption, including the consumption of non-protected products. This fall in consumption may lead to a fall in employment which outweighs the rise in employment in the protected industries.

### 19.33 *A Change in Exchange Rates*

In our initial discussion of Table 19.3 we showed how a change in the exchange rate (to 1s = 0.8d), would cause the pattern of international trade to become more balanced. We now explore how a change in the exchange rate might be brought about. It is, in fact, necessary to distinguish between floating and fixed exchange rates systems, since their mechanisms differ.

### 19.331 *Floating Exchange Rates*

The term 'floating' indicates that the exchange rate is allowed to move freely in response to the forces of demand and supply. The higher the demand for, and the lower the supply of, a currency, the higher will be its value in terms of other currencies. The demand and supply reflect the level and pattern of international trade.

In Figure 19.1, with initial demand $D_1$ and supply $S_1$, the equilibrium rate of exchange is £1 = $1·50. If American demand for British goods were to increase, the demand for Sterling, to pay for imports into the U.S.A. would increase. This would be represented by a shift in the demand curve from $D_1$ to $D_2$, which causes the equilibrium rate of exchange to rise to £1 = $1·75.

If British demand for American goods were now to fall, the earning of American exporters would fall. This would be reflected in a fall in the amount of Sterling supplied by these exporters to the foreign exchange market. This would be represented by a shift of the supply curve from $S_1$ to $S_2$ causing the equilibrium rate of exchange to rise to £1 = \$2·00.

Currencies are also demanded for investment purposes. If an American company decided to build a factory in the U.K. it would require Sterling to pay the contractors, etc. If American investors wished to buy shares in a British company or U.K. government securities, they would be required to pay in Sterling. In all of these instances the increased demand for Sterling would be represented in Figure 19.1 by a shift of the demand curve to the right.

In subsequent years these transactions would probably give rise to an increase in the supply of Sterling. The American owners of a British factory would wish to remit some of the profits to the U.S.A. The owners of shares and stock would wish to remit dividends and interest received. They would therefore offer Sterling to be exchanged for dollars. This would be represented in Figure 19.1 by a shift of the supply curve to the right.

One factor influencing decisions as to the country in which investment, and in particular short-term investment, should be made is investors' views of how the external values of different countries' currencies are going to change over the life of the investment. To see why this factor is so important, consider an investment at 10 per cent for a period of three months. The interest received

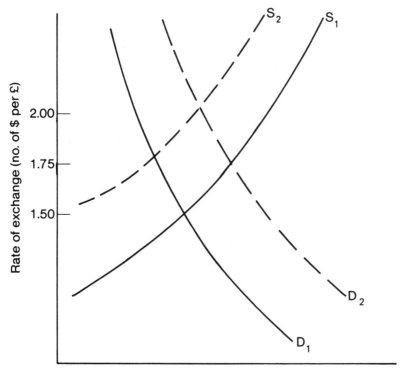

Fig. 19.1 Equilibrium rate of exchange

after three months will be $2\frac{1}{2}$ per cent (= 10 per cent per annum), which may seem to be a satisfactory rate of return. However, if the currency has in the meantime depreciated by $2\frac{1}{2}$ per cent in terms of other currencies, the investor's gain will be wiped out.

Investors' expectations of changes in the value of a currency will be subject to many influences. But especially important is the balance between that country's exports and imports. Investors will normally favour countries that have a favourable trade balance – one in which exports exceed imports – and whose currencies are experiencing a strong trading demand.

### 19.332 *Fixed Exchange Rates*

Under a system of fixed exchange rates the rate at which one currency can be exchanged for another is officially guaranteed. In practice rates are usually fixed with reference to a lower and upper limit, within which they are allowed to move. (It has become customery to relate the value of other currencies to the U.S. dollar.) These official guarantees (in so far as they can be relied upon) result in a stability of exchange rates that is valuable to companies engaged in international trade, since it reduces the degree of uncertainty concerning the future value of contracts.

### 19.333 *Devaluation and revaluation*

Fixed rates prevent the exchange rate from responding to market forces. This may have advantages in some instances, e.g. when a country has an adverse trade balance that will soon be reversed; but when there is a more fundamental disequilibrium (and this is the situation with which we are concerned in this section), fixed rates may simply delay the adjustment process. Then, when the government finally decides to change the value of its currency, it will do so by a considerable amount. In the postwar period devaluations (downward changes in the external value of a currency) have normally been of at least 10 per cent. Revaluations (upward changes in the external value of a currency) have usually been more modest, at around 5 per cent.

### 19.334 *Managed Floating*

Currently most major currencies are floating. However the authorities do intervene from time to time, mainly in order to prevent extreme fluctuations in exchange rates. The term managed or dirty floating has been applied to this situation.

### 19.34 *The Adjustment Mechanisms Compared*

In comparing the various adjustment mechanisms that we have discussed it is appropriate to adopt the viewpoint of the country that is suffering an adverse balance of trade and payments, since the main burden of adjustment would normally fall on this country. Although in this comparison we shall obviously be concerned with the efficiency of each mechanism in correcting this adverse balance, we first consider the effects of the mechanisms in the light of two other important objectives of government policy, namely price stability and a high level of utilization of resources, especially labour.

### 19.341 *Price Stability*

Of the four adjustment mechanisms, the one most likely to contribute to an objective of price stability is clearly a fall in relative prices. An absolute reduction in the general price level seldom occurs in modern economies. Nevertheless the price-adjustment mechanism at least operates to moderate any tendencies to price increases, whereas the other mechanisms contribute towards such increases.

The primary effect of these other mechanisms is an increase in the price of imports, but there is also likely to be a secondary effect in the form of an increase in the prices of home-produced goods. This may happen because domestic producers use imported raw materials and components. Furthermore, as noted above, domestic producers of goods that are directly competitive with imports may take advantage of the higher price of imports to raise their own prices. These effects are clearly likely to be greatest following the devaluation or depreciation of the currency, since this affects the price of all imports, although they also occur following the imposition of tariffs or quotas which are applied selectively. Also, as pointed out above, quotas affect prices only indirectly.

### 19.342 *Resource Utilization*

As noted above, quotas, tariffs and VERs, by raising prices lead to higher output and employment in the protected industries. On the other hand these gains might be outweighed by losses arising from the fall in consumers' real income.

However, an increase in resource utilization is virtually certain to follow from a fall in the exchange rate. For now not only do the prices of imports rise, the prices of exports fall.

If price adjustment requires policies designed to restrict the level of economic activity, then its short-term effects on resource allocation will clearly be unfavourable.

### 19.343 *The Balance of Payments*

The effect on the balance of payments is easiest to evaluate in the case of tariffs and quotas. These measures reduce the volume of imports – quotas directly and tariffs indirectly – and so reduce the outflow of capital.

Devaluation and depreciation, via higher prices, also reduce the *volume* of imports, but the effect on the total *value* of imports will depend upon the elasticity of demand. Similarly, the change in the value of exports, following a fall in their price, will depend upon the elasticity of demand in export markets. Given that supply can respond to changes in demand (i.e. given spare production capacity), devaluation (or depreciation) will lead to an improvement in the balance of payments, provided that the *sum of the elasticities of demand for imports and for exports exceeds unity.*

Finally, the price adjustment mechanism is likely to lead to an improvement in the balance of payments. The exceptions will be where import prices increase and demand is inelastic, so that the total import bill increases, and where export prices fall and demand is inelastic, so that export receipts fall.

### 19.35  *The Impact on Producers' Policies*

In the discussion above we have been concerned mainly with the impact on the economy as a whole of exchange rate movements. We now consider briefly the impact on producers' policies, especially relating to price and output.

### 19.351  *A Fall in the Exchange Rate*

When the exchange rate falls, exporting normally becomes more profitable. Take the example of a British firm exporting whisky to the U.S.A. If it wishes to obtain £6 a bottle and the exchange rate is £1 = $3 it will set a price of $18. If the exchange rate falls to £1 = $2 a price of $18 would yield £9 a bottle. The exporter might maintain this price and take the benefit in the form of a higher profit per bottle sold. The firm might use some of the additional revenue to boost advertising or other marketing expenditures. Another alternative would be to reduce the dollar price and take the benefit in the form of higher sales. A price of $12 would yield £6 a bottle at the new exchange rate and might be expected to lead to a substantial increase in the volume of sales.

Which of these alternatives was chosen would depend upon a number of factors, including the estimated price elasticity of demand of the product, the responsiveness of sales to advertising or other marketing expenditures, and the ability of the producer to increase supply to match an increase in demand.

If the fall in the exchange rate is substantial and seems likely to persist, some producers may enter export markets for the first time.

A fall in the exchange rate causes a rise in the price of imports. This can have both favourable and unfavourable effects. For those firms producing goods in competition with imported goods the price rise affords a measure of protection. Such firms may take advantage by raising their prices, or by increasing sales to customers who would previously have bought imported products, or both.

On the other hand those firms purchasing raw materials and components from overseas experience an increase in their costs. To minimize this they will seek alternative sources of supply and in some instances may even start to make the components themselves.

### 19.352  *A Rise in the Exchange Rate*

A rise in the exchange rate has the opposite effects to those discussed in the previous section. To maintain a given sterling price, overseas prices have to be raised, but this is likely to cause a fall in the volume of sales. Overall, therefore, exporting become less profitable, as does production in competition with imports whose price has fallen. The only beneficiaries are those producers whose costs fall because of the fall in the price of imported raw materials and components.

## 19.36 *The Terms of Trade*

The terms of trade is the ratio of the average price of a country's exports of goods to the price of its imports of goods. The ratio in the base year (1980 in Table 19.4) is expressed as 100. A fall in the ratio (as between 1981 and 1986) is described as a deterioration or worsening, and a rise in the ratio (as between 1986 and 1988) as an improvement in the terms of the trade.

*Table 19.4 The Terms of Trade*

| | Unit value indices (average prices) | | |
| | Exports | Imports | Terms of trade |
|---|---|---|---|
| 1981 | 76 | 74 | 103 |
| 1982 | 81 | 80 | 102 |
| 1983 | 88 | 88 | 100 |
| 1984 | 95 | 96 | 100 |
| 1985 | 100 | 100 | 100 |
| 1986 | 92 | 96 | 96 |
| 1987 | 96 | 99 | 97 |
| 1988 | 97 | 99 | 98 |

*Source: Economic Trends*

The term improvement refers to the fact that as the price of exports rises, relative to that of imports, a given *volume* of exports (and hence of labour and other resources) can buy a larger volume of imports, with a consequent improvement in our standard of living. However a rise in the relative price of exports can also have undesirable consequences. It tends to make British goods less competitive, which leads to a fall in the volume of exports and hence of employment. Moreover if the rise in price of British exports is accompanied by a rise in price of British goods sold on the domestic market, imports will become more competitive and this will also cause a reduction in domestic employment.

## 19.4 The United Kingdom Balance of Payments

Having discussed in terms of a simple model the meaning of equilibrium and disequilibrium in the balance of payments, and having indicated what steps might be taken to correct a disequilibrium, we now put flesh on the bare bones of the discussion by examining the composition of the U.K. balance of payments. Table 19.5 gives a summary of the balance of payments in 1988. We examine in turn each of the main items in the table. The figures in brackets after each of the items correspond to those in Table 19.5.

### 19.41 *Visible Trade (1)*

Visible trade refers to goods of all kinds. The U.K. has traditionally had a deficit on visible trade, a surplus on manufactures being outweighed by a deficit on trade in foodstuffs and raw materials. The development of North Sea oil and gas

Table 19.5  U.K. Balance of Payments, 1988 (£ million)

| | |
|---|---:|
| 1 Visible trade | −20,557 |
| 2 Invisibles | + 5,892 |
| 3 Current balance | −14,665 |
| 4 Net transactions in (external) assets and liabilities | −562 |
| 5 (of which, change in official reserves (drawings +; additions −) | −2,761 |
| 6 Balancing item | +15,227 |

Source: Economic Trends

led to visible surpluses in three consecutive years, 1980, 1981 and 1982, something unknown within living memory. But since then the balance has been in deficit. Moreover, even the balance in manufactures, a category in which the U.K. has traditionally enjoyed a surplus, has recently been in deficit by as much as £14 billion (1988).

### 19.42 *Invisible Trade (2)*

Invisible trade comprises three major categories. The most important is services, which includes overseas earnings of shipping companies, air lines, insurance companies, banks and other financial institutions, and spending on travel. The U.K. has consistently earned a surplus on services, in particular on financial services. The second category is interest, profits and dividends, flows which result from past investment overseas. Taking one year with another, cash inflows under this heading exceed cash outflows. The final category of invisible trade is transfers, on which the U.K. invariably has a deficit. Transfers comprise expenditure on overseas aid, contributions to the European Community etc. It can be seen from Table 19.5 that the net result of these three sets of transactions was a surplus of almost £5.9 billion on invisible trade.

### 19.43 *The Balance on Current Account (3)*

Adding together the balance on visible and invisible trade gives the balance on current account. It can be seen that the (record) deficit on visible trade far outweighed the surplus on invisibles, giving a substantial current account deficit. Considerable importance is attached to the current balance, since it indicates the extent to which the U.K. is paying its way on a day-to-day basis in the international economy. If the current balance is seriously in deficit for any length of time, the government will feel obliged to take remedial action.

### 19.44 *Net Transactions in External Assets and Liabilities (4)*

In principle a deficit on the current account (leading to an outflow of money) should be matched by a surplus (an inflow of money) on the capital account (transactions in external assets and liabilities). This did not happen because there was a substantial volume of unrecorded items, the *balancing item* (6). This could mean that the current deficit was much less than recorded, or that there was a big surplus on the capital acount, or both.

The existence of such a large balancing item makes it difficult for the government to decide what policy to adopt. Normally a current account deficit of the size recorded would call for remedial action, e.g. increases in taxation and/or in the rate of interest in order to dampen expenditure. But the government would be reluctant to take such action if it felt that the situation was not as unfavourable as suggested by the official statistics.

If the U.K. did have a big surplus on the capital account, this would involve a growth in overseas assets. In subsequent years the yield on these assets, in the form of interest, dividends etc., would contribute to the inflow on the U.K.'s current account.

### 19.45 *Change in Official Reserves (5)*

This is one of the flows included in item 4. We have identified it separately in Table 19.5 because it receives special attention by the government. The official reserves are holdings of gold and convertible currencies, Special Drawing Rights and reserves with the International Monetary Fund (see Chapter 20). These reserves are immediately available to settle our international indebtedness, and the increase in these reserves was a welcome feature of the year's transactions.

## 19.5 Government Policy and the Balance of Payments

Under a system of fixed exchange rates a major policy variable is the decision whether to maintain or alter the exchange rate. Under a system of floating rates this option is not open to the government. The most that the monetary authorities can do, by buying or selling in the currency markets, is to reduce the magnitude of short-term price fluctuations. (As, noted above, when the authorities intervene in this way we are said to have a system of managed or dirty floating.)

Most governments have also relinquished the right, except in exceptional circumstances, to use barriers to trade to significantly influence the balance of payments. As noted above, national tariffs and quotas have tended to be reduced in recent years.

In the absence of these two weapons governments have two other methods of correcting an adverse balance of payments. They may seek to reduce aggregate expenditure in order to reduce the demand for imports and encourage exports. (This point was mentioned during our discussion of demand management policies in Chapter 15.)

Alternatively they may try to engineer a rise in interest rates, as noted in Chapter 17. A rise in interest rates is, of course, one method of reducing aggregate expenditure. In addition higher interest rates can attract foreign money into the U.K., with an immediately favourable effect on the exchange rate and the balance of payments.

Finally, decisions on joining international organisations, such as the European Community, have a major impact on a country's international trade and balance of payments. This point is discussed at length in the following chapter.

### 19.6 Summary and Conclusions

International trade arises because different countries have different resources. The gains from international trade are maximized when countries specialise in those products in which they have a comparative advantage. To enable trade to take place the exchange rate has to be at an appropriate level. A disequilibrium exchange rate can be corrected by a change in relative prices. It can also be corrected by imposing barriers to trade. (However, these barriers may sometimes be imposed simply to protect domestic producers.) The exchange rate changes very infrequently under a system of fixed exchange rates, but much more frequently when the rate is allowed to float.

The U.K. balance of payments was examined in some detail. Although the U.K. recorded a record current account deficit in 1988 this was difficult to interpret because of an unusually large balancing item.

### Further Reading

Artis, M. J., Ed., *The U.K. Economy* (London: Weidenfeld and Nicolson, 11th Edn, 1986), Ch. 3.

Begg, D., Fischer, S. and Dornbusch, R., *Economics* (London: McGraw-Hill, 2nd Edn, 1987), Ch. 31.

Griffiths, A. and Wall, S., *Applied Economics* (London: Longman, 2nd Edn, 1986), Chs 22–4.

Hardwick, P., Khan, B. and Langmead, J., *An Introduction to Modern Economics* (London: Longman, 2nd Edn, 1986), Chs 28 and 29.

Lipsey, R. G. and Harbury, C., *First Principles of Economics* (London: Weidenfeld and Nicolson, 1988), Ch. 43.

Livesey, F., *A Textbook of Economics* (London: Longman, 3rd Edn, 1989), Ch. 17.

Maunder, P., Myers, D., Wall, N. and Miller, R. L., *Economics Explained* (London: Collins, 1987), Ch. 31.

### Revision Exercises

1 Discuss the benefits to be gained from international specialization and trade.
2 State what you understand by the term 'equilibrium rate of exchange', and discuss the factors that may cause the rate to change.
3 How may a balance of payments deficit be corrected?
4 Compare and contrast tariffs and devaluation as methods of correcting a balance of payments deficit.
5 What are the relative advantages and disadvantages of fixed and floating exchange rates?
6 In what circumstances is a country most likely to revalue its currency? What unfavourable consequences may follow from revaluation?
7 In what circumstances might a surplus on the balance of payments current account have undesirable consequences?
8 Define the terms of trade and discuss the implications of changes in its value.

9 Distinguish between natural and artificial barriers to international trade, and explain why artificial barriers are erected.

10 Explain why a country may experience a surplus or a deficit on its balance of payments current account.

# 20. *International Institutions and Development*

## 20.1 Introduction

This chapter begins with a discussion of the major international economic institutions – their objectives, regulations, financing, etc. Many of these institutions have as one of their objectives the provision of assistance to less developed countries. But despite this assistance many of these countries still face serious problems, and the second part of the chapter considers what further steps might be taken in order to try to solve these problems.

## 20.2 The International Monetary Fund

Founded in 1945, the I.M.F. has a membership of 146 countries. The central aims of the I.M.F. are exchange rate stability, the removal of restrictions on foreign exchange operations, and international monetary co-operation.

The I.M.F.'s resources are provided by members according to a system of quotas related to the size of their economies; in addition the group of Ten (see below) provide resources under the General Arrangements to Borrow. Seventy-five per cent of a country's quota can be contributed in its own currency, the remainder being in gold or reserve assets.

Any member experiencing a balance of payments deficit can obtain from the Fund supplies of the currency it requires, in exchange for its own currency. A member can borrow up to 125 per cent of its quota, although borrowing above 50 per cent is permitted only after a detailed programme of macroeconomic policy measures has been agreed and begun to be implemented by the member. Money borrowed from the Fund is normally repaid within three to five years, by which time it is expected that the balance of payments problems will have responded to the new policies.

As international trade expanded, a decline occurred in the ratio of the world's official reserves and foreign exchange to the value of world trade, and in order to boost world liquidity, the I.M.F. established Special Drawing Rights. The S.D.R. is in effect an entry in a member's bank balance with the I.M.F., and is available for settlements between central banks and with the I.M.F. Recently there has been an upsurge in the use of S.D.R.s in private transactions, and in the 1980s several banks introduced S.D.R. current accounts to facilitate the settlement of S.D.R. transactions.

The main use of I.M.F. funds has been to help countries deal with temporary balance of payments difficulties. However, this type of assistance has become less important as countries have increasingly met their need for temporary finance by borrowing from commercial banks without submitting to the policy conditions imposed by the I.M.F.

The I.M.F. has responded by offering assistance on longer maturities and with less strict conditions. Moreover, some of these new forms of assistance have led the I.M.F. to meet needs more traditionally met by the World Bank (see below). In 1988 it established the Enhanced Structural Adjustment Facility (E.S.A.F.), with about £4½ billion, which can be borrowed by the poorest, debt-distressed countries, which cannot afford to borrow at market rates of interest. Subsidies provided by the richer nations enable the I.M.F. to lend under E.S.A.F. at an interest rate of only ½ per cent. About sixty low income countries are eligible, but borrowers are expected to implement programmes to strengthen their economies.

## 20.3 The International Bank for Reconstruction and Development

The I.B.R.D. (also known as the World Bank) was established at the same time as the I.M.F. and has virtually the same membership. Its purpose is to encourage capital investment for the reconstruction or development of its member countries, either by acting as a channel for private funds or by making loans from its own resources. These resources comprise partly the subscriptions of member countries and partly money raised by selling bonds on the world market. The Bank usually makes loans – at market related rates of interest – either direct to governments or with governments as the guarantor. Today almost all the Bank's lending is to the less developed countries (L.D.C.s). The Bank also provides various kinds of technical assistance.

The lending of the Bank increased substantially in the 1980s, as it began to participate in joint ventures with the commercial banks. The aim of this co-operation was to provide loans for longer periods than would normally be available directly from the private sector.

### 20.31 *The International Finance Corporation*

Affiliated to the I.B.R.D., the International Finance Corporation was created in 1956 in order to stimulate the provision of international aid from private sources, especially to the less developed countries. It obtains funds from eighty or so members, and can borrow from the I.B.R.D. to re-lend to private investors without government guarantee. The fact that a government guarantee is not required gives an element of added flexibility to the use of funds. Further flexibility results from the fact that the I.F.C., in addition to providing loans, can hold shares in companies.

### 20.32 *The International Development Association*

Also affiliated to the I.B.R.D., the International Development Association was established in 1960. It provides loans at little or no interest for projects in L.D.C.s that would not be feasible if finance had to be obtained at normal commercial rates of interest. These projects are normally concerned with the improvement of the country's infrastructure, e.g. roads, power supplies. Such projects are usually very capital-intensive and have a long life, so that they would normally attract a heavy burden in interest payments. Maturities on I.D.A. credits are fifty years, as against twenty years or less for I.B.R.D. loans.

## 20.4 Bank for International Settlements

The main purpose of the B.I.S., which was founded in 1930, is to promote co-operation among central banks, including the provision of short-term liquidity to central banks in need. It also organises regular meetings of the central banks of the Group of Ten countries – the U.S.A., Japan, West Germany, France, the U.K., Canada, Italy, Belgium, the Netherlands and Sweden.

## 20.5 The General Agreement on Tariffs and Trade

GATT, an international organization with its headquarters in Switzerland, was established in 1948. Ninety-five countries, accounting for 80 per cent of world trade in goods, are now parties to the Agreement, with many more countries applying its rules in practice. Members are pledged to the reduction of barriers to trade, including tariffs, quotas and preferential trade agreements.

Central to the Agreement is members' obligation to apply equality of treatment ('Most Favoured Nation' or MFN status) to trade with other members. Exceptions are allowed in the case of customs unions, free-trade areas, and the Generalised System of Preferences (GSP) granted by industrial countries to L.D.C.s

Under the auspices of GATT several rounds of multilateral negotiations – the most recent being the 'Uruguay Round' initiated in 1986 – have reduced trade barriers.

## 20.6 Regional Groupings

There are two main types of regional grouping, the free-trade area and the customs union.

### 20.61 *Free-Trade Areas*

A free-trade area is an association of countries among which all trade barriers are removed. Each country is, however, permitted to retain any barriers that it wishes to impose in respect of trade with non-members. Until the U.K. joined the European Community in 1973 it was a member of the European Free Trade Association.

### 20.62 *Customs Unions*

Although a free-trade area brings about a reduction in trade barriers among members, it also implies discrimination, since members are permitted to retain barriers against non-members. In a customs union discrimination is formalized, since all its members agree to adopt a common external tariff against non-members. The most important customs union, in terms of value of trade, the detailed nature of its provisions, and the range of its objectives, is the European Community, sometimes known as the Common Market.

## 20.7 The European Community

Created in 1957 under the Treaty of Rome, the founder-members of the E.C. were France, West Germany, Italy, Belgium, Holland and Luxembourg. The membership has since increased to twelve with the entry of the U.K., Ireland, Denmark, Greece, Spain and Portugal.

In addition to the elimination of trade barriers among members and the adoption of a common external tariff, the E.C.'s objectives include mobility of labour and investment funds within the Community, common agricultural and transport policies and, eventually, the harmonization of members' fiscal and monetary policies.

### 20.71 *The Single European Act*

The Single European Act 1986 set a target date of 31 December 1992 for the creation of a single European market, which will have a population in excess of, and a GDP almost as great as, that of the U.S.A. It is intended that within the single market the movement of goods, services, people and capital should be free from artificial restrictions. This will require some 300 separate measures designed to remove physical, technical and fiscal barriers to trade.

The measures proposed include: removing barriers created by differences in trade mark and patent laws; removing frontier controls (subject to retaining necessary safeguards for security, social or health reasons); further opening up of the purchasing of public supplies; mutual recognition of higher education qualifications.

### 20.72 *The Common Agricultural Policy*

The basis of the C.A.P. is the guaranteed price. Domestic producers are assured of the prices they will receive and can plan the running of their businesses in the light of this information. In order to prevent price falling below the guaranteed level two mechanisms have been established. First, the possibility that cheaper imports might force the price down is avoided by a system of levies, which bring the external price up to the internal guaranteed level. Second, if within the Community supply exceeds demand at the guaranteed price, thus threatening to force down the price, the surplus is taken off the market and retained as a 'buffer stock'. If the guaranteed or target price remains above the equilibrium price for a long period of time, however, the buffer stock may become unmanageably large. During the 1970s and 1980s massive stocks were accumulated under the C.A.P., first of butter and beef and then of dried milk, wine and apples. In 1984 quotas, designed to reduce the output of milk and milk products, were introduced. More recently, farmers have been compensated for taking land out of production.

One of the primary objectives of the policy is to protect the incomes of the farming community, and the build-up of large surplus stocks is a clear indication that their incomes have been maintained at a higher level than they would otherwise have been. Corresponding costs have been incurred by the purchasers of those products, who have paid a price above the free-market equilibrium price. The additional costs have been estimated to amount to £550 a year for a family of four. When allowance is made for the fact that a reformed C.A.P. would cause a fall in European production and exports, and hence a rise in world prices, the true cost is probably less than this. Nevertheless it remains substantial.

Moreover, all taxpayers share in the cost to the Community budget. This cost includes export refunds, which bridge the gap between internal prices and the lower prices for exports to the rest of the world; the purchase and storing of products; subsidies to output and farm restructuring. In total expenditure on agriculture accounts for two-thirds of the E.C. budget.

### 20.73 *The European Investment Bank*

The European Investment Bank was created by the Treaty of Rome, and came into force in 1958. Its principal role is to make loans available to public- and private-sector borrowers in member countries for projects that fall into one or more of the following categories:

1 Projects for benefiting less developed regions.
2 Projects concerned with modernization or developments that are of such a size or nature they cannot be entirely financed by the means available in individual member countries.
3 Projects of common interest to several members that cannot be entirely financed by the various means available in individual member countries, e.g. improving cross-border communications.

The finance for these loans comes from two sources. First, there is the Bank's capital, subscribed by the member countries. Second, the Bank issues bonds on national and international markets. Since the Bank does not pay interest on the capital subscribed, it obtains its funds at an overall cost that is slightly below the commercial free-market cost. The Bank's current cost of borrowing is reflected in the rate of interest charged to borrowers, irrespective of both the type and the riskiness of the project being financed. Borrowing from the Bank will therefore best suit those projects for which the highest commercial rate would have been charged.

The greater part of the Bank's lending has gone to 'regional development and conversion' schemes. The bulk of the remainder is accounted for by the financing of projects for the production and distribution of energy. The main beneficiary has been Italy, a reflection of the serious regional problems faced by that country, followed by the U.K. Loans were initially confined to members of the Community, but by 1980 about one-sixth of the loans were made to non-members, mainly to the sixty signatories of the Lomé Convention – for the most part former colonies of E.C. members such as the U.K. and France.

### 20.74 *Other European Community Institutions*

The *European Regional Development Fund* was established in 1975 to help to correct regional economic imbalances in member countries. The U.K. has received about a quarter of the Fund's expenditure, the money being applied to projects receiving U.K. regional aid (see Chapter 21). The *European Social Fund* was established in 1957 'to improve the employment opportunities for workers in the Common Market and to contribute thereby to raising the standard of living [by] rendering the employment of workers easier and increasing their geographical and occupational mobility'. Assistance is provided towards the costs of training and retraining schemes; the resettlement of workers and their families who have to move home to gain or retain employment; schemes to improve access to employment for disabled workers and workers over the age of fifty; job creation schemes for unemployed young people. The U.K. is currently the main beneficiary.

Not all Community institutions are concerned primarily with the interests of their own members. *The European Development Fund* was established in 1971 to provide loans and non-repayable credits for specific projects in the developing countries, such as the building of roads and bridges, and radio and telecommunications networks.

### 20.75 *The European Monetary System*

The E.M.S. was established in 1979 to create a zone of monetary stability in Europe. The members created a *European Currency Unit* (ECU or Ecu), a 'basket' containing fixed amounts of the currencies of all E.C. currencies, as the common denominator used in fixing parities.

Under the *Exchange Rate Mechanism* a set of bilateral exchange rates is established. Members are expected to prevent exchange rate fluctuations of more than $2\frac{1}{2}$ per cent (6 per cent for the Italian lira) on either side of these agreed rates.

Although the U.K. declined to join the E.M.S. at its inception, sterling is one of the Ecu's basket currencies. It seems possible that U.K. co-operation will be extended to membership of the E.M.S. in the near future.

### 20.76 *The Impact on U.K. Membership of the European Community*

The impact on the U.K. of membership of the E.C. is easiest to assess with respect to the budgetary contribution and the pattern of trade.

### 20.761 *The U.K.'s Budgetary Contribution*

The Community's revenue or 'own resources' comes from three sources: duties levied on imports entering the Community under the common external tariff; levies charged on agricultural product imports to bring their prices up to the levels prevailing under the C.A.P. price support scheme; 1.4 per cent of members' V.A.T. receipts (around two-thirds of total Community revenue). Because of its structure of industry and pattern of trade the U.K. makes a larger contribution to the Community budget than it would if each country's contribution was determined by its national income.

As noted above, about two-thirds of the Community's budget is spent on agriculture. Since the U.K. has a relatively small agricultural sector, her share of Community expenditure is also relatively small.

The government has argued that the budgetary procedures would result in the U.K. making an unjustifiably high net contribution. An agreement was reached whereby the U.K. received a rebate, which in 1988, for example, reduced its net contribution from £3 billion to £1 billion.

### 20.762 *The Impact on the Pattern of Trade*

Figure 20.1 shows that there has been a substantial increase in the share of U.K. trade accounted for by the other members of the Community. There has been a corresponding fall in the share of North America and the rest of the world (especially important here being Commonwealth countries with whom the U.K. used to have very strong trading links). Since the U.K. joined the Community, the rate of increase in imports has steadily exceeded the rate of increase in exports, giving rise to an ever-widening trade deficit.

### 20.77 *The Economic Effect of Regional Groupings*

Regional groupings can be evaluated in terms of their effects on the total welfare of all countries, the welfare of their members as a whole and the welfare of individual members. It might be thought that total welfare would be increased by the formation of a regional grouping since the abolition of barriers to trade among members encourages, within that grouping, specialization and trade in accordance with the principle of comparative advantage. However on a wider international scale, regional groupings – and especially customs unions – may be inconsistent with that principle. One member of the grouping may have a comparative advantage in a particular product when compared to other members, but not when compared to non-members. To put the matter slightly differently, a low-cost producer may be excluded from a market, leaving it to be supplied by a relatively high-cost producer.

The total welfare of all the nations in the world may not, therefore, increase as a result of the formation of a regional grouping. Moreover, even when we confine our attention to the members of the grouping it is not inevitable that total welfare should increase. The high-cost producer will benefit by being sheltered from the competition of low-cost non-members, but this is at the expense of consumers, who have to pay higher prices.

Finally the producers of some member countries may benefit at the expense of producers in other member countries. As noted above, there is some evidence to suggest that on the whole U.K. industry has lost rather than gained sales as a result of our entry into the E.E.C.

### 20.8 Less Developed Countries

Table 20.1 shows recent changes in GDP. It can be seen that overall the low and

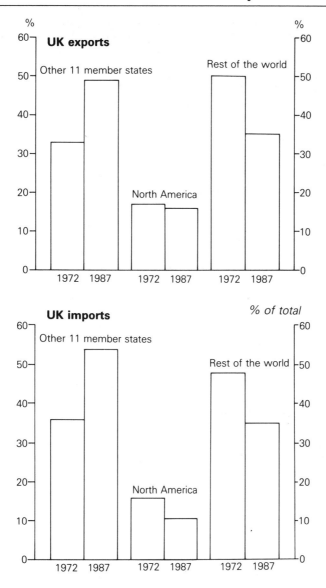

Fig. 20.1 U.K. trade patterns since joining E.C.
*Source: Economic Progress Report*, October 1988

mid-income countries grew more rapidly than the high income O.E.C.D. countries (Germany, U.K., U.S.A., Japan etc.). However, there was a vast range of experience within the low and mid-income group. On the one hand G.D.P. per head grew by 5½ per cent a year in Asia (Hong Kong, Thailand etc.); on the other hand it fell by 2½ per cent a year in Sub-Saharan Africa.

*Table 20.1 Annual Change in G.D.P. 1980–8*

| Country group | Change in G.D.P. | Change in G.D.P. per head |
|---|---|---|
| Low and mid income | 4·0 | 2·0 |
|   excluding China and India | 2·6 | 0·2 |
|   Sub-Saharan Africa | 0·5 | −2·5 |
|   Asia | 7·3 | 5·5 |
|   Europe, Mid East, N. Africa | 2·9 | 0·7 |
|   S. America, Caribbean | 1·7 | −0·6 |
| 17 highly indebted countries | 1·3 | −1·2 |
| High income O.E.C.D. | 2·7 | 2·1 |

*Source: World Bank Development Report, 1989*

In order to try to attain a higher rate of growth, many L.D.C.s have sought financial assistance in the form of official aid, commercial bank loans and direct investment. However, in many instances the recipients have found it difficult to make repayments and hence large-scale indebtedness has been added to their other problems.

### 20.81 *International Debt*

Between 1982 and 1988 the exposure of the commercial banks to the major debtor countries rose by 17 per cent (after allowing for debt reduction that had already taken place, principally via debt/equity swaps). However, the exposure of public bodies – governments, export credit agencies and the international financial institutions – rose far more, by 107 per cent. Consequently the share of debt owned by these public bodies increased from less than a quarter to over a third. Given on the one hand the dangers of default by some countries and on the other hand the increased responsiveness of the I.M.F. to the needs of the poorest countries, it is difficult to see any reduction of the public sector's share in the near future.

### 20.82 *Aid versus Trade*

The case for increased economic aid – advanced in such documents as the Brandt Report – is not accepted by all economists. Some, such as Professor Peter Bauer, argue that international aid is often used highly inefficiently, in projects that contribute more to the prestige than the development of the country. It is also argued that foreign funds are often substituted for, rather than added to, domestic funds. Moreover the receipt of aid may sap local initiative, so that the net effect of aid on development may actually be negative.

Whatever the respective merits of the two sides of this argument, both groups would agree that the L.D.C.s can be helped by improving their access to world markets. Under the 1975 Lomé Agreement, subsequently renewed, the European Community and the A.C.P. (a group of African, Caribbean and Pacific countries) were constituted as a preferential trading area in which the E.C. relinquished the right of reciprocity. It was estimated that under the agreement 94 per cent of the agricultural products of the A.C.P. states would enter the Community free of duty.

Nevertheless the World Bank has remained highly critical of the E.C. Common Agricultural Policy, and of the subsidisation of uncompetitive industries in rich countries.

## 20.9 Policy towards Multinational Enterprises

We noted in Chapter 4 that multinational enterprises now account for about one-fifth of world output. Moreover their output is estimated to be growing at twice the rate for the world economy as a whole. The rise of the multinationals has caused concern for a number of reasons.

The first point concerns the balance of payments. When an overseas company invests in a country, the initial impact on that country's balance of payments is favourable, for money flows into the country. But subsequently profits are remitted to the parent company overseas, causing a drain on the balance of payments. It is the long-term outflow of funds that causes concern.

The second point is the fear that overseas companies may become so strongly entrenched and obtain such economies of scale, that their domestic competitors may suffer, and may even be forced out of business. I.B.M., for example, has over half the European computer market.

Third, overseas companies may become so large that their decisions have an impact comparable to decisions taken by parliaments. For example, a decision to build, or not to build, a new petro-chemical plant might have the same impact on the level of demand as a change in tax rates. This problem may also arise with large domestic firms, though it is easier for governments to influence their decisions. In the last resort the multinational can threaten to run down its business in one country and expand elsewhere.

However, against these potential disadvantages of multinational companies must be set the potential benefits, many of which arise simply from the investment undertaken by the multinationals – the creation of additional employment, an increase in efficiency, etc. Additional benefits may arise because the companies are multinational. New products or processes may be introduced into one country after they have been developed by the company in other countries. More generally, overseas subsidiaries may benefit from the research and development work undertaken by the parent company.

Different countries have taken different attitudes towards multinationals. France has at times proved hostile, whereas U.K. governments have normally been eager to attract overseas companies. Many of these companies have been offered assistance under the regional policies discussed in the following chapter.

## 20.10 Summary and Conclusions

Uneven rates of economic growth have resulted in wide differences in international living standards. Numerous institutions have been created in order to expand the flow of aid from richer to poorer nations. Other institutions have been established to serve the interests of regional groupings of countries, the European Community being the best developed.

**Further Reading**

Artis, M. J., Ed., *The U.K. Economy* (London: Weidenfeld and Nicolson, 11th Edn, 1986), Ch. 3.

Begg, D., Fischer, S. and Dornbusch, R., *Economics* (London: McGraw-Hill, 2nd Edn, 1987), Ch. 3.

Griffiths, A. and Wall, S., *Applied Economics* (London: Longman, 2nd Edn, 1986), Ch. 26.

Livesey, F., *A Textbook of Economics* (London: Longman, 3rd Edn, 1989), Ch. 25.

Maunder, P., Myers, D., Wall, N. and Miller, R. L., *Economics Explained* (London: Collins, 1987), Ch. 35.

**Revision Exercises**

1 Outline the functions of the International Monetary Fund, the International Bank for Reconstruction and Development, the European Investment Bank and the General Agreement on Tariffs and Trade.

2 Distinguish between a customs union and a free-trade area, outlining the relative advantages of each.

3 Evaluate the costs and benefits of the E.C.'s Common Agricultural Policy with respect to (a) producers and (b) consumers.

4 Assess the costs and benefits to the U.K. of membership of the E.C.

5 Discuss the major developments that have occurred in the international economy in the postwar period.

6 'Trade, not aid, is the best solution to the problems of the underdeveloped countries.' Discuss.

7 What criteria might be adopted in drawing up a programme of investment in an underdeveloped country?

8 'The consequences of the Common Agricultural Policy illustrate the foolishness of interfering with the free play of market forces.' Discuss.

9 Discuss the functions of the major European economic institutions.

10 Why is it sometimes argued that overseas aid can reduce economic growth?

# 21. Government Policies to Influence the Type and Location of Investment

## 21.1 Introduction

In previous chapters we have discussed policies intended to influence the level of investment, and hence the level of expenditure, output and employment. In this chapter we consider policies intended to influence the type and location of investment. The type of investment is influenced mainly by industrial policy, and the location of investment by regional policy. But it will be seen that there is a slight overlap between the two sets of policies.

## 21.2 Industrial Policy

The justification advanced for industrial policy is that for one reason or another market forces would not result in the most desirable pattern of investment, so that the government must intervene in order to effect an improvement. Some governments have been more persuaded than others about the benefits of intervention.

### 21.21 *Innovation*

Innovation is the introduction of new products and processes. It is usually the culmination of a programme – large or small – of spending on research and development. Almost one half of the total cost of research and development is met by the government. Government spending has been heavily concentrated on industries of national strategic importance, and in particular on defence including aerospace and nuclear energy. While government support in these areas may be appropriate, it has been argued that these industries have absorbed too high a share of spending, and in particular that they have employed too great a proportion of highly qualified scientists and engineers.

The government runs its own research establishments, funds research in universities and through Research Councils, and supports co-operative research associations in a number of industries. Government support for research and development is usually justified on strategic grounds, as noted above, or on the grounds that the social benefits arising from innovation exceed the private benefits.

## 21.22 *Sectoral Assistance*

Governments have frequently encouraged – by providing financial and other types of assistance – investment in certain sectors of the economy. (Insofar as this investment includes spending on research and development there is an overlap with the assistance considered in the previous section.) Sectoral assistance has been provided in two sets of circumstances.

### 21.221 *Expanding Industries*

When industries are expanding, a shortage of capacity in one industry or sector may limit output in other industries. For example a shortage of microelectronic chips could limit the production of equipment incorporating chips. With this possibility in mind, £70 million of government money was made available to supplement private investment in the production of chips. In addition the N.E.B. invested an initial £50 million in INMOS, a British microelectronics company. (After further public investment, INMOS was returned to the private sector in 1984.) The government also launched a microelectronics industry support programme (M.I.S.P.) with funds of £55 million over the period 1978–85 and £120 million in 1985–90. The money enabled a 20 per cent subsidy to be provided on purchases of plant and equipment.

Not all investment takes the form of spending on plant and equipment. Under the microprocessor application project (M.A.P.), administered by the Department of Industry, funds were made available to increase awareness and training at senior levels in industry and the trade unions, and towards the costs incurred in commissioning consultants and developing specific microprocessor applications.

Under Section 8 of the 1972 Industry Act, discretionary grants were made towards the cost of re-equipment in a number of industries, an important aim again being to prevent potential bottlenecks. The most expensive scheme was that for ferrous foundries which cost £45 million over a two year period, and aimed to promote investment of £480 million.

### 21.222 *Contracting Industries*

Assistance has also been provided to contracting industries. Where it is clear that the trend of demand is such that contraction is inevitable the aim has been to hasten the process, but limit the scale, of contraction. Once capacity has been reduced, the remaining firms are better placed to undertake investment and hence increase their efficiency. The Cotton Industry Act 1959 and the Shipbuilding Industry Act 1967 provided compensation for firms which reduced their capacity, or left the industry entirely, and assistance for re- equipment by the surviving firms.

### 21.3 **Indicative Planning**

In principle, and indeed in practice in the U.K., indicative planning does not involve executive action by the government. The theory behind indicative planning is that if the plans of producers – with respect to output, investment, etc. – are known, potential imbalances between demand and supply can be identified and corrected. It can therefore be seen as a means of ensuring that investment is undertaken where it is most needed.

The first attempt at indicative planning was undertaken by the National Economic Development Council, set up in 1962 with a brief to study the country's economic performance, and to suggest how the country's resources might best be used to further economic growth. N.E.D.C. produced a number of reports in the 1960s, including a National Plan in 1965, in which the implications of economic growth were explored. However the growth rates chosen turned out to be unrealistically high, and the exercise was of little value.

Since then indicative planning has assumed a less ambitious and less centralized form. The task of identifying obstacles to improvement in the performance of particular industries or sectors of the economy, and of suggesting ways of overcoming these obstacles, has been given to forty Sector Working Parties (or in a few instances Economic Development Committees). The activities of the S.W.P.s include identifying imports that could be replaced by domestic markets, suggesting improved ordering procedures, and studying possible applications of advanced technology, especially micro-electronics.

## 21.4 An Evaluation of Industrial Policy

It is extremely difficult to evaluate industrial policy, if only because it has so many different aspects. There is little doubt that the return from investment is lower in the U.K. than in many other industrialized nations, and measures to increase this return would be welcome. But it is not clear that industrial policy has succeeded in this respect.

As noted above indicative planning, at least in its early form, was a failure. Although some of the lame ducks rescued by the government subsequently regained their health, e.g. Ferranti, which was returned to the private sector in 1983, others did not, e.g. Alfred Herbert the manufacturer of machine tools, that went into liquidation after a series of losses.

The emphasis given to industrial policy varies from one government to the next. Governments have been markedly less enthusiastic in the 1980s than in the 1970s, as illustrated by the following statement by Leon Brittan made in 1981 when he was a Treasury Minister: 'It is neither possible nor desirable for government to determine our future industrial structure. I do not believe that some group of wise men sitting in Whitehall or some kind of national investment bank can identify the industries, companies and projects which will become the key growth points as the economy moves out of recession.' And yet it must be remembered that this government increased financial support for micro-electronics.

## 21.5 The Location of Investment: Regional Policy

The major reason leading governments to seek to influence the geographical location or distribution of investment spending is the fact that the rate of economic growth and development varies from one part of the country to another. Given the uneven distribution of economic resources, differential rates of growth are almost inevitable, and may sometimes be necessary if a satisfactory rate of growth at the national level is to be achieved. However differential growth frequently gives rise to a number of serious economic problems.

In areas of low growth, job opportunities may increase less quickly than the working population, so that unless workers are willing to move to find work, these areas suffer from above-average unemployment. This often leads to other disadvantages, such as lower incomes and a substandard social fabric. Table 21.1 shows that income per head is well below, and unemployment well above, the national average in Scotland, Wales, Northern Ireland and Northern England.

*Table 21.1 Regional Differentials in Unemployment and Income*

|  | Unemployment % 1989 (second quarter) | Personal income per head 1986 £ million | Index |
|---|---|---|---|
| North | 10·3 | 5,305 | 92·2 |
| Yorkshire and Humberside | 7·8 | 5,381 | 93·5 |
| East Midlands | 5·9 | 5,511 | 95·8 |
| East Anglia | 3.5 | 5,649 | 98·2 |
| South East | 4·0 | 6,668 | 115·9 |
| South West | 4·9 | 5,649 | 98·1 |
| West Midlands | 6·5 | 5,293 | 92·0 |
| North West | 9·1 | 5,367 | 93·2 |
| Wales | 8·6 | 4,997 | 86·8 |
| Scotland | 9·8 | 5,446 | 94·6 |
| Northern Ireland | 15·6 | 4,304 | 74·8 |
| United Kingdom | 6·6 | 5,756 | 100.0 |

*Source: Economic Trends*

In the areas of above-average growth the problems are of a different nature. Rapid growth often (although not always) leads to external costs of various kinds: overcrowding, congestion, lack of green spaces, long and tiring journeys to work, overloading of some social services, etc.

Moreover, significant differences in regional unemployment rates may make the government's task of controlling inflation more difficult. The government may feel that a reduction in expenditure would, via a reduction in the demand for labour, help to moderate the rise in costs and prices. But most controls on expenditure are applied nationally, and if expenditure were reduced to an 'appropriate' level in areas of high growth, this might cause an unacceptably high rate of unemployment in areas of low growth.

## 21.6 The Free Market Solution

It is argued that each firm is in the best position to judge which location would be the most efficient. In arriving at its decision it takes into account a wide range of factors: the availability of labour of various types; the wage rates prevailing in the area; the state of labour relations in the area; the nearness to suppliers of raw materials, components etc.; the nearness to markets, transport links with other plants operated by the firm etc. As firms make their individual choices, the forces of demand and supply will operate so as to bring about an efficient allocation of resources. If the costs of congestion, etc., in the high-growth areas become so great that firms' costs become higher than they would be in other areas, this will prove a disincentive to further growth in the former areas, so that the differential in growth between the areas will be reduced.

Again, if external costs bear so heavily on workers in high-growth areas that they outweigh the advantages of working in those areas (greater job opportunities and probably higher earnings), workers will be more ready to look for work in other areas. Shortage of labour will then tend to raise the costs of employers in the high-growth areas, as they have to offer higher wages to attract sufficient workers. This will again tend to reduce geographical differentials in growth rates.

To turn to the low-growth areas, the argument is that if the cost to the workers in terms of poor employment prospects is greater than the advantages of living in the area (nearness to relatives and friends, supporting the local football team, pleasant surroundings, etc.), workers will move to other areas to seek employment. Thus eventually the 'surplus' unemployment will disappear.

To look finally at the implications for the government's anti-inflationary policy, it is argued that the free market approach would *not* put obstacles in the way of this policy, since differences in unemployment rates would eventually disappear, either because of the movement of industry into what were low-growth areas or the movement of workers into high-growth areas, or a combination of the two processes.

### 21.61 *An Evaluation of the Free Market Approach*

The free market approach ignores the fact that when workers leave an area, the expenditure in that area falls. Moreover this initial fall in expenditure is magnified by the operation of the (local) multiplier. While the outflow of workers would tend to reduce unemployment in the area, the loss of their spending power would act to create additional unemployment. Consequently it might take a very long time indeed before unemployment in the area fell to an average level.

In the inter-war period Wales lost a considerable number of workers through migration. Despite this fact, there was no improvement in Wales's unemployment record in relation to that of the United Kingdom as a whole. In 1929 Wales's unemployment rate was almost double that of the U.K. (19·3 per cent compared with 10·4 per cent). In 1934 the relation was the same, although both rates had increased (to 32·3 per cent compared with 16·7 per cent). By 1938 unemployment had fallen somewhat, but the Welsh rate was now more than double that of the U.K. (25·9 per cent compared with 12·9 per cent).

In order to explain the second deficiency of the free market approach it is necessary to discuss in rather more detail the meaning of 'resources' and 'advantages' in the particular context of regional economic development. A broad distinction can be made between the inherent and the acquired advantages of an area. One area has an inherent advantage over another if it is better endowed with natural resources, including the natural abilities of its workers. 'Better endowed' has, of course, to be interpreted in relation to the needs of the process of production.

Once an area begins to develop, it acquires additional advantages: its workers acquire a range of skills, new firms set up in the area and become customers of and suppliers to other firms in the area, local educational and training facilities are established, the infrastructure (roads, railways, etc.) is developed. The more pronounced are these external economies, the more conducive to growth will the situation be. (An external economy is one that benefits more than one firm. External economies are often acquired, i.e. they arise from the growth of a region or an industry, but may sometimes be inherent in a region, e.g. a river that provides water for a number of firms.)

The implications of this fact for the free market argument are clear. In the absence of government intervention there would be a tendency for highly developed areas to develop further and for the less developed areas to remain less developed. If, on the other hand, the government intervened so as to accelerate the rate of growth of some of the less developed areas, these areas might in time be expected to acquire advantages that would lead to further 'natural' growth.

We now introduce the distinction between private (or internal) costs and external costs. When a firm is deciding where to build a factory it will normally take into account only internal costs and benefits. However, its decision may well have an impact on other firms. If it settles in a high-growth area, it may put further pressure on a tight labour market, create additional congestion, and utilize very scarce open space. If a large number of firms settle in such an area, this could give rise to substantial external costs. Despite these additional costs, firms already established in the area may still be better off than they would be if they uprooted themselves and moved elsewhere, since they might then incur substantial 'removal' costs; the fact that they stay does not mean that their costs and efficiency are not affected by the entry of new firms. Incidentally, precisely the same arguments apply to individuals. They too may prefer to stay in an area despite extra congestion, etc., because of the removal costs.

Finally, we should point out that one of the assumptions behind the free market approach, that an individual firm will choose the most efficient and least expensive location, is also open to challenge. Numerous studies have revealed that the process of searching for new locations is often limited. Firms have frequently been found to settle for a 'satisfactory' location rather than prolong their search. Furthermore in a number of industries there are many locations that could be chosen without any appreciable effect on the firms' costs. Consequently there is little chance that government intervention will cause firms in those so-called foot-loose industries to choose a location at which their costs are appreciably higher than they would be elsewhere.

## 21.7 Alternative Forms of Government Intervention

Having examined the arguments for and against the free market approach, we now consider the various forms government intervention might take. The first broad distinction is between the imposition of controls designed to limit development in some areas and the provision of incentives in order to encourage firms to settle in other areas.

The imposition of controls, e.g. firms at one time had to obtain an Industrial Development Certificate, has the advantage of being relatively cheap to administer, and of avoiding the problems that arise in deciding which areas should qualify for assistance. On the other hand, firms whose development in one area is prevented are not necessarily encouraged to develop in another area. Without such encouragement these firms might decide not to develop at all, or to develop in other countries; in either case the domestic rate of economic growth will suffer.

### 21.71 *Government Incentives*

In order to avoid this danger most countries have offered positive incentives of one kind or another, often in conjunction with controls. These incentives can be classified as follows:

1 Subsidies related to the total costs and/or revenue of the firms, e.g. remission of tax on profits.
2 Subsidies related to the cost of capital inputs – buildings, plant and equipment.
3 Subsidies related to the cost of labour.
4 The provision of facilities, especially factories, for firms. These facilities are sometimes provided below cost.
5 The provision of facilities that might benefit several or indeed all of the firms in an area, e.g. central training facilities, an improved communications network.

A 'subsidy' may take the form of tax relief, a low-cost loan or a grant. A further distinction can be made (for all forms of assistance) between assistance available only to firms when they first locate in an area and assistance available to all firms in the area, including those established there for many years. Finally, the government may lay down other conditions that must be met before assistance is made available, e.g. that the development creates additional employment.

## 21.8 The Impact of Regional Policy

Table 21.2 shows how regional unemployment rates have changed. It can be seen that as national unemployment rises, the differentials in the *absolute* level of unemployment tends to increase, the South and East of England having suffered

*Table 21.2 Regional Unemployment*

| | Percentages | | | | Index (U.K. = 100) | | | |
|---|---|---|---|---|---|---|---|---|
| | 1966 | 1978 | 1984 | 1989 | 1966 | 1978 | 1984 | 1989 |
| North | 2·5 | 8·0 | 17·1 | 10·3 | 145 | 146 | 136 | 156 |
| Yorkshire and Humberside | 1·1 | 5·4 | 13·5 | 7·8 | 73 | 99 | 107 | 118 |
| East Midlands | 0·8 | 4·5 | 11·6 | 5·9 | 66 | 83 | 92 | 89 |
| East Anglia | 1·4 | 4·7 | 9·8 | 3·5 | 93 | 85 | 78 | 53 |
| South East | 0·9 | 3·8 | 9·3 | 4·0 | 61 | 70 | 74 | 61 |
| South West | 1·7 | 5·9 | 11·1 | 4·9 | 117 | 109 | 88 | 74 |
| West Midlands | 0·7 | 5·0 | 14·6 | 6·5 | 51 | 91 | 116 | 98 |
| North West | 1·4 | 6·6 | 15·4 | 9·1 | 95 | 120 | 122 | 138 |
| Wales | 2·7 | 7·3 | 15·3 | 8·6 | 186 | 132 | 121 | 130 |
| Scotland | 2·7 | 7·3 | 14·3 | 9·8 | 183 | 133 | 113 | 148 |
| Northern Ireland | 5·8 | 10·1 | 20·4 | 15·6 | 395 | 183 | 162 | 236 |
| United Kingdom | 1·5 | 5·5 | 12·6 | 6·6 | 100 | 100 | 100 | 100 |

*Source: Economic Trends*

less than other parts of England, Scotland, Wales and Northern Ireland. On the other hand the differentials tend to decline when expressed in index number form. (The most marked change occurred in the West Midlands, where the absence of assistance prior to 1984 was associated with a shift from below to above average unemployment.)

It is impossible to make a precise evaluation of regional policy, if only because we do not know what would have happened if a different policy had been adopted. But there is little evidence that policy has reduced regional differentials. Of course in the absence of government intervention the differentials might well have increased. Nevertheless, given that each new job created in the Assisted Areas is estimated to have cost £35–40,000, the effectiveness of policy must be open to question.

Three particular deficiencies in policy can be noted. First, the emphasis on subsidies for capital investment has meant that industries thought to be most responsive to regional policy in terms of job creation, such as electrical engineering and clothing, have received a relatively small share of regional assistance. On the other hand the industries receiving most aid, chemicals and metal manufacture, showed very little or even a negative return in terms of direct job creation in the Assisted Areas.

Second, regional aid has been largely concentrated on the manufacturing sector. The incentives for service industries, first introduced in 1973, could be described as being too little too late. The bias towards manufacturing has proved especially unfortunate in view of the shift of employment from manufacturing to the service sector.

Third, regional policy has been associated with the establishment of many branch plants in the Assisted Areas. These plants, externally controlled, and frequently involved in the manufacture of standardized products, became only weakly integrated into the local economy. Consequently their multiplier effect was limited. Moreover they often proved vulnerable in times of economic downturn.

## 21.9 Policy Changes

In 1983 the government issued a White Paper in which it argued that regional policy was not cost-effective and proposed a number of changes in policy. Under existing policy the principal forms of regional industrial assistance were regional development grants under Part II of the Industrial Development Act 1982 and selective financial assistance under Section 7 of the same Act. The balance of expenditure was weighted heavily in favour of the more automatic regional development grants (and was strongly biased towards manufacturing industries). The White Paper stated that 'The Government intend that in the future automatic assistance will account for a smaller proportion of expenditure; will be targeted more closely on job creation; and will be extended to include appropriate service activities.'

In November 1984 the government announced a change from a three to a two-tier system of Assisted Areas. Development Areas, accounting for 15 per cent of the working population, are eligible for both regional development grants and selective assistance. Intermediate Areas, accounting for 20 per cent of the working population, are eligible for selective assistance only. (In addition all Assisted Areas are eligible for support from the European Regional Development Fund.) The coverage of the Assisted Areas is shown in Figure 21.1.

Two changes were made which were designed to correct imbalance in the previous policy. First, many service industries (although not tourism) became eligible for assistance on the same terms as manufacturing industry. Second, in an attempt to gain the maximum benefit from expenditure in terms of job creation, a cost per job limit of £10,000 was imposed. (This limit does not apply to firms employing less than 200 workers.) Alternatively, if it is to their advantage, firms can claim a grant of £3,000 for each job created. The government also hoped to increase the policy's cost-effectiveness by increasing the proportion of spending on selective assistance, as noted above. However spending overall was planned to decline. Between 1983–4 and 1987–8 spending in real terms fell by about a half. Moreover, in 1988 the government announced its intention to replace R.D.G.s in the Development Areas with a system of discretionary grants available only to firms with less than 25 employees.

## 21.11 Summary and Conclusions

In an attempt to influence the type and geographical location of investment governments have offered a wide range of assistance. Geographical location has also at times been influenced by the imposition of controls in certain areas. The recipients of assistance are, of course, individual firms. But the policy has been justified on the grounds that it leads to an overall increase in economic efficiency.

Regional policy has also been justified as making for more equal opportunities as between one region and another. However there has been considerable debate about the cost effectiveness of the policy, and the scale of assistance has recently been reduced.

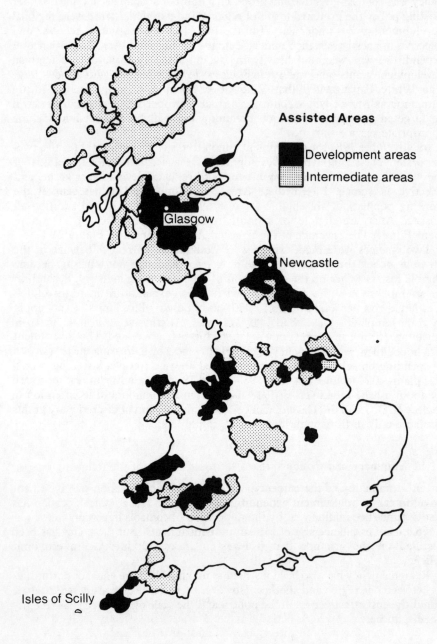

Fig. 21.1 The Assisted Areas

**Further Reading**

Artis, M. J., Ed., *The U.K. Economy* (London: Weidenfeld and Nicolson, 11th Edn, 1986), Ch. 4.
Griffiths, A. and Wall, S., *Applied Economics* (London: Longman, 2nd Edn, 1986), Ch. 19.
Livesey, F., *A Textbook of Economics* (London: Longman, 3rd Edn, 1989), Ch. 19.
Regional Studies Association, *Report of an Inquiry into Regional Problems in the United Kingdom* (London: Geo Books, 1983).

**Revision Exercises**

1 Explain what you understand by the term industrial policy.
2 Why have governments thought it necessary to give financial assistance to certain sectors of the economy?
3 How would you decide which sectors of the economy should receive government subsidies to investment?
4 'The growth and decline of industries should be a matter for market forces, not government action.' Discuss.
5 What are the advantages and disadvantages of indicative planning?
6 'Businessmen are in a much better position than government ministers or civil servants to decide where factories and offices should be built.' Discuss.
7 What information would be required for a comprehensive evaluation of regional policy?
8 On the basis of the information contained in this chapter, evaluate regional policy.
9 Explain the statement that the existence of external costs and benefits justifies government intervention in location decisions.
10 Outline the main aims of government economic policy and the means by which these aims might be achieved.

**Objective Test Questions: Set No. 6**

For answers see p. 274.

1 Unemployment is likely to rise as a result of each of the following *except*

A devaluation of the currency
B a fall in government expenditure
C a rise in taxation
D a fall in the average propensity to consume

2 Which of the following policies would be most appropriate if the government wished to reduce the pressure of demand without causing prices to rise further?

A an increase in both V.A.T. and tariff barriers
B an increase in V.A.T. and a reduction in tariff barriers
C an increase in both direct taxation and tariff barriers
D an increase in direct taxation and a reduction in tariff barriers

3 The table below shows four combinations of goods that could be produced in two countries if each country were to allocate half its resources to the production of each good.

|   | Country R Good X | Good Y | Country T Good X | Good Y |
|---|---|---|---|---|
| A | 3 | 3 | 4 | 6 |
| B | 3 | 1 | 1 | 3 |
| C | 1 | 4 | 2 | 6 |
| D | 2 | 3 | 6 | 9 |

The only situation in which the output of both goods could not be increased as a result of specialization in accordance with the principle of comparative advantage is

A     B     C     D

4    *Price in U.K. (£)*          *Price in U.S.A. ($)*
   X      Y           X      Y
 1·00   1·33     2·00  3·20

The above table shows the domestic prices of two products, X and Y, in the U.K. and the U.S.A. Assuming that producers wish to obtain the same revenue per unit in overseas markets as in the domestic market and that transport costs are negligible, full specialization in accordance with the principle of comparative advantage will occur with an exchange rate of £1 =

A  $2·50
B  $2·25
C  $1·75
D  $1·35

5 Visible exports include the overseas earnings of the suppliers of all of the following products *except*

A  foodstuffs
B  raw materials
C  freight services
D  machinery

6 The U.K. balance of payments on current account will benefit from all of the following *except*

A  an increase in the overseas earnings of British insurance companies
B  a reduction in investment abroad by British firms
C  an increase in the volume of foreign trade carried by British ships
D  a reduction in spending by British tourists abroad

7 In which of the following situations is devaluation most likely to lead to an improvement in the balance of payments?

*Elasticity of demand for*

| | Imports | Exports |
|---|---|---|
| A | 0·0 | 0·0 |
| B | 0·2 | 0·6 |
| C | 0·1 | 0·0 |
| D | 0·6 | 0·6 |

8 The main difference between a customs union and a free-trade area is that

A foreign trade is regulated by means of tariffs in the former, and in the latter by means of quotas

B exchange rates are fixed in the former, while in the latter they can be varied

C a common external tariff is adopted in the former, while in the latter different external tariffs are permitted for trade with non-members

D barriers to trade between members are encouraged in the former, and discouraged in the latter.

Questions 9 and 10 are based on the following types of unemployment:

A frictional
B residual
C structural
D cyclical

Indicate which type of unemployment is referred to in each of the questions below. (Each type may apply once, more than once or not at all.)

9 The gap in employment that may occur when workers voluntarily change their jobs

A  B  C  D

10 Unemployment that arises when some industries are declining while others are expanding, and which is associated with an imbalance in the supply of, and demand for, certain types of skills

A  B  C  D

11 In a situation of very low unemployment and rapidly rising prices which of the following policies would be appropriate?

1 Reducing the rate of personal taxation
2 Reducing import barriers
3 Increasing the level of special deposits lodged by the clearing banks at the Bank of England

A 1, 2 and 3
B 1 and 2 only
C 1 and 3 only
D 2 and 3 only

12 Special Drawing Rights constitute an entry in a member country's bank balance with the

A Bank for International Settlements
B International Monetary Fund
C European Monetary Union
D International Bank for Reconstruction and Development

13 If national income increases from £1,000 million to £2,400 million while prices double, the growth in real national income is

A 120 per cent
B 100 per cent
C 40 per cent
D 20 per cent

14

| | Price index of exports | Price index of imports |
|---|---|---|
| Year 1 | 100 | 100 |
| Year 2 | 121 | 110 |

The terms of trade in year 2 were

A 121
B 111
C 110
D 90

15 An increase in real expenditure on the running costs of motor vehicles might reflect an increase in

1 the price of motor vehicles
2 the price of petrol
3 the level of car ownership

A 1 and 2 only
B 2 and 3 only
C 1 only
D 3 only

16 If the terms of trade change from 105 to 110 we can conclude that

A the total value of exports has risen
B the total value of imports has risen
C the total value of exports has risen more than the total value of imports
D the average price of exports has risen relative to the average price of imports.

17 Which of the following is part of the balance of payments current account?

A Spending by foreign tourists
B Short term overseas lending by banks
C The building of factories overseas
D Portfolio investment overseas

18 Which of the following institutions was/were established primarily to provide financial assistance to the less developed and developing countries?

1 International Monetary Fund
2 European Development Fund
3 International Bank for Reconstruction and Development

A 1, 2 and 3
B 1 and 2 only
C 1 and 3 only
D 2 and 3 only

19 Which of the following policies is designed mainly to influence the type of investment?

A Monetary policy
B Fiscal policy
C Industrial policy
D Regional policy

20 The largest item of expenditure in the U.K. is

A consumers' expenditure
B investment expenditure
C government expenditure on goods and services
D transfer payments

*Answers to Objective Test Questions*

| Q | Set No. 1 | Set No. 2 | Set No. 3 | Set No. 4 | Set No. 5 | Set No. 6 |
|---|---|---|---|---|---|---|
| 1 | A | C | C | D | C | A |
| 2 | D | D | C | D | D | D |
| 3 | A | D | A | C | B | D |
| 4 | B | B | A | C | B | B |
| 5 | C | B | B | D | C | C |
| 6 | B | D | C | B | C | B |
| 7 | C | B | C | D | C | D |
| 8 | D | D | A | B | A | C |
| 9 | C | C | D | D | A | A |
| 10 | C | A | B | B | B | C |
| 11 | B | A | D | C | B | D |
| 12 | B | C | C | A | D | B |
| 13 | C | A | C | B | A | D |
| 14 | C | D | B | A | C | C |
| 15 | C | D | C | D | D | D |
| 16 | B | A | A | D | D | D |
| 17 | A | D | C | D | C | A |
| 18 | B | C | D | C | A | B |
| 19 | C | B | D | D | B | D |
| 20 | A | D | A | B | C | A |

# Index